HUMAN WILDLIFE CONFLICT AND MANAGEMENT

GRAVITY AND INTERVENTIONS

DR. REJI D. NAIR

BlueRose ONE.com
Stories Matter
NewDelhi • London

BLUEROSE PUBLISHERS
India | U.K.

For permissions requests or inquiries regarding this publication, please contact:

BLUEROSE PUBLISHERS
www.BlueRoseONE.com
info@bluerosepublishers.com
+91 8882 898 898
+4407342408967

ISBN: 978-93-7310-663-2

Cover design: Daksh
Typesetting: Tanya Raj Upadhyay

First Edition: November 2025

Aabout the Author

Reji D. Nair has a PhD in Economics from Kerala University (1997), India. He has authored 20 books, including 10 academic works and 10 literary pieces. He has published over 70 research papers in national and international journals. His important books include Land Economics: Issues in Land Use (2003), Emerging Africa: Potential and Challenges (2009), Natural Resources Management and Agrarian Development (2010), Role of Indigenous Communities in Forest Conservation: Lessons from Africa (2010), Farm Management: Theory and Practice (2011), Employee Empowerment and Job Satisfaction (2015), Graduate Employability in GCC Countries (2020), Managing Climate Change (2025), and Zero to Hero & Hero to Super Star: Igniting Young Minds (2025).

His works are cataloged in esteemed libraries such as the US Congress Library and the Australian Parliament Library. With vast experience in higher education, Dr. Nair has worked at universities and Higher Education Institutions in India, the UAE, Saudi Arabia, and Ethiopia. He has collaborated with various national and international professional organizations. He is also a motivational speaker and a certified trainer in Teaching and Learning Methods from CPI, New Zealand. His area of study mostly focuses on environmental issues, forest conservation, sustainable development, natural resource management, education, and the economies of the Middle East and Africa.

His books have been translated into multiple languages, including French, German, Spanish, Italian, and Russian. In addition to his academic contributions, he is a writer in Malayalam, having published novels, short stories, children's literature, and science fiction. Some of his literary works have been translated into English and Kannada.

PREFACE

Human-wildlife conflict (HWC) has become one of the most important sustainable development challenges today, driven largely by the relentless expansion of human activities into natural ecosystems. As forests shrink and farmlands expand, wild animals are increasingly pushed into human-dominated landscapes, leading to inevitable clashes. Climate change and urbanization further intensified the issues. These confrontations endanger both human settlements and wildlife survival, with root causes including habitat destruction, unsustainable farming, competition for resources, and climate disruptions. This book delves into the intricate dynamics of HWC, examining its dimensions and exploring ways to foster harmony between people and wildlife.

The impacts of HWC are severe and wide-ranging. For people living near wildlife habitats, conflicts can mean destroyed crops, lost livestock, injuries, and even fatalities—threatening food security and economic stability. At the same time, wild animals suffer from retaliatory killings, habitat loss, and declining populations, further destabilizing fragile ecosystems. This destructive cycle not only endangers species but also undermines the natural systems that sustain human life, making conflict resolution a critical priority.

Addressing HWC demands a holistic approach, combining policy reforms, community involvement, and creative problem-solving. Solutions such as creating wildlife corridors, compensating farmers for losses, and empowering local conservation groups have shown promise. Technological innovations—including AI-based monitoring and non-lethal deterrents—are also proving effective in preventing clashes. The goal is to strike a balance where both human livelihoods and wildlife conservation can thrive.

Different countries offer valuable lessons in managing HWC. In Asia, community-driven efforts have successfully reduced tensions between farmers and elephants, demonstrating the power of grassroots involvement. Africa's conservancy model has turned wildlife into an economic asset for local communities, fostering coexistence with species like lions and elephants. Meanwhile, South America's agroforestry systems blend farming with forest conservation, reducing habitat conflicts. These examples highlight adaptable, context-specific solutions.

India's experience with HWC is particularly instructive, given its high biodiversity and dense human populations. The country has pioneered innovative strategies, from solar-powered fences to community awareness campaigns, blending modern science with traditional knowledge. Indigenous practices and cultural reverence for wildlife have also played a key role in mitigating conflicts, proving that conservation must respect local values.

Kerala's unique ecological and cultural landscape presents both challenges and breakthroughs in HWC management. With its mix of forests, farmlands, and waterways, the state sees frequent human-wildlife encounters. Yet, Kerala has led the way in community-based monitoring, using technology like camera traps and GPS tracking to predict and prevent conflicts. By involving locals in conservation decisions, the state has built trust and resilience, offering a replicable model for other regions.

Ultimately, each conflict is an opportunity—to educate, innovate, and collaborate. The path to coexistence requires shared responsibility, blending science, policy, and community wisdom. Only by working together can we ensure a future where humans and wildlife thrive side by side.

This book brings together global insights to illuminate the complexities of HWC and inspire actionable solutions. By learning from diverse case studies, we can develop strategies that protect both people and wildlife.

DR. REJI D. NAIR

Table of Contents

CHAPTER: 1 INTRODUCTION 1

CHAPTER: 2 DRIVERS OF HUMAN WILDLIFE CONFLICT 19

CHAPTER: 3 IMPLICATIONS OF CLIMATE CHANGE 35

CHAPTER: 4 IMPLICATIONS OF HUMAN WILDLIFE CONFLICT 57

CHAPTER: 5 HUMAN WILDLIFE CONFLICT AND MANAGEMENT 71

CHAPTER: 6 WILDLIFE AND CO-EXISTENCE 95

CHAPTER:7 GRAVITY OF HUMAN WILDLIFE CONFLICT ... 117

CHAPTER: 8 AFRICAN LESSONS IN THE MANAGEMENT OF HUMAN WILDLIFE CONFLICT 138

CHAPTER: 9 HUMAN WILDLIFE CONFLICT IN INDIA 160

CHAPTER:10 HUMAN WILDLIFE INTERFACE IN KERALA . 172

CHAPTER: 11 CONCLUSION AND RECOMMENDATIONS.... 191

APPENDICES 201

BIBLIOGRAPHY 219

List of Figures:

Figure: 1.1 Economic Losses due to HWC, 2020-23 ($ Million) 4
Figure: 1.2 Framework of Social-Ecological System (SES) 16
Figure: 2.1 Causes of HWC 22
Figure: 2.2 Relationship between HWC and their Associated Interventions 25
Figure: 2.3 Factors Affecting Intensity of HWC – A Model 28
Figure: 3.1 Relation between Forest and Climate Change 38
Figure: 4.1 Causes & Impact of HWC – A Model 60
Figure: 4.2 Annual Deaths due to HWC, 2022-23 62
Figure: 5.1 Areas of overlap between wildlife and people (%) 76
Figure: 5.2 Effectiveness of HWC Mitigation Strategies (%) 77
Figure: 7.1 A Model of HWC 118
Figure: 7.2 Annual Economic Loss due to HWC, 2010-23 (million$) 120
Figure: 8.1 Annual Economic Loss due to HWC, 2023 (USD) 141
Figure: 8.2 Human and wildlife causalities reported, 2020-23 146
Figure: 9.1 Human death due to wildlife attack, 2018-23 160
Figure: 9.2 Causes of HWC in India (%) 162
Figure: 10.1 Causality and reported incidents due to HWC in Kerala, 2017-18 & 2022-23 174
Figure: 10.2 Compensation paid in HWC in Kerala, 2017-18 & 2022-23 (Rs Crore) 175
Figure: 10.3 Intensity of HWC in Kerala, 2022 183

List of Table:

Table:1.1 Gravity of HWC in selected countries, 2019-2024 2
Table: 1.2 Recent HWC Incidents, 2020-2023 3
Table: 1.3 Reflection of HWC on SDGs 11
Table: 2.1 Key drivers and pressures leading to HWC 23
Table: 3.1 Recent Climate-Related HWC Incidents (2018–2023) 37
Table: 3.2 Climate Adaptive Actions in Forest Management 40
Table: 3.3 Habitats at Risk Due to Climate Change 44
Table: 3.4 Impact of Climate Change on Wildlife 47
Table:4.1 Gravity of HWC around the world, 2020 57
Table:4.2 Costs of HWC 58
Figure: 4.1 Causes & Impact of HWC – A Model 60
Table: 4.3 Species Affected by HWC, 2023 62
Table: 4.4 Nature of Impact of HWC 63
Table: 4.5 Stages in the evolution of wildlife damage 64
Table: 6.1 Global Wildlife Co-existence Initiatives 97
Table: 6.2 Review of Coexistence Strategies 109
Table: 7.1 Major Causes of HWC 118
Table: 7.2 Reported HWCs by Region, 2010-2023 120
Table: 7.3 Gravity of HWC in South America 123
Table: 7.4 Gravity of HWC in North America 125
Table: 7.5 Gravity of HWC in Asia 127
Table: 7.6 Implications of HWC 128
Table: 7.7 Major Impacts of HWC by Continent 130
Table: 7.9 Major lessons from HWC around the World 134

Table: 8.1 Reported Wildlife Conflicts in African Countries, 2018–2023 139
Table: 8.2 Major Causes of HWC in African Countries 143
Table: 8.3 Retaliatory Wildlife Killings in Africa (2020–2022) 146
Table: 9.1 HWC fatalities by State, 2023 164
Table: 9.2 Crop Damage by Wildlife in Selected States, 2022 (₹ Crores) 165
Table: 10.1 Gravity of HWC in Kerala, 2022 & 2023 174
Table: 10.2 Human Fatalities in HWC in Kerala (2020–2024) 176

List of Box:

Box: 3.1 Indicators of Climate Warming in Western Antarctic: Chinstrap Vs Adélie penguins 45

Box: 3.2 Zimbabwe's Elephant Conflicts 46

Box: 7.1 Human – Elephant Conflict Management in Kui Buri district of Thailand 125

Box: 7.2 Human – Elephant Conflict Management in Sabah, Malaysia 127

Box: 7.3 Integrated approach to HWC in Nepal 129

Box: 8.1 Kavango-Zambezi (KAZA) Trans frontier Conservation Area (TFCA) in Angola, Botswana, Namibia, Zambia, and Zimbabwe 152

Box: 8.2 Community-based ecotourism in Bwindi, Uganda 153

Box: 8.3 Community centred management of HWC: Success stories from Namibia 154

Box: 9.1 Human – Elephant Conflict Management in Valparai and Hassan areas in Karnataka State, India 165

Box: 10.1 HWC in Wayanad 185

CHAPTER: 1
INTRODUCTION

1.1 Introduction

Human Wildlife Conflict (HWC) has grown worse in recent times worldwide, causing significant loss of life among both people and animals, economic challenges, and obstacles to conservation efforts. This conflict arises when interactions between humans and wildlife lead to adverse consequences for either or both groups. It typically occurs when the behaviors or needs of wildlife interfere with human activities, or vice versa. With expanding human populations increasingly encroaching into natural ecosystems, encounters with wildlife are on the rise—posing serious threats to biodiversity, food security, and public safety (WWF, 2023). Contributing factors such as deforestation, climate change, and habitat loss have intensified these conflicts, endangering both ecosystems and human livelihoods.

According to a joint report by the World-Wide Fund for Nature (WWF) and the United Nations Environment Programme (UNEP), more than 75% of wild cat species globally are impacted by killings linked to such conflicts. African countries are facing serious HWC challenges. In a case in Malawi, the relocation of 263 elephants to Kasungu National Park in July 2022 triggered increased conflict, resulting in at least 10 human deaths and widespread property damage (Hill, 2004). Local communities have taken legal action against the International Fund for Animal Welfare (IFAW) for failing to implement effective conflict mitigation strategies. Similarly, in Zambia, communities bordering conservation zones have reported loss of crops and human lives due to elephant intrusions, leading to growing tensions between residents and conservation authorities.

HWC is not confined to developing countries. In France, for example, an 81-year-old hunter was prosecuted for killing a protected bear in self-defense, underscoring the complex interplay between wildlife protection laws and human safety (Gross, 2021). Table 1.1 presents an overview of recent HWC incidents across various regions. Between 2019 and 2024, India alone recorded 3,076 human fatalities due to wildlife conflict, elephants being the leading cause of such causalities in most countries.

Table:1.1 Gravity of HWC in selected countries, 2019-2024

Region/Country	*Period*	*Human Fatalities*	*Species Involved*
India	2019-2024	3,076	Elephants, Tigers
Malawi	2022-2024	10	Elephants
Zambia	2022-2024	9	Elephants
France	2021	0	Bear

Source: WII (2022), SEPA (2023), WWF (2023)

HWC is an escalating global issue as expanding human settlements encroach on natural habitats, resulting in competition for resources and risks to both human and animal safety. This book explores the status of HWC, provides worldwide account on conflict cases, analyzes primary causes, and evaluates potential solutions. The discussion underscores the critical need for sustainable approaches that promote harmony between conservation efforts and human well-being.

Key species frequcntly involved in HWC are elephants, large felines (such as lions, tigers, and leopards), wolves, crocodiles, and primates. Major concerns include crop destruction by elephants and primates, livestock attacks by predators, and human fatalities. India recorded over 12,000 HWC incidents between 2020 and 2023, followed by Kenya (8,000+) and Brazil (2,000+). For more information, see Table-1.2.

Table: 1.2 Recent HWC Incidents, 2020-2023

Region	*Country*	*Key Species Involved*	*Reported Incidents (Annual Avg.)*	*Human Fatalities (Annual)*
Asia	India	Tigers, Leopards	12,000+	500+
Africa	Kenya	Elephants, Lions	8,000+	200+
South America	Brazil	Jaguars, Capybaras	3,500+	50+
North America	USA	Wolves, Bears	2,000+	10+
Europe	Sweden	Wolves, Boars	1,200+	<5

Sources: KWS, 2023, WII, 2022, USFWS, 2023, SEPA, 2023.

The reported primary factors contributing to HWC, in general include (Gross, 2021):

i. *Habitat loss & fragmentation:* Agricultural expansion and urban development shrink natural wildlife habitats.
ii. *Climate change:* Shifts in animal migration routes lead to increased human-wildlife interactions.
iii. *Human population growth*: Rising numbers of people settling near wildlife zones heighten conflict risks.
iv. *Livestock encroachment:* Grazing animals in forested areas draw predators closer to human settlements.

The consequences of HWC are wide-ranging and most important include (Redpath, et al. 2013):

i. *Economic losses:* Farmers suffer from destroyed crops and livestock, severely affecting incomes. Figure 1.1illustrates the financial toll of HWC in selected nations. Between 2020 and 2023, India recorded losses worth of $20.5 million, while Kenya faced $15.2 million in damages.
ii. *Biodiversity decline:* Retaliatory actions by humans, such as killing wildlife, endanger vulnerable species.

iii. *Human fatalities:* Attacks by large predators like big cats and elephants result in loss of human lives.

Figure: 1.1 Economic Losses due to HWC, 2020-23 ($ Million)

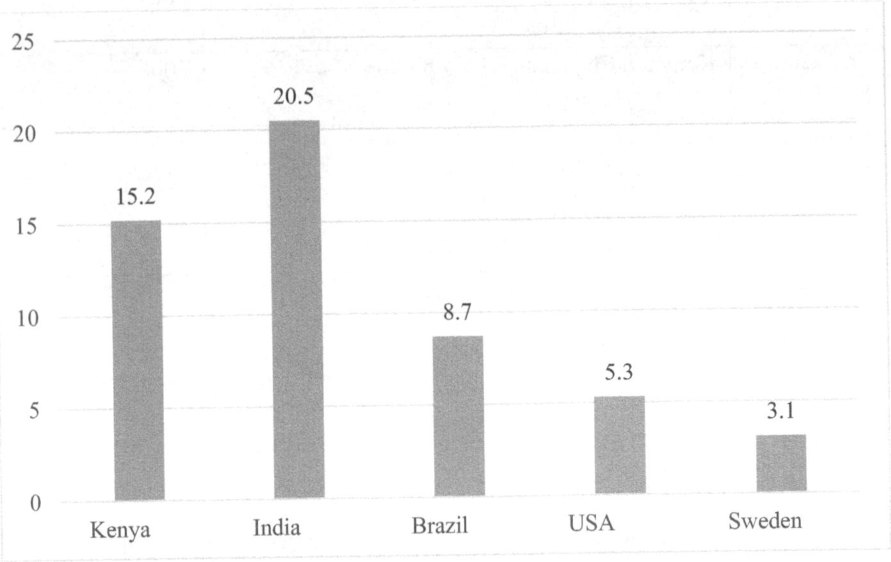

Sources: KWS, 2023, WII, 2022, USFWS, 2023, SEPA, 2023.

1.2 Managing HWC

Managing HWC is a multifaceted challenge that spans numerous disciplines, including animal behavior, conservation biology, ecology, genetics, zoology, anthropology, economics, environmental science, geography, history, political science, psychology, technology, and natural resource management (For more details refer Appendix-1). As a result, addressing HWC requires innovative approaches in areas such as economics, ecology, governance, land use planning, forest conservation, infrastructure development, environmental justice, and human rights. Technological advancements offer valuable tools for identifying emerging patterns of conflict and developing new strategies tailored to diverse ecosystems.

One of the most pressing drivers of HWC is climate change, which significantly threatens both human populations and wildlife, as well as broader conservation efforts. Effectively addressing HWC calls for a comprehensive and integrated strategy in the following areas (IUCN, 2023).

i. *Community involvement:* Engaging local populations in conservation efforts ensures their needs, safety, and livelihoods are considered and respected.
ii. *Habitat protection and restoration*: Conserving and rehabilitating wildlife habitats helps prevent animals from encroaching into human-dominated areas.
iii. *Technological interventions*: Tools such as motion detectors and alert systems can provide timely warnings of wildlife presence, thereby reducing risk.
iv. *Financial compensation*: Offering monetary relief to those who suffer losses due to wildlife helps reduce the economic burden on affected communities.

Over the past two decades, the importance of HWC management has gained widespread recognition, as these conflicts increasingly pose obstacles to conservation and sustainable development efforts around the world (Guerra, 2019). Environmental degradation, habitat destruction, and climate change are expected to further intensify these issues (Mason et al., 2018). HWC contributes to a broad array of environmental, economic, social, and political challenges globally, making its management especially intricate.

Practically proven and successful intervention strategies to counter HWC included the following (Manfredo, et al. 2009):

i. *Preventive Approaches*:
    - Electric Fences: Help deter crop raiding; proven effective in countries like Kenya and India (KWS, 2023).
    - Early Warning Systems: For example, Sri Lanka successfully uses SMS alerts to inform communities about elephant movements (Karanth, et al. 2002).

- Compensation Programs: Governments in countries like Namibia reimburse farmers for losses caused by wildlife in the most effective way (Hill, 2004).

ii. Community-Based Strategies:

- Predator-Proof Livestock Enclosures: Reduce attacks from big cats and in places like Tanzania it was quite successful (WWF, 2023).
- Beehive Fences: Used in Botswana to discourage elephants from entering farmland was reported to be effective (Karanth, et al. 2002).

iii. Policy and Planning Initiatives:

- Land-Use Zoning: Establishes buffer zones to minimize human-wildlife interactions.
- Wildlife Corridors: Facilitate safe movement of animals across fragmented landscapes, as seen in India's Project Elephant was a popular initiative (WII, 2022).

Detailed account on approaches to HWC management is provided in Appendix-3.

1.3 HWC and Human Wildlife Interaction

Human interactions with wildlife yield both positive and negative outcomes, though public discourse often emphasizes the latter. Positive aspects—such as recreation, education, psychological benefits, and ecosystem services—are frequently overlooked. Historically, traditional societies competed with wildlife for resources, leading to the extinction of some species while domesticating others.

HWC arises when the actions of wildlife negatively impact humans or vice versa, manifesting as threats to safety, economic losses, and food insecurity (Redpath et al., 2013). Some scholars argue for distinguishing between conflict and impact, suggesting 'human-wildlife coexistence' as a more constructive framework (Peterson et al., 2010).

Effective HWC management requires understanding its three defining features (IUCN, 2023):

i. *Direct and Recurring Interactions:*
   a. Conflicts stem from real or perceived harm caused by wildlife, ranging from minor nuisances to severe economic or life-threatening damage.
   b. The intensity of conflict often depends less on the actual impact and more on human perceptions and reactions, especially when incidents recur.

ii. *Underlying Social Conflicts:*
   a. HWCs frequently reflect deeper disputes among human groups over wildlife management.
   b. Stakeholders—such as affected communities, conservationists, government, and policymakers—often hold divergent values and priorities.
   c. In some cases, wildlife complaints mask unrelated social tensions (e.g., power struggles or cultural clashes). Rarely, animals themselves may become active participants, as seen in retaliatory elephant attacks.

iii. *Involvement of Species of Conservation Concern:*
   a. Conflicts often involve threatened or protected species, where lethal control is legally or ethically restricted.
   b. This limitation escalates tensions, as affected communities lack recourse while conservationists prioritize species survival, complicating conflict resolution.

1.4 Complexity of the Issue

HWC is not a recent phenomenon—it has been occurring for thousands of years, with humans historically taking measures to protect themselves and their property from wild animals (Karanth & Madhusudan, 2002). Today, the term HWC typically refers to any adverse interaction between people and wildlife, whether perceived or actual, and whether the impact is economic, aesthetic, social, or political. When wildlife causes damage that exceeds what individuals or communities can tolerate, it often changes their perceptions of those animals (Karanth & Madhusudan, 2002). In many cases, the response has been retaliatory—killing wildlife or destroying their habitats to prevent future harm.

Historically, humans lived in relatively harmonious relationships with nature. But this balance began to shift during the colonial era, when a utilitarian mindset and commercialization led to widespread forest encroachment for agriculture and human development. This period saw extensive deforestation and the extinction of numerous plant and animal species. After World War II, the establishment of the United Nations and its affiliated organizations brought renewed global attention to nature conservation. Since then, HWC has intensified, particularly in the context of accelerating climate change.

Large carnivores such as African lions, spotted hyenas, tigers, African wild dogs, Florida panthers, and grey wolves are experiencing population declines globally, largely due to human activity along the edges of forests (Michalski et al., 2006). These species are particularly vulnerable to intentional killings, shootings, poisoning, road accidents, and other indirect threats. Conflicts with carnivores typically arise because their large territorial ranges often overlap with human-dominated landscapes, especially in areas where livestock farming is widespread.

During the 20th century, many wildlife populations rebounded due to increased protection, scientific research, and the application of effective wildlife management strategies (Trefethen, 1975). However, what was once a straightforward rivalry between humans and wildlife has now evolved into a more complex conflict—often between individuals and institutions like forest departments, environmental agencies, and wildlife protection authorities (Hill, 2004). In many forest-adjacent communities, frustration and resentment toward these authorities are common.

Addressing HWC today requires transparent, inclusive, and democratic planning methods that consider the current socio-economic and political landscape.

According to Guynn (1997), a successful HWC management process should ensure the following:

i. Clearly defined goals and outcomes;
ii. Clear delineation of responsibilities to avoid unrealistic expectations;
iii. Consensus-based decision-making among stakeholders;
iv. Team-building activities to foster collaboration;
v. Consistent participation, avoiding replacement of members;
vi. Use of strategies that promote active listening; and
vii. Tackling smaller, manageable issues as stepping stones to larger solutions.

Determining the ideal wildlife population size and appropriate management strategies is highly complex. Wildlife professionals must gather detailed information about animal behavior, the scale and causes of conflict, historical context, socio-economic changes in affected areas, and community involvement to develop effective solutions.

1.5 Sustainable Development Challenge

The pillars of sustainability—economic, social, and ecological dimensions—are deeply interconnected and cannot function in isolation. The United Nations' 2030 Agenda for Sustainable Development outlines 17 Sustainable Development Goals (SDGs) with 169 targets, integrating biodiversity conservation under Goal 14 (Life below water) and Goal 15 (Life on land). HWC directly and indirectly impacts multiple SDGs, as summarized in Table-1.3.

To foster harmonious coexistence between humans and wildlife, all stakeholders—including governments at various levels—must collaborate to ensure the benefits of shared landscapes outweigh the costs. The consequences of HWC extend beyond local communities and wildlife, posing risks to global conservation efforts and sustainable development programs. In fact, HWC is linked directly or indirectly to all SDGs.

A holistic approach to HWC opens doors for partnerships between conservation and development sectors. Joint initiatives in these fields promote long-term sustainability by engaging diverse stakeholders. Such collaborations yield dual benefits:

i. *Ecological:* Preserving ecosystems and wildlife populations.
ii. *Social:* Encouraging community-led stewardship of conservation efforts.

Establishing shared goals among stakeholders—such as conservationists, local communities, and policymakers—is crucial for fostering a unified approach to mitigating negative interactions between people and wildlife. To effectively address these conflicts, employing evidence-based strategies grounded in research is essential; these approaches can identify successful interventions that balance human needs with wildlife conservation. Furthermore, clearly defined roles for each stakeholder ensure that responsibilities are understood, whether in implementing preventive measures, conducting community outreach, or enforcing regulations. Together, these elements create a comprehensive framework for achieving sustainable solutions in HWC management. These elements ensure biodiversity protection while supporting sustainable development.

Human-wildlife coexistence is not just a conservation issue but also a humanitarian and socio-economic concern. Effective HWC management demands multi-sectoral collaboration, integrating coexistence strategies into business operations, economic policies, and social development programs (WWF, 2023).

To achieve lasting solutions, HWC mitigation must be woven into sustainable development frameworks—particularly in regions, where humans and wildlife share habitats.

Table: 1.3 Reflection of HWC on SDGs

SDGs	*Impact of HWC*
SDG-1: No Poverty	HWC affects the income of farmers, herders, artisanal fishers, and indigenous peoples, particularly those living in poverty and without resilience.
SDG-2: Zero Hunger	Wildlife damages food stores, crops, and livestock and puts subsistence farmers at risk of hunger.
SDG-3: Good Health and wellbeing	HWC impacts people's health – both directly, when attacks lead to injury, and more indirectly, for example, when malaria rates increase as a result of farmers' need to protect their crops through the night.
SDG-4: Quality education	Children are often responsible for time consuming crop and livestock guarding, which decreases school attendance and lowers education standards for pupils in HWC-impacted areas, creating potentially lifelong inequalities.
SDG-5: Gender equality	Women carry the highest burden of HWC due to their role in society and culturally defined tasks and responsibilities; for example, not only are they vulnerable to attack by wildlife while collecting natural resources but also, if they are widows, they may suffer high losses because it is culturally unacceptable for them to guard at night.
SDG-6: Clean water and sanitation	In arid parts of the world, water access may be reduced and risky for people as they compete with wildlife for water sources.
SDG-8: Decent work and economic growth	HWC can drive the vicious circle of poverty and low livelihood diversity, resulting in the unavailability of occupational work in HWC hotspots.
SDG-9: Industry, innovation and infrastructure	HWC can increase as a result of linear infrastructure development that fails to consider the migratory routes and spatial distribution of wildlife, resulting in vehicle collisions with wildlife or displacement of wildlife.
SDG-10: Reduced inequalities	HWC drives inequality of cost and benefit distribution if those who pay the price for living with wildlife do not receive the benefits of coexistence.
SDG-11: Sustainable cities and communities	Facing shrinking natural habitats, wildlife increasingly utilizes green spaces in urban areas and pursues non-traditional food

	sources, which leads to urban HWC, such as human-leopard conflict in the city of Mumbai.
SDG-13: Climate Action	Climate change alters habitats and drives human and wildlife behaviour changes, bringing humans and wildlife into closer proximity to each other, which can lead to HWC.
SDG-14: Life below water	Marine HWC negatively impacts the survival of many marine species, including sharks, whales, sea turtles, seals, and polar bears.
SDG-15: Life on land	The survival of multiple terrestrial species, particularly apex predators and mega herbivores, depends on successful HWC management and coexistence.
SDG-16: Peace, justice and strong institutions	Carnivores and mega-herbivores create immediate safety concerns. Also, HWC can lead to demoralizing conflicts between groups of people and result in inequities and societal destabilisation.
SDG-17: Partnerships for the goals	Human-wildlife coexistence and sustainable development both require integrated decision making, participation, and good governance at international, national, and regional levels, plus the involvement of civil society.

Source: Gross E, et. al, 2021

1.6 Historical Perspective of HWC

HWC is not a recent issue. It began around 13,000 B.C. when humans started farming and around 8,000 B.C. when they began raising animals for food (Hillman G, et. al., 2016). Throughout history, societies have tried to reduce encounters with wildlife that result in damage to crops and livestock and pose risks to personal safety.

The story of human civilization is deeply intertwined with our interactions with flora and fauna. Facing harsh climates and scarce resources, early humans competed fiercely with wildlife for survival. Through intelligence and innovation, humans overcame physically stronger species—such as lions, elephants, and sharks—eventually emerging as the planet's dominant super-predator (Worm, 2015). This dominance led to large-scale hunting and habitat destruction, driving numerous species to extinction. Evidence suggests human activity contributed to the disappearance of Pleistocene megafauna (Surovell et al., 2016).

For early hominids, avoiding predators was a critical survival challenge. Strategies such as group cooperation, tool use, and weaponry helped humans defend themselves (Hart & Sussman, 2009). Ancient cave paintings and records from civilizations like the Indus Valley, China, Greece, and Egypt document early human-wildlife conflicts, particularly over crop protection, livestock safety, and human survival (Guthrie, 2005). Historical accounts from 300 BC in Asia describe elephant raids on farmland (Sukumar, 1989).

As societies grew, kingdoms and colonial powers implemented predator eradication programs, leading to the near-extinction of species like Chinese tigers, European wolves, American jaguars, African lions and wild dogs, and Falkland wolves (WWF, 2023). Historically, in Western countries like the United States and nations across Europe, the common response to wildlife conflicts—especially involving carnivores—was to eliminate these animals and destroy their habitats (Woodroffe, 2000). However, such actions led to serious ecological consequences, including overpopulation of herbivores and the resulting damage to vegetation.

Across civilizations, wildlife and nature have profoundly shaped cultural traditions, beliefs, and religious practices. For instance (Hill, 2004):

i. The Nanai and Udege peoples of Russia's Far East consider sightings of the Amur tiger a sign of good fortune.
ii. In Hinduism, the goddess Durga is depicted riding a lion while battling evil forces.
iii. The Mesoamerican Mayans revered the jaguar as a sacred bridge between the physical and spiritual realms.
iv. In Hindu culture, the elephant symbolizes Lord Ganesha, the deity who removes obstacles.

Throughout human civilization's development, our species has consistently competed with wildlife for essential needs - sustenance, materials, and living areas. This ongoing struggle has frequently resulted in the disappearance of numerous plant and animal species. However, as societies progressed, they gradually recognized that preserving biodiversity was not just beneficial but critical for their own long-term survival. This realization prompted the creation of innovative coexistence approaches, implemented through updated legal frameworks, policy reforms, institutional support, technological advancements, and evolving societal values.

In the modern era, governments worldwide have shifted toward legal and policy frameworks to better manage human-wildlife interactions, balancing conservation with human needs. Key milestones in HWC management are outlined in Table-1.4, tracing developments since 1987.

Table: 1.4 Important global milestones in the development of HWC management

Year	*Events/mile stones*
1987	The International Bear Association and the International Union for the Conservation of Nature (IUCN) Bear Specialist Group starts to focus on HWC.
1990-2005	IUCN African elephant specialist group gave recommendations on human-elephant conflict management.
2004	IUCN World Parks Congress, South Africa, recognises the need to address growing challenges of HWC.
2005	Book titled, 'People and Wildlife: Conflict or Coexistence?' broadens the discussion on HWC.
2008	Pathways Conference discusses the need to better integrate the human dimension into HWC management.
2009	HWC collaboration, later renamed CPeace, launches capacity building programme on conflict transformation.
2010-2015	Scientists and conservation practitioners recognize HWC as conflicts among different groups of people on wildlife.

2016	IUCN SSC HWC Task Force is set up to support professionals working on HWC.
2019	Book titled, 'HWCs and the need to include Coexistence' broadens the discussion of coexistence concepts.

Source: Gross E, et. al, 2021

Beyond their ecological roles, wildlife holds immense aesthetic, cultural, religious, economic, and educational importance. Therefore, the loss of wildlife can negatively impact overall human well-being (Manfredo et al., 2009). This highlights the interconnectedness of human and wildlife welfare, emphasizing the need for an integrated approach that combines both social and natural sciences to better understand human-wildlife interactions. This integrated perspective is referred to as a socio-ecological system—or human-environment system—where each component depends on the other. Changes in one part of the system, such as human interventions in wildlife management, can lead to unforeseen consequences across the entire system (Folke et al., 2010). A conceptual model of this Socio-ecological system is shown in Figure 1.2.

Large carnivores are particularly vulnerable to human activities due to biological traits like low population densities and slow reproductive rates, as well as social challenges such as inadequate protection and poaching (Carter & Linnell, 2016). As human populations expand and development increases, there is growing overlap in space and time between people and wildlife, often pushing animals to adapt to and coexist within human-altered landscapes.

Figure: 1.2 Framework of Social-Ecological System (SES)

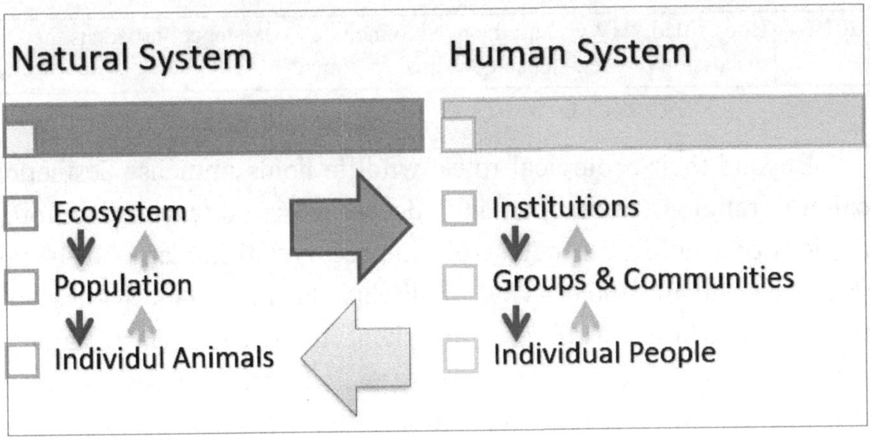

Source: Carter, N.H, et. al. (2016)

1.8 Conclusion

The rising intensity of HWC presents serious obstacles to both conservation efforts and human welfare. As a critical global concern, HWC demands holistic and coordinated solutions. It is essential to develop well-rounded strategies that protect ecosystems while ensuring human safety. Effective conflict mitigation relies on strong partnerships among governments, conservation groups, and local communities to foster peaceful coexistence between humans and wildlife. Although current mitigation approaches offer encouraging results, their long-term effectiveness hinges on sustained habitat protection, active community participation, and consistent implementation of relevant policies. Looking ahead, research should prioritize developing conflict management strategies that are adaptable to climate change.

References

1. Carter, N H & Linnell, J D C (2016), 'Co-adaptation is key to co-existing with large carnivores,' *Trends in Ecology and Evolution*, Vol. 31, No.8, pp. 575-578.

2. Folke, C, et.al. (2010), 'Resilience thinking: Integrating resilience, adaptability and transformability,' *Ecology and Society*, Vol.15, No.4, p.20
3. Gross E, et.al. (2021), *A Future for All: The Need for Human-Wildlife Coexistence*, WWF, Gland, Switzerland.
4. Guerra, A.S. (2019), 'Wolves of the sea: Managing human–wildlife conflict in an increasingly tense ocean', *Marine Policy*, Vol. 99, pp. 369–373.
5. Guthrie, RD (2005), *The Nature of Paleo-lithic Art*, University Chicago Press, Chicago, IL.
6. Guynn, D.E (1997), 'Miracle in Montana- Managing Conflicts over Private Lands and Public Wildlfe Issues,.' *Transactions of the North American Wildlife and Natural Resources Conference,* Vol. 62, pp.146-154
7. Hart D & Sussman, W (2009), Man the Hunted: Primates, *Predators and Human Evolution*, Westview Press, Boulder.
8. Hill, C.M (2004), 'Farmers' perspectives of conflict at the wildlife-agriculture boundary: Some lessons learned from African subsistence farmers,' *Human Dimensions of Wildlife*, Vol.9, pp.279-286.
9. IUCN (2023), *IUCN SSC guidelines on HWC and coexistence*, First Edition, Gland, Switzerland: IUCN
10. Karanth, K.U & Madhusudan, M. D (2002), Mitigating HWCs in Southern Asia, in J. Terborgh, C.P Van Schaik, M. Rao & L. C Davenport (eds.), *Making park work: identifying key factors to implementing parks in the tropics* (pp. 250-264). Convelo, CA: Island Press.
11. Kenya Wildlife Service (KWS). (2023). *Annual HWC Report.*
12. Manfredo, M J, et. al. (2009), 'Linking society and environment: A multilevel model of shifting wildlife value orientations in the western US,' *Social Science Quarterly*, Vol. 90, No. 2, pp. 407-427.

13. Mason et al., (2018), 'Wicked conflict : Using wicked problem thinking for holistic management of conservation conflict,' Conservation Letters, Vol.
14. Michalski, et.al. (2006), 'HWCs in a Fragmented Amazonian Forest Landscape: Determinants of Large Felid Depredation on Livestock,' *Animal Conservation*, Zoological Survey of India, Vo..9, pp.179-188.
15. Peterson, et. al. (2010), 'Rearticulating the Myth of HWC,' *Conservation Letters,* Vol. 3, pp. 74-82.
16. Redpath, SM, et.ail. (2013), 'Understanding and Managing Conservation Conflict's, *Trends in Ecology and Evolution*, Vol.28, pp.100-109.
17. Sukumar, R (1989), *The Asian Elephant: Ecology and Management*, Cambridge University Press, Cambridge.
18. Surovell, TA, et. al. (2016), 'Test of Martin's overkill Hypothesis using Radiocarbon Dates on Extinct Mega fauna,' *Proceedings of the National Academy of Sciences*, Vol. 113, pp.886-891.
19. Trefethen. J.B (1975), *An American Crusade for Wildlife*, Boone and Crockett Club, Alexandria, Virginia.
20. US Fish & Wildlife Service (USFWS). (2023). *Wolf Conflict Statistics*.
21. Wildlife Institute of India (WII). (2022). *National Database on Human-Animal Conflict*.
22. Woodroffe, R (2000), 'Predators and People: Using human densities to interpret declines of large carnivores,' *Animal conservation*, Vol. 3, No.2, pp. 165-173.
23. Worm, B, (2015), 'A Most unusual Super-predator,' *Science*, Vol. 349, pp.784-785.
24. WWF. (2023). *HWC: A Global Challenge*. Retrieved from https://www.wwf.org

CHAPTER: 2
DRIVERS OF HUMAN WILDLIFE CONFLICT

2.1 Introduction

HWC poses a major global challenge, causing loss of life, injuries, and economic losses, while also endangering wildlife populations. HWC arises when human-wildlife interactions lead to harmful outcomes, including crop destruction, livestock attacks, or even human casualties. As people move further into wildlife territories, conflicts escalate, endangering biodiversity and human well-being. To develop successful mitigation measures, it is crucial to understand the underlying factors driving HWC. This chapter analyzes the main causes, emphasizing ecological, economic, and social influences, and stresses the importance of holistic conservation strategies. Chapter also explores the causes such as habitat encroachment and changes in land use. The growing overlap between human settlements and wildlife habitats has worsened conflicts, harming both people and animals. Identifying the root causes of HWC is vital for creating effective solutions.

HWC stems from both natural and human-induced factors. Ecological drivers include seasonal shifts, natural disasters, and wildlife behavioral patterns, while anthropogenic causes include habitat destructions, land-use changes, livestock and farming practices, climate change, resource management, infrastructure expansion, and urbanization (Konig H.J., et al., 2020). When humans and wildlife coexist near forests, shrinking habitats due to human encroachment often lead to increased conflict. Historical, cultural, and perceptual factors further complicate these conflicts, making them harder to predict.

Cultural values, traditions, and personal experiences shape people's tolerance toward wildlife. Public attitudes depend on the extent of damage caused by wildlife, past interactions (positive or negative), social influences, education, and awareness. Urban residents, who rarely encounter wildlife, often hold more favorable views (Triguero-Mas M., et al., 2010). In contrast, rural communities, facing greater exposure and risks from wildlife, tend to have more negative perceptions. Indigenous groups, whose livelihoods are closely tied to nature, traditionally maintain a complex relationship with wildlife and their environment (Goldman M.J., et al., 2010).

2.2 Drivers of HWC

The causes of HWC are highly varied, as illustrated in Figure 2.1. Among them, agricultural expansion accounts for the largest share (30%), followed by the spread of human settlements (24%) and deforestation (IUCN SSC, 2020). These key factors are detailed as below:

i. *Habitat Loss and Fragmentation:* Transforming natural landscapes into farmland, urban centers, and infrastructure is a primary driver of HWC. Deforestation and alterations in land use bring wildlife into closer contact with human populations, raising the likelihood of conflict. According to the World Wildlife Fund, the world has lost about 10% of its forest cover since 2000, heightening tensions in regions such as Sub-Saharan Africa and South Asia (WWF, 2023). Fast-growing human populations are expanding into forested zones, resulting in significant habitat intrusion. For instance, in Kerala, India, the Forest Department has identified 1,004 areas with high conflict potential (MoEFCC, 2023). The clearing of forests for farming and settlements has intensified human-wildlife encounters.

ii. *Climate Change:* Shifts in climate patterns have altered the behavior and distribution of wildlife, contributing to increased conflicts. Droughts and irregular rainfall often push animals to enter human habitations in search of food and water. Nyhus (2023) observed a 30% rise in elephant-related conflicts in Kenya during extended drought periods.

iii. *Agricultural Expansion:* The intrusion of farmland into wildlife habitats often leads to incidents of crop raiding by elephants, wild boars, and primates. According to the Food and Agriculture Organization, roughly 60% of rural communities in India and Nepal suffer crop losses annually due to wildlife activity (FAO, 2022). The closeness of cultivated fields to forests makes them easy targets, especially for elephants. The presence of attractive crops near forest edges draws animals, causing agricultural damage and financial harm to farmers.

iv. *Human Population Growth:* The rapid increase in human numbers places greater demand on natural ecosystems, resulting in the displacement of wildlife. Projections from the United Nations (2023) suggest that Africa's population will double by 2050, potentially worsening conflicts in biodiversity hotspots.

v. *Decline in Natural Prey Populations:* Unsustainable hunting and poaching reduce the availability of wild prey, prompting predators like leopards and lions to attack livestock. A study from Tanzania by Mkonyi et al. (2022) revealed that 45% of lion attacks on livestock occurred in areas where wild prey had become scarce.

vi. *Conservation Translocations and their Consequences:* Though conservation relocations are intended to safeguard wildlife, they can sometimes unintentionally lead to increased HWC. In Malawi, the relocation of 263 elephants to Kasungu National Park in 2022 resulted in at least 10 human deaths and widespread property destruction (Gross, 2021). This event sparked legal action from local communities against the responsible NGO, underlining the importance of thorough planning and community engagement in conservation efforts.

Figure: 2.1 Causes of HWC

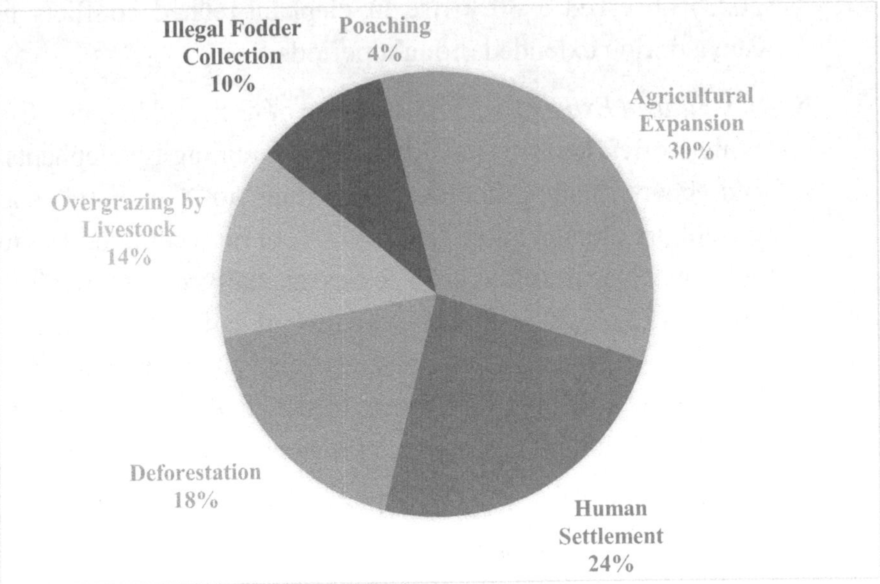

Source: IUCN SSC, 2020

The economic and psychological costs of coexisting with wildlife primarily fall on communities living near forests, while the benefits of species conservation are often enjoyed more broadly. This imbalance exists at both local and global levels. In nations with abundant wildlife, rural and indigenous communities bear the brunt of HWC, whereas urban populations reap the advantages of wildlife preservation. Accordingly, HWC must be differentiated into two types:

i. *Human-Wildlife Impacts:* Direct negative interactions, such as predation, crop damage, livestock loss, attacks, disease transmission, and retaliatory killings.

ii. *Human-Human Conflicts:* Disputes between local communities and conservation authorities over wildlife management, often rooted in historical tensions, competing values, or socio-political inequalities (Madden & McQuinn, 2014).

HWC is a social phenomenon shaped by human interactions, sometimes manifesting as disagreements over wildlife conservation priorities. Multiple ecological and social factors trigger to HWC, including rising human populations and agricultural expansion, increased demand for land, transportation and energy, wildlife population growth and habitat encroachment, climate change, leading to food and water scarcity in forests, and behavioral shifts in wildlife due to environmental pressures.

Urbanization is a major anthropogenic driver, fragmenting habitats through infrastructure development. Vehicle-wildlife collisions are among the most common forms of HWC (Conover, 2002). In regions like Brazil, the decline of natural predators has turned herbivores like capybaras and wild boars into agricultural pests (Marchini & Crawshaw, 2015). As human populations grow, farmland expansion continues to displace wildlife. In Africa, increasing livestock numbers have significantly altered wildlife habitats, with grazing systems covering nearly 30% of the Earth's ice-free land (Thornton, 2010).

Additional contributing factors included the following (Duncan et al., 2014).

i. Growth in outdoor recreation and human settlements,
ii. Wildlife adapting to urban environments,
iii. Natural resource extraction (mining, oil exploration) threatening ecosystems.

A summary of key HWC drivers and impacts is provided in Table 2.1.

Table: 2.1 Key drivers and pressures leading to HWC

Drivers	Pressures	Impacts
1. Human population dynamics 2. Human resource requirements 3. Land use changes 4. Extractive industries	1. Habitat loss and fragmentation 2. Disturbance of wildlife 3. Blocking of wildlife corridors 4. Extreme weather events 5. Natural calamities	1. Crop damage 2. Property damage 3. Livestock damage 4. Food and livelihood insecurity 5. Human loss of life and injuries

5. Linear infrastructure 6. Perceptions of nature 7. Market forces 8. Policy effects 9.Wildlife population dynamics 10. Wildlife behaviour 11. Climate change	6. Invasive species 7. Economic hardship 8. Attractants such as waste, human food, highly palatable crops, and livestock	6. Decreased human wellbeing and health 7. Change in tolerance of wildlife 8. Non-lethal control of wildlife 9. Translocation of wildlife 10. Culling of wildlife 11. Retaliatory or defensive killing of wildlife

Source: Gross E, et. al, 2021

Biological factors, including the age, health, and gender of wild animals, as well as their spatial distribution, play a significant role in influencing HWC. Research indicates that older, injured, or sick animals may struggle to hunt wild prey, and in certain species, younger individuals may exclude weaker members from their groups (Lambert et al., 2006). As a result, carnivores often target livestock as easier prey, while herbivores raid nearby crops. Male animals tend to exhibit more aggressive behaviour, posing a greater threat to communities living near forests. For instance, male elephants are frequently involved in crop raiding across both Asia and Africa (Sukumar & Gadgil, 1988). Social learning also contributes to conflict patterns, as demonstrated in studies from Kenya's Amboseli National Park, where just ten elephants were responsible for over half of all crop raids (Chiyo et al., 2011a). Similarly, male big cats are more likely to prey on livestock when venturing into human settlements (Patterson, 2004). The relationship between HWC and their associated interventions is illustrated in Figure 2.2.

Figure: 2.2 Relationship between HWC and their Associated Interventions

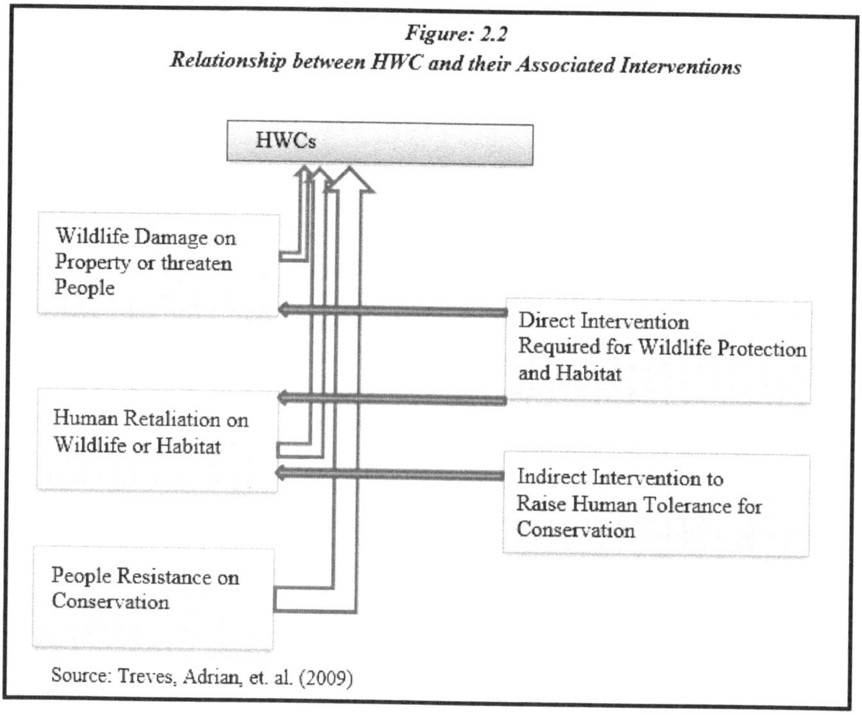

Human-related factors, including cultural beliefs, emotional experiences, economic conditions, governance structures, and community engagement, also shape the nature of HWC. Public perceptions of wildlife are further influenced by cultural values, historical interactions, ideological beliefs, innate fears, and the perceived novelty of risk (Dickman, 2010). Gender also plays a significant role in HWC, particularly in rural areas of developing countries where women often bear a disproportionate burden due to their daily interactions with natural resources.

2.3 Socio-cultural Dimensions of HWC

HWC is often a reflection of deeper human-human tensions, such as disputes between local communities and authorities, or between groups with differing cultural backgrounds. Research indicates that communities are generally more accepting of the risks and challenges posed by wildlife when they arise organically, rather than being imposed by external forces (Roskaft et al., 2003). People with long-standing experience of coexisting with wildlife usually show lower levels of fear towards animals.

Societal reactions to wildlife incidents vary significantly across regions, and even minor events can lead to disproportionate responses. For instance, in Hokkaido, Japan, a bear alert in 1966 led to the killing of 39 bears (Knight, 2000). Similarly, an incident in Namibia during the 1980s prompted the killing of 700 cheetahs in retaliation (Marker, 2002). In some Asian and African countries, cultural and spiritual beliefs also shape attitudes toward wildlife. In Mozambique, a belief exists that certain ethnic groups can use sorcery to turn twigs into spirit-lions to attack rival communities, leading to mass lion killings (West, 2001). Many HWCs arise from clashing goals among various stakeholders and interest groups, particularly when wildlife is seen as a resource to be exploited for economic or cultural gains (White & Ward, 2010). These conflicts are further complicated by rapid population growth and developmental pressures that threaten wildlife conservation.

Culturally, human attitudes toward nature can generally be categorized into two perspectives: one that sees humans as being subject to nature, and another that promotes human dominance over it. These differing views are rooted in the transition from hunter-gatherer societies to pastoral ones. Some cultures view this shift as a sign of progress through the control of nature (Ingold, 1994). Western religions have been associated with fostering a divide between humans and nature, supporting the idea of human superiority over the environment (White, 1967). In contrast, many Eastern religions advocate for the interconnectedness and equality of all life forms, often revering nature as a nurturing force (Dwitvedi, 2001). Furthermore, some scholars argue that the emergence of scientific rationalism combined with Calvinist ideologies encouraged capitalist expansion and colonization, particularly in North America (Weber, 1948).

Generally, individualistic cultures tend to promote competition for natural resources and wildlife, while collectivist cultures focus on sharing and cooperative use of these resources.

Environmental factors also contribute to HWC, including features of the landscape (such as forest-edge zones) and the presence or absence of alternative food sources for wild animals. Additionally, societal beliefs and values significantly influence how communities perceive and respond to such conflicts. For example, Hazzah (2006) found that Evangelical Christian values were associated with increased hostility towards wildlife, whereas Ale (1998) noted that Buddhist herders in Nepal historically viewed snow leopard attacks as divine retribution, accepting them without retaliation.

People's values and how they express them shape their perspectives on wildlife. While some view killing wildlife for human benefit as justified, others regard it as cruel and unacceptable. These differing attitudes are rooted in fundamental beliefs formed early in life. To better understand these viewpoints, the concept of Wildlife Value Orientation (WVO) was developed, highlighting two contrasting perspectives: Wildlife Protection Orientation (WPO) and Wildlife Use Orientation (WUO). WPO holds that wildlife has intrinsic rights, like humans, and is embraced by cultures that prioritize coexistence. In contrast, WUO supports the idea that wildlife should serve human needs, often promoting a more exploitative approach to nature. A comprehensive model outlining the factors influencing HWC is presented in Figure 2.3.

Figure: 2.3

Factors Affecting Intensity of HWC – A Model

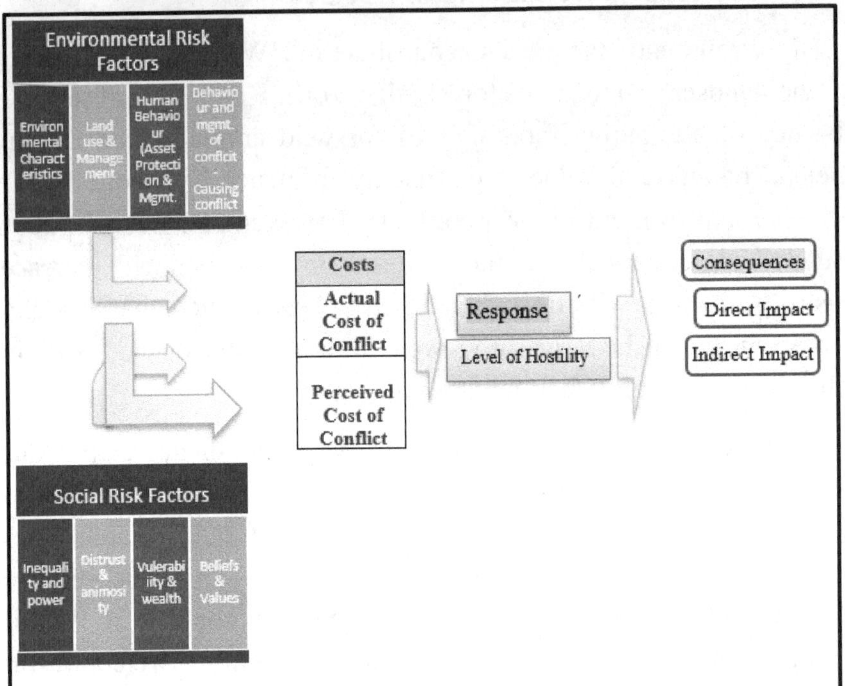

Source: Dickman AJ (2010)

In a post-materialistic society, the focus shifts towards improving quality of life and personal fulfillment. A key distinction between materialist and post-materialist values is seen in their approach to wildlife: materialists typically align with the Wildlife Use Orientation (WUO), emphasizing the utilitarian value of animals, while post-materialists are more inclined toward the Wildlife Protection Orientation (WPO), prioritizing the intrinsic rights of wildlife (Manfredo & Ashley, 2004).

Emerging trends present two major challenges for wildlife professionals. First is the paradigm shift from conservation—aimed at increasing wildlife populations—to management, which often involves regulating or reducing those populations (Marchini & Crawshaw, 2015). Second is the evolving nature of human tolerance toward wildlife, emphasizing the importance of understanding the human dimension in wildlife management. These shifts reflect a growing interdisciplinary approach that incorporates ecological, social, and behavioral sciences into conservation strategies and public policy.

Human attitudes toward wildlife are shaped by numerous factors, including social groups and their influence on policymaking, which is often constrained by their proximity to power structures within the government (Lute et al., 2014). Economic development has also influenced societal values, moving from subsistence-based mindsets to those centered on self-expression, significantly impacting how wildlife is perceived. Cultural variations play a role as well—for example, traditional societies in India and Mongolia often demonstrate high tolerance for wildlife (Athreya et al., 2013). These findings indicate that human tolerance toward wildlife conflict is not solely based on perception but is dynamic, shifting with cultural change and modernization.

Accordingly, the social dimensions of HWC can be examined across three distinct levels:

i. *Level I Conflict:* This level involves immediate emotional reactions such as anger and frustration due to wildlife-induced damages. These responses typically represent the surface-level disputes that arise directly from loss or harm.

ii. *Level II Conflict:* When individuals repeatedly experience negative impacts from HWC, deeper concerns emerge—often highlighting inadequate government intervention, insufficient compensation, or ineffective conflict resolution mechanisms. These issues complicate and escalate the situation.

iii. *Level III Conflict:* This level delves into more entrenched conflicts that are shaped by broader socio-cultural and historical factors. Examples include forced resettlement of communities, restricted access to culturally significant sites, or the criminalization of traditional hunting practices (Gross, 2019).

2.4 Conclusion

HWC has become a major global conservation and socio-economic issue, driven by interrelated ecological, human, and climatic factors. Key contributors include habitat loss and fragmentation due to agriculture, urbanization, and infrastructure, which push wildlife into human settlements, leading to increased crop raiding and livestock attacks. Climate change worsens the situation by reducing natural food and water sources, forcing animals to seek resources in human areas. Anthropogenic activities like land-use change and overgrazing further intensify competition for space and food between humans and wildlife. Infrastructure such as roads and railways also disrupt animal movement and raise collision risks.

Socio-cultural factors influence how communities perceive and respond to HWC. Rural populations often have negative attitudes due to direct losses, while urban groups tend to be more supportive of wildlife. Gender, governance, and community involvement also shape conflict dynamics, with weak policies and exclusion from conservation decisions fueling resentment. Biological aspects such as animal age, injury, and behavior also affect conflict patterns. Some animals, like lone elephants or old predators, are more likely to cause damage, and social learning among wildlife can perpetuate conflict.

In summary, HWC arises from a complex mix of environmental degradation, climate pressures, human actions, and cultural attitudes. Solutions require integrated approaches, including habitat restoration, community engagement, and equitable conservation policies, to foster peaceful coexistence between humans and wildlife.

References

1. Ale, S (1998), 'Culture and Conservation: the Snow Leopard in Nepal,' *International Snow Leopard Trust Newsletter*, Vol. 16, p.10.

2. Athreya V, et. al. (2013), 'Big cats in our backyards: Persistence of large carnivores in a human dominated landscape in India', *PLoS ONE*, Vol. 8, No.3, pp. 57-72
3. Carpenter et al. (2000), 'Stakeholder acceptance capacity in wildlife management,' *Human Dimensions of Wildlife*, vol. 5, pp. 5–19.
4. Chartier, et. al (2011), 'Habitat Loss and Human-elephant Conflict in Assam, India: Does a Critical Threshold Exist?,' *Oryx*, Vol. 45, pp.528-533.
5. Chiyo, P I, et. al. (2011a), 'Using Molecular and Observational Techniques to Estimate the Number and Raiding Patterns of Crop-raiding Elephants,' *Journal of Applied Ecology*, Vol. 48, pp. 788-796.
6. Conover (1997), 'Monetary and intangible valuation of deer in the United States,' *Wildlife Society Bulletin,* Vol. 25, pp. 298–305.
7. Conover, M.R (2002), *Resolving HWCs: the Science of Wildlife Damage Management,* Lewis Publishers, Boc Raton, Florida, USA.
8. Dickman AJ (2010), 'Complexities of Conflict: the Importance f Considering Social Factors for Effectively Resolving HWC,' *Animal Conservation*, Vol. 13, pp.458-466.
9. Duncan, C, et. al. (2014), 'Oil in the Sahara: Mapping Anthropogenic Threats to Saharan Biodiversity from Space,' *Philosophical Transactions of the Royal Society* B369:20130191.
10. Dwitvedi O.P (2001), 'Satyagraha for Conservation: Awakening the Spirit of Hinduism,' in L.P Pojman (Ed.), *Environmental Ethics*, Wadsworth/Thomson Learning, Belmont, pp. 29-50.
11. FAO. (2022). *Crop Damage by Wildlife: Global Assessment.* Rome: FAO.

12. Fulton, et. al. (1996), 'Wildlife Value Orientations: A Conceptual and Measurement Approach,' *Human Dimensions of Wildlife*, Vol. 1, No. 2, pp. 24-47.
13. Goldman M.J., Roque De Pinho J. Perry J (2010), 'Maintaining Complex Relations with Large Cats: Maasai and Lions in Kenya and Tanzania,' *Human Dimensions of Wildlife*, Vol. 15, No. 5, pp. 332-346.
14. Gross E.M (2019), *Tackling routes to coexistence. Human-elephant conflict in sub-Saharan Africa*, GIZ Partnership against Poaching and Illegal Wildlife Trade, Eschborn, Germany.
15. Gross E, et.al. (2021), *A Future for All: The Need for Human-Wildlife Coexistence*, WWF, Gland, Switzerland.
16. Hazzah, L.N (2006), *Living among Lions: Coexistence or Killing? Community Attitude towards Conservation Initiatives and the Motivations behind Lion Killing in Kenyan Maasailand*, University of Wisconsin-Madison .
17. Ingold T (1994), 'From Trust to Domination: An Alternative History of Human-animal Relations,' in A. Manning & J. Serpell (eds.), *Animals and Human Society*, Routledge, New York, pp. 1-22.
18. IUCN. (2023). *Red List of Threatened Species*. Gland, Switzerland.
19. IUCN Species Survival Commission (SSC) HWC Task Force. (2020). *IUCN SSC position statement on the management of HWC*. HWCTF.
20. Knight, J (2000), 'Culling Demons: the Problem of Bears in Japan,' *Natural enemies- People-wildlife Conflicts in Anthropological Perspective*, Routledge, London, pp.145-169.
21. Konig H.J., et. al. (2020), 'Human-wildlife coexistence in a changing world,' *Conservation Biology*, Vol. 34, No. 4, pp. 786-749.

22. Lambert CMS, et. al. (2006), 'Cougar Population Dynamics and Viability in the Pacific Northwest,' Wildlife Management, Vo. 70, pp. 246-254.
23. Lute, M.L & Gore, M L (2014), 'Knowledge and power in wildlife management,' *The Journal of Wildlife Management,* Vol. 78, No. 6, pp.1060-1068.
24. Madden, F., McQuinn, B. (2014), 'Conservation's blind spot: The case for conflict transformation in wildlife conservation,' *Biological Conservation*, Vol. 178, pp. 97–106.
25. Manfredo, M J & Ashley A D (2004), 'Concepts of Exploring the Social Aspects of HWC in a Global Context,' *Human Dimensions of Wildlife*, Vol. 9, pp. 317-328.
26. Marchini S & P. G Crawshaw (2015), 'HWCs in Brazil: A Fast-growing Issue,' *Human Dimensions of Wildlife*, Vol. 20, pp. 323-328.
27. Marker, L (2002), *Aspects of Cheetah – Biology, Ecology and Conservation Strategies on Namibian Farmlands*, University of Oxford, Oxford.
28. Mkonyi, F., et al. (2022). "Livestock Predation and Prey Depletion in Tanzania." *Journal of Wildlife Management,* 86(4), 789-801.
29. MoEFCC. (2023). *Human-Elephant Conflict Report*. New Delhi: Government of India.
30. Nyhus, P. (2023). "Climate Change and HWC in Africa." *Conservation Biology*, 37(2), 112-125.
31. Patterson B D, et. al. (2004), 'Livestock Predation by Lions and Other Carnivores on Ranches Neighbouring Tsavo National Park, Kenya,' *Biological Conservation*, Vol. 119, pp. 507-516.
32. Roskaft, et. al. (2003), 'Pattern of Self-reported Fear towards Large Carnivores among the Norwegian Public,' *Evolutionary Human Behaviour*, Vol. 24, pp. 184-198.
33. Shen Z & K. Ma (2014), 'Effects of Climate Change on Biodiversity,' *Chinese Science Bulletin*,pp.1-2.

34. Sukumar, R & Gadgil M (1988), 'Male-Female Differences in Foraging on Crops by Asian Elephants,' *Animal Behaviour*, Vol. 36, pp.1233-1235
35. Thornton, P.K (2010), 'Livestock Production: Recent Trends, Future Prospects,' *Philosophical Transactions of the Royal Society of London Royal Society of Biological Science*, Vol. 365, pp.2853-2867.
36. Treves, Adrian, et.al. (2006), 'Co-managing HWCs: A Review,' *Human Dimensions of Wildlife,* Vol.11, pp.383-396.
37. Triguero-Mas M., et. al. (2010), 'Urban and rural perceptions of protected areas: a case study in Dandeli Wildlife Sanctuary, Western Ghats, India,' *Environmental Conservation*, Vol. 36, No. 3, pp. 208-217.
38. UN. (2023). *World Population Prospects*. New York: United Nations.
39. Weber M (1948), *The Protestant Ethics and the Spirit of Capitalism*, Scribner, New York.
40. West, H (2001), 'Sorcery of Construction and Socialist Modernisation- Ways of Understanding Power in Post-Colonial Mozambique,' *American Ethnologist*, Vol. 28, pp. 119-150.
41. White L (1967), 'The Historical Roots of our Environmental Crisis,' *Science*, Vol. 155, No. 3767, pp. 1203-1207.
42. White, P C. L. & Alastair I. Ward (2010), 'Interdisciplinary approaches for the management of existing and emerging human–wildlife conflicts,' *Wildlife Research*, Vol. 37, No.8, pp. 623-629.
43. WWF. (2023). *Living Planet Report*. Gland, Switzerland.

CHAPTER: 3
IMPLICATIONS OF CLIMATE CHANGE

3.1 Introduction

Climate change is worsening HWC globally, creating serious risks for both ecosystems and human populations. As temperatures rise, precipitation patterns shift, and habitats degrade, wildlife increasingly encroaches on human settlements, resulting in more frequent cases of crop destruction, livestock attacks, and even human casualties. HWC arises when wildlife behavior negatively affects human livelihoods or when human activities harm wildlife (Nyhus, 2016). Climate change intensifies these conflicts by disrupting habitats, reducing food sources, and changing species distributions (IPCC, 2022). Extreme weather events, shifting temperatures, and altered rainfall patterns push animals into human-occupied areas, escalating competition over resources and conflict frequency.

Addressing HWC demands a collaborative effort from various fields, including climate science, animal behaviour, conservation biology, ecology, genetics, wildlife management, zoology, anthropology, economics, environmental studies, geography, history, natural resource management, political science, psychology, and technology (Nair, 2009). Over the last twenty years, managing HWC has become a greater priority due to its worldwide impact on communities and its hindrance to conservation and sustainable development goals.

This chapter investigate how climate change influences HWC and examine how climate change affects forest ecosystems and biodiversity, contributing to species extinction. For instance, due to shifts in rainfall patterns, elephants in Kenya are encroaching on agricultural lands, resulting in considerable crop destruction and clashes with farmers. In another case, warmer winters and shorter hibernation periods are prompting bears in North America to search for food earlier in the year, leading to more frequent interactions with humans.

According to recent estimates (IPCC, 2022), around 25% of the world's mammal species and 12% of bird species face a high risk of global extinction. While climate change plays a significant role, it is just one of many threats to wildlife. Other major challenges include overexploitation, pollution and toxic chemical exposure, wildlife diseases, collisions with man-made structures like towers, barriers that limit animal movement, and human conflicts such as war. These factors collectively heighten the risk of species becoming rare or extinct. Additionally, habitat loss and degradation impact nearly 89% of threatened bird species and 83% of threatened mammal species.

The 2024 WWF Living Planet Report indicates that global wildlife populations have decreased by 73% over the last five decades, with the most severe declines seen in Latin America and the Caribbean (95%), followed by Africa (76%) and the Asia-Pacific region (60%). This reduction is primarily due to habitat destruction, overexploitation, pollution, invasive species, and climate change (Le Monde).

HWC can endanger human lives, cause financial problems, and threaten access to food (Redpath et al., 2013). Factors like climate change, habitat loss, and deforestation are predicted to worsen HWC (Mason et al., 2018). This issue has widespread effects, impacting the environment, society, the economy, and even political stability in many developing countries (Guerra, 2019). A survey conducted by the World Bank found that 73% of countries are experiencing a rise in HWC, with low-income nations being the hardest hit. The main issues reported include crop damage (79%), livestock predation (60%), and human injuries or deaths (57%) (World Bank). A summary of climate change and HWC globally is presented in Table-3.1.

Table: 3.1 Recent Climate-Related HWC Incidents (2018–2023)

Region	*Wildlife Species*	*Conflict Type*	*Climate Drivers*
Arctic (Canada)	Polar bears	Human encounters	Sea ice loss
East Africa	Elephants	Crop raiding	Drought
South Asia	Tigers	Livestock attacks	Mangrove loss
Amazon (Brazil)	Jaguars	Predation on livestock	Deforestation & fires
North America	Black bears	Urban foraging	Reduced natural food

Sources: Atwood et al. (2020), Thirgood et al. (2021), Mukherjee et al. (2022), Marchini et al. (2021), Baruch-Mordo et al. (2021)

3.2 Climate Change and Forest Management

Forests and climate change maintain a deeply interconnected and reciprocal relationship. Climatic elements such as temperature, solar radiation, rainfall patterns, and atmospheric CO_2 concentrations play a fundamental role in shaping forest ecosystems. At the same time, forests actively influence climate dynamics through carbon storage, solar energy absorption, cooling via evapotranspiration, and aerosol emissions that affect cloud formation. This two-way interaction is visually represented in Figure 3.1.

Projections indicate that climate change will significantly transform forest ecosystems, requiring adaptive management approaches. These changes may include large-scale biome shifts or more gradual alterations in forest growth and productivity (Aber et al., 2001). Increasing temperatures and prolonged droughts pose serious threats to forest biodiversity while diminishing forests' capacity to deliver crucial ecosystem benefits (Gnacadja & Lesch, 2009).

Human activities - particularly land-use changes, deforestation, fossil fuel consumption, and industrial operations - stand as primary drivers of climate change, alongside natural factors like solar variability and volcanic eruptions. Forest destruction and degradation alone contribute nearly 20% of global greenhouse gas emissions (GHGs), making them significant climate change accelerators.

Conversely, climate change itself intensifies deforestation pressures, creating a destructive feedback loop.

Historically, forests blanketed about 45% of the earth's terrestrial surface, but agricultural expansion and other human activities have reduced this coverage to approximately 30% (Khaine, et al. 2015). Contemporary deforestation persists at an alarming rate of 0.14% annually, equating to the loss of 5.2 million hectares each year (FAO, 2012). This continuous depletion of forest cover not only exacerbates climate change but also represents a critical decline in vital ecosystem services that support life on earth.

The complex interplay between forest systems and climatic conditions underscores the urgent need for integrated conservation strategies that address both environmental protection and climate change mitigation. Sustainable forest management practices must be implemented to preserve these vital ecosystems while maintaining their climate regulation functions (Ravindranath, et al. 2010). Only through such comprehensive approaches can we hope to break the destructive cycle between forest degradation and climate change.

Figure: 3.1 Relation between Forest and Climate Change

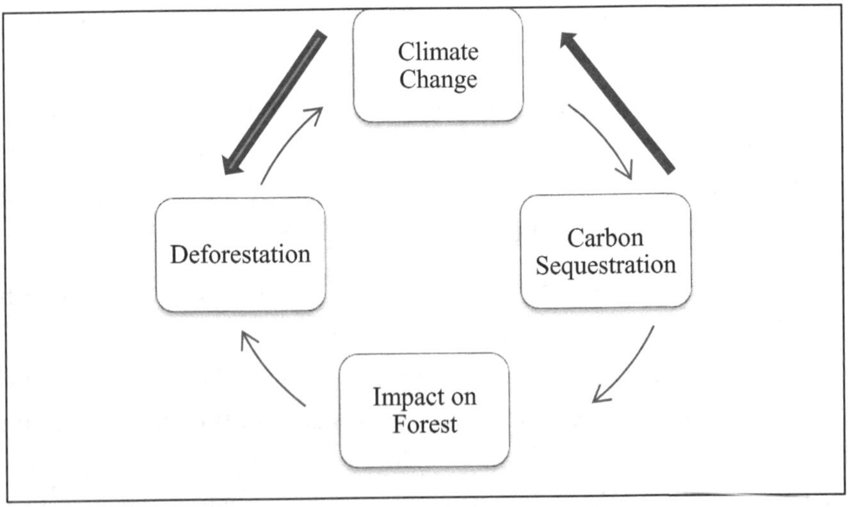

Source: Khaine, Inkyin & Su Young Woo (2015)

Forest growth is strongly tied to climate, especially how much water is available (Toledo et al., 2011). Warmer temperatures and more rainfall can boost tree growth, while long periods of dryness hinder it. Even sunlight plays a role. Forests are crucial for taking care of the environment by storing carbon, conserving water, and protecting soil. How well we conserve the environment greatly affects how much carbon forests can hold. Globally, forests contain over 650 billion tons of carbon, with about 44% in the trees themselves, 45% in the soil, and 11% in dead wood and fallen leaves (FAO, 2010).

Recent research suggests a worrying future for forests. Global warming might cause forests to lose their ability to regulate carbon, and by the end of this century, land ecosystems could actually release more carbon dioxide than they absorb (Seppala et al., 2009). Studies indicate that climate change will lead to significant changes in vegetation and biodiversity. Research in India suggests that around 39% of its forested areas are susceptible to climate change (Chaturvedi et al., 2011). Climate impact predictions estimate that by 2085, 68% to 77% of India's forest regions could undergo major transformations, including the disappearance of current forest types and the emergence of new ones (Ravindranath et al., 2010). Climate change threatens unique forest ecosystems and biodiversity, potentially causing species to go extinct.

Sustainable forest management has become an important way to adapt to climate change. It ensures that actions to adapt to and reduce climate change consider the economic, social, and environmental value of forests (Nair, 2010). Using a landscape-wide approach can improve forest-based efforts to adapt to and reduce climate change, leading to the best possible outcomes for the environment, society, and the economy. Adaptation involves changing ecosystems, communities, and economies in response to the effects of climate change (Smit et al., 2000). Successful adaptation in forest management requires planning ahead, setting future goals for forests under changing conditions, raising awareness, assessing how vulnerable forests and societies are, developing cost-effective ways to adapt, reducing risks, and continuously monitoring forest health (Holling, 2001).

Strategies for adapting to climate change should be included in broader plans to manage risks and minimize future losses. The way we manage forests today is largely based on past climate conditions. Policymakers and forest managers need to recognize that climate change is a real danger to forests and communities (Nair, 2022). Effective adaptation involves assessing research and education needs, evaluating forest management strategies, identifying existing obstacles, updating forest policies, setting up monitoring systems, and deciding on appropriate levels of intervention (Spittlehouse & Stewart, 2003). A detailed plan for climate adaptation in forest management is provided in Table-3.2.

Table: 3.2 Climate Adaptive Actions in Forest Management

Areas	*Actions*	*Remarks*
1. Gene Management	i. Determining the responses of species and genotypes to climate and the limits of their transferability, and developing climate-based seed zones that will change over time ii. Breeding for pest resistance and for a wider tolerance to a range of climate stresses and extremes in specific genotypes iii. Re-evaluating seed orchard locations. iv. Planting a mixture of provenances at a site v. Re-evaluating conservation and recovery programs.	Climate change will affect the geographic extent of the zones
2. Forest Protection	i. Any future increases in wildfire are expected to overwhelm the ability of fire management agencies to respond to all occurrences.	Rapid changes are the outcome of fire, wind, ice storms, and pests.

	ii. Altering forest structure (e.g., tree spacing and density, standing dead trees, or coarse woody debris on the forest floor) to reduce the risk and extent of disturbance; increasing use of prescribed burning to minimize fuel loading. iii. Developing "fire-smart" landscapes by using harvesting, regeneration, and stand-tending activities that manage fuels to control the spread of wildfire. iv. Enhancing Forest recovery after fire disturbances. v. Partial cutting or thinning to increase stand vigour and lower the susceptibility to attack. vi. Reducing disease losses through sanitation cuts that remove infected trees. vii. Shortening the rotation length to decrease the period of stand vulnerability to damaging insects and diseases and facilitating change to more suitable species. viii. Using insecticides and fungicides in situations where silvicultural activities for insect pest management are ineffective or inappropriate. ix. Using genotypes bred for improved resistance to pests.	
3. Forest Regeneration	i. Identifying drought-tolerant genotypes. ii. Assisting the migration of commercial tree species from their present to future ranges through artificial regeneration. iii. Planting provenances that grow adequately under a wide	Existing forests are quite resistant to climate variability, it is the regeneration phase that will initially be susceptible to the changed climate.

	range of conditions and planting stock from a range of provenances at a site. iv. Controlling undesirable plant species, which become more competitive in a changed climate, through vegetation management treatments.	
4. Silvicultural Management	i. Pre-commercially thinning or selectively removing suppressed, damaged, or poor quality individuals to increase light, water, and nutrient availability to the remaining trees. ii. Reducing vulnerability to future disturbances by managing tree density, species composition, forest structure iii. Under-planting with other species or genotypes where the current advanced regeneration is unacceptable as a source for the future forest. iv. Reducing the rotation age followed by planting to speed the establishment of better-adapted forest types.	Nutrient availability and acclimation by trees are likely to limit the potential for increased growth due to higher concentration of atmospheric carbon dioxide. Warmer sites may see increased respiration, offsetting any gains.
5. Forest Operations	i. Increasing the amount of timber from salvage logging of fire- or insect-disturbed stands. ii. Advanced planning for climate change allows for infrastructure replacement as part of the normal replacement cycle. iii. Mitigating the impacts on infrastructure, fish, and potable water supplies, of changes in the timing of peak flow and volume in streams resulting from increased precipitation.	Biological and climate changes have implications for forest operations.

	iv. Including adaptation planning in forest certification as part of a risk management strategy. v. Mitigating climate change through forest carbon management, and evaluating the risk of climate change to carbon stocks. vi. Increasing the use of forests for biomass energy. vii. Developing policies to facilitate the creation and implementation of adaptive management responses to climate change.	
6. Non-timber Resources	i. Minimizing fragmentation of habitat and maintaining connectivity. ii. Maintaining representative forest types across environmental gradients and protecting primary forests. iii. Maintaining diversity of functional groups as well as species within groups.	Climate change will affect habitat quality and availability for wildlife and influence predator/ prey synchrony
7. Wilderness Area Management	i. Managing to delay, ameliorate, and direct change. ii. Identifying and planting alternate tree species. iii. Conserving biodiversity and maintaining connectivity in a varied, dynamic landscape to aid vegetation and wildlife migration as the climate changes.	Traditional measures may not be feasible under changed climate, given that the values and attributes the park or wilderness areas were designed to protect may no longer exist within the protected area.

Source: Spittlehouse D L & R B. Stewart (2003)

3.3 Climate Change as Drivers of HWC

Climate change involves long-term shifts in global temperature and weather conditions. Although natural variations occur, human activities—particularly greenhouse gas emissions—have significantly accelerated these changes. According to the IPCC, if emissions continue unchecked, global temperatures may rise by 1.5°C to 2°C above pre-industrial levels by 2100. Research indicates a 40% rise in HWC incidents across Africa (2010–2022) due to climate variability (WWF, 2023). Similarly, in South Asia, 60% of HWC cases result from climate-induced habitat changes (Dave & Jhala, 2023). While HWC has historically been driven by habitat loss and resource competition, climate change is now amplifying these conflicts by altering ecosystems and wildlife behavior. Recognizing the link between climate change and HWC is essential for crafting effective conservation measures and ensuring community safety. Some of the important habitats affected due to climate change are given in Table 3.3.

Table: 3.3 Habitats at Risk Due to Climate Change

Habitat Type	*Projected Changes by 2050*	*Regions Affected*
Forests	Increased mortality from pests	Amazon, Southeast Asia
Wetlands	Increased flooding and droughts	North America, Africa
Coastal Areas	Sea-level rise	Pacific Islands, Bangladesh
Grasslands	Altered rainfall patterns	Africa, Central Asia

Source: World Bank. (2023), WWF. (2023)

Climate change and increasing climate variability significantly influence HWC by altering the availability of food and water resources for wildlife, particularly during prolonged droughts (Shen & Ma, 2014). The scarcity of the essential resources, along with other ecological factors, can escalate conflicts between humans and wildlife. For instance, the decline in natural prey populations or the seasonal migration of herbivores often leads to increased raids on crops and livestock by wild animals. Research from India highlights how shrinking forest cover and habitat loss have intensified conflicts involving elephants (Chartier et al., 2011). The timing and frequency of these conflicts vary widely across species and even within the same species. Additionally, the spatial distribution of wildlife and human settlements plays a crucial role in shaping HWC dynamics, with proximity to protected areas serving as a key predictor of conflict occurrence.

Africa is witnessing a dangerous escalation in HWC as climate change reshapes ecosystems and forces unprecedented interactions between people and animals. Rising temperatures and erratic weather patterns are transforming habitats, disrupting wildlife behavior, and driving species into human-dominated landscapes in their search for sustenance. This collision between human needs and wildlife survival is creating a crisis that undermines livelihoods, threatens food security, and jeopardizes decades of conservation progress.

Box: 3.1 Indicators of Climate Warming in Western Antarctic: Chinstrap Vs Adélie penguins

Over the past 50 years, midwinter surface air temperatures in the Western Antarctic Peninsula (WAP) have risen by 4–5°C. Research indicates that this warming has significantly altered the timing and distribution of winter sea-ice formation in the region. Over the last 25 years, populations of Chinstrap and Adélie penguins—two species with similar diets and overlapping breeding areas—have shown contrasting trends. While Adélies rely on pack ice for survival, Chinstraps prefer open water and tend to avoid ice-covered areas. During this period, Adélie penguin numbers have declined by 22%, whereas Chinstrap populations have surged by over 400%. This stark difference highlights how the warming climate and resulting increase in open water are benefiting the ice-averse Chinstraps while disadvantaging the ice-dependent Adélies.

Source: IPCC (2022)

The climate crisis manifests most dramatically through prolonged droughts that devastate both wildlife and human communities. As water holes dry up and vegetation disappears, massive herbivores like elephants, buffalo, and hippos increasingly raid crops—sometimes destroying a season's harvest in a single night. Countries including

Kenya, Tanzania, and Botswana report surging elephant incursions during dry periods, leaving subsistence farmers with nothing (Roe, 1998). These encounters frequently turn deadly, as frightened or angry communities resort to killing animals that threaten their survival.

Carnivores face equally dire challenges as climate change disrupts their food chains. Lions, leopards, and hyenas, struggling to find their natural prey due to habitat degradation, increasingly target livestock instead (Pillai, et. al. 2010). For pastoralist communities already grappling with climate stresses, each lost cow or goat represents an economic catastrophe—often triggering retaliatory killings that push vulnerable predator populations closer to extinction.

Box: 3.2 Zimbabwe's Elephant Conflicts

In Zimbabwe, extended droughts have forced elephants to enter villages in search of food and water, leading to damaged crops, destroyed infrastructure, and even human fatalities. To address this, a GPS tracking system has been implemented to monitor elephant movements and alert communities in advance. These early warning systems, like wildlife GPS tracking, can help communities better prepare for and prevent potential conflicts. In Zimbabwe, this approach has shown potential in minimizing interactions between humans and elephants.

Source: AP News

Climate change is scrambling the ancient migratory clocks of African wildlife. Species are altering their movement routes and timing, sometimes appearing unexpectedly in human settlements (Western, et al. 2009). Traditional wildlife corridors are vanishing due to combined pressures of climate shifts and human expansion, creating new conflict hotspots across the continent.

Table: 3.4 Impact of Climate Change on Wildlife

Wildlife	*Region*	*Climate related driver*	*Climate change effects on Wildlife*
Venomous jellyfish	Global	Ocean warming	Increased jellyfish blooms
Venomous snakes	South Asia, South America, southern US	Increased heavy rainfall events and flooding	Snakes are forced into the open and into closer contact with humans
Bull shark	Coastlines worldwide	Ocean warming	Poleward range expansion
Great white shark	Sundarbans mangrove forest	SLR & extreme weather events	Humans forced to enter deeper into forests for livelihoods
Venomous snakes	Himalayas	Higher average temperatures	Uphill shift of tree line and habitat lines
Tiger	Across tigers' range	Environmental stress (droughts, flooding)	Loss of prey; short-term displacement leading to tigers intruding into human-dominated areas
Tiger	Vidarbha, India	Higher average temperatures	Shift in tiger movement, often utilising agricultural land
Leopard	Leopard's range	Environmental stress (droughts, flood)	Loss of prey; short-term displacement leading to leopards intruding into human-dominated areas
Lion	African grasslands	Drought	Livestock herders encroaching on protected areas
Jaguar	South America	Drought	Loss of natural prey brings jaguars into closer human contact in search of livestock/ anthropogenic food sources and may even trigger predatory attacks
Brown bear	Across species range	Higher seasonal temperatures	Shortened hibernation period
Asiatic/Himalayan black bear	Across species range	Higher seasonal temperatures	Shortened hibernation period

Polar bear	Arctic	Loss of Arctic Sea ice	Change in seasonal migration, polar bears spend more time on land
Hyena	Botswana, Zimbabwe	Drought	Increased attacks on livestock and even humans as natural food sources dwindle
African elephant	African grasslands	Drought	Livestock herders encroaching on protected areas
Asian elephant	South-East Asia	1. Changes to monsoon 2. Drought	1. Range extension into higher altitudes in the Himalayas 2. Increased encroachment of elephants into human habitats in search of food and water
Wild boar	North-East Asia	Higher average temperatures	Wild boar's range in Asia expands north and north-eastward
Hippopotamuses	Hippopotamuses African range	Drought	Increased competition for water with humans

Source: Amy Newsom, Zita Sebesvari, Ine Dorresteijn. (2023)

Nowhere are these dynamics more devastating than in climate-vulnerable regions like the Sahel, East Africa, and southern Africa. Here, desertification and resource scarcity pit desperate human populations against equally desperate wildlife in a zero-sum struggle for survival. As climate impacts intensify, both people and animals become trapped in a vicious cycle of conflict and deprivation.

Breaking this cycle requires innovative, integrated solutions that address both ecological and human needs including (WWF, 2022b):

i. Protecting and restoring critical wildlife corridors,
ii. Promoting drought-resistant farming techniques,

iii. Developing early warning systems for animal movements, and

iv. Empowering local communities in conservation planning.

The climate-HWC nexus presents one of Africa's most complex challenges—one that demands immediate, coordinated action. By treating HWC as both a conservation priority and a climate adaptation strategy, we can work toward solutions that protect both biodiversity and vulnerable communities in our warming world.

Habitat Changes and Range Shifts

Climate change can result in alterations to habitats, compelling wildlife to move into areas dominated by humans. This migration often leads to conflicts as animals seek food and shelter. Additionally, ongoing urbanization and agricultural development further diminish available habitats. As ecosystems are modified by climate change, species are forced to relocate. For example, polar bears in the Arctic are entering human communities due to the loss of sea ice (Atwood et al., 2020). Similarly, African elephants are encroaching on farmland as droughts limit water resources (Thirgood et al., 2021).

Resource Shortages

The reduction of food and water resources caused by climate change heightens competition between humans and wildlife. In India, for instance, Nilgai antelope and wild boars are increasingly raiding crops due to a decline in natural forage (Dave & Jhala, 2023). Likewise, in Nepal, snow leopards are preying more frequently on livestock as wild ungulate populations decrease (Chettri et al., 2022). As climate change impacts both water availability and food production, wildlife may intrude upon agricultural lands, resulting in crop damage and livestock losses.

Extreme Weather Events

Extreme weather events such as floods, droughts, and wildfires displace both humans and wildlife. For example, the Australian bushfires of 2019–2020 forced kangaroos and koalas into urban areas (Lunney et al., 2021). Similarly, Cyclone Idai in Mozambique in 2019 resulted in increased crocodile attacks as floodwaters expanded their habitat (Dunham et al., 2020).

Changes in Animal Behavior and Migration

Climate change influences the availability of natural resources, prompting wildlife to migrate in search of food and water. In the Himalayas, for instance, diminished grass cover at high altitudes due to climate change has led bharal (wild sheep) to forage closer to human settlements, which in turn attracts predators like snow leopards and increases livestock predation (Population Connection).

3.4 Conclusion

Climate change is transforming global ecosystems, leading to an increase in HWC that have resulted in casualties on both sides. Worldwide initiatives are being implemented to address this growing problem through various intervention strategies. These approaches focus on either enhancing human tolerance toward wildlife or reducing the occurrence and intensity of dangerous encounters. Climate change is a major factor contributing HWC, requiring a comprehensive approach that integrates technological solutions, community participation, and policy reforms. Tackling these conflicts is crucial for the conservation of biodiversity and the welfare of human communities.

Globally, climate change significantly influences human-wildlife interactions, resulting in heightened conflicts that jeopardize both wildlife preservation and human livelihoods. Addressing these issues necessitates a multifaceted strategy that encompasses community engagement, effective management practices, and sustainable development. By merging climate adaptation strategies with wildlife conservation efforts, we can reduce conflicts and promote coexistence. Future research should concentrate on predictive modeling and community-driven solutions to tackle this growing challenge. To minimize climate-induced HWC integrated approaches should focus on the following areas:

i. *Habitat restoration:* Revitalizing degraded ecosystems to support wildlife populations.
ii. *Early warning systems*: Utilizing AI and satellite data to anticipate wildlife movements (Dinerstein et al., 2022).
iii. *Community-based conservation*: Engaging local populations in conflict resolution (e.g., implementing beehive fences to deter elephants).
iv. *Policy integration:* Coordinating climate adaptation initiatives with wildlife management strategies (IPBES, 2023).

Preventive measures include physical barriers, protective structures, and deterrent systems, along with relocation programs for both animals and human communities. Modifications to agricultural practices, such as adjusting cropping patterns, have also proven effective in minimizing interactions. In extreme cases where human lives are lost, lethal removal of problematic animals becomes necessary as a last resort.

Effective long-term solutions typically require a multifaceted approach combining several strategies simultaneously. Programs offering compensation for damages, economic incentives for coexistence, environmental awareness campaigns, and regulated wildlife harvesting can collectively foster greater tolerance among affected communities. However, achieving sustainable resolution of HWC in forest-adjacent areas remains challenging, as current mitigation efforts often prove inadequate and sometimes conflict with broader conservation objectives. The complexity of these issues suggests that permanent solutions will require more innovative and integrated approaches to balance human safety with wildlife preservation.

References

1. Aber, J., et al. (2001). Forest processes and global environmental change: Predicting the effects of individual and multiple stressors. *BioScience, 51*(9), 735–751.
2. Amy Newsom, Zita Sebesvari, Ine Dorresteijn. (2023). Climate change influences the risk of physically harmful human-wildlife interactions. *Biological Conservation.* Volume 286, October 2023. https://www.sciencedirect.com/science/article/pii/S0006320723003567
3. AP News. (2025). *Zimbabwe is full of elephants and conflict with villagers is growing.* Retrieved from https://apnews.com/article/e0685f64a82be3847730bbad66d4dcfd
4. Atwood, T., et al. (2016). Rapid environmental change drives increased land use by an Arctic marine predator. *PLoS ONE, 11*(6).
5. Atwood, T. C. (2017). Implications of rapid environmental change for polar bear behavior and sociality. In A. Butterworth (Ed.), *Marine mammal welfare: Human-induced change in the marine environment and its impacts on marine mammal welfare* (pp. 445–462). Springer International Publishing.
6. Atwood, T. C., et al. (2020). *Nature Climate Change*. Vol. 10. No. 9. Pp. 844-850.
7. Barua, M., et al. (2013). The hidden dimensions of HWC: Health impacts, opportunity, and transaction costs. *Biological Conservation, 157*, 309–316.
8. Baruch-Mordo, S., et al. (2021). *Global Ecology and Conservation*. 25, e01413.
9. Chartier, et. al (2011), 'Habitat Loss and Human-elephant Conflict in Assam, India: Does a Critical Threshold Exist?,' *Oryx*, Vol. 45, pp.528-533.
10. Chaturvedi, R. K., et al. (2011). Impact of climate change on Indian forests: A dynamic vegetation modeling approach.

Mitigation and Adaptation Strategies for Global Change, 16, 119–142.

11. Chettri, N., et al. (2022). *Biological Conservation.* 265, 109399.
12. Climate Fact Checks. (2025). *Human-Wildlife conflict in Kerala: Over 100 deaths in the past year, experts cite Climate Change as a factor.* Retrieved from https://climatefactchecks.org/human-wildlife-conflict-in-kerala-over-100-deaths-in-the-past-year-experts-cite-climate-change-as-a-factor/
13. Dave, C., & Jhala, Y. (2023). *Journal of Applied Ecology*. Vol. 60. No. 2. pp. 301-312.
14. DeMotts, R., & Hoon, P. (2012). Whose elephants? Conserving, compensating, and competing in northern Botswana. *Society and Natural Resources, 25*(9), 837–851.
15. Dickman, A. J. (2010). Complexities of conflict: The importance of considering social factors for effectively resolving HWC. *Animal Conservation, 13*, 458–466.
16. Food and Agriculture Organization of the United Nations (FAO). (2010). *Global forest resources assessment*. FAO.
17. Frontiers. (2024). *Editorial: Climate change, human-wildlife interactions and sustainable tourism nexus in protected areas.*
18. Fulton, D. C., et al. (1996). Wildlife value orientations: A conceptual and measurement approach. *Human Dimensions of Wildlife, 1*(2), 24–47.
19. Gnacadja, L., & Lesch, W. (2009). *Running dry: Climate change in drylands and how to cope with it.* München, Germany.
20. Gross, E. M. (2019). *Tackling routes to coexistence: Human-elephant conflict in sub-Saharan Africa.* GIZ Partnership against Poaching and Illegal Wildlife Trade.
21. Guerra, A. S. (2019). Wolves of the sea: Managing human–wildlife conflict in an increasingly tense ocean. *Marine Policy, 99*, 369–373.

22. Guthrie, R. D. (2005). *The nature of Paleolithic art*. University of Chicago Press.
23. Hart, D., & Sussman, R. W. (2009). *Man the hunted: Primates, predators, and human evolution*. Westview Press.
24. Hazzah, L. N. (2006). *Living among lions: Coexistence or killing? Community attitude towards conservation initiatives and the motivations behind lion killing in Kenyan Maasailand* (Doctoral dissertation, University of Wisconsin-Madison).
25. Holling, C. S. (2001). Understanding the complexity of economic, ecological, and social systems. *Ecosystems, 4*, 390–405.
26. IPCC. (2022). *Climate Change 2022: Impacts, Adaptation, and Vulnerability*.
27. Intergovernmental Panel on Climate Change (IPCC). (2023). *Climate Change 2023: Impacts, Adaptation, and Vulnerability*.
28. Khaine, I., & Woo, S. Y. (2015). An overview of interrelationship between climate change and forests. *Forest Science and Technology, 11*(1), 1–11.
29. Khumalo, K. E., & Young, L. A. (2015). Women, HWC, and CBNRM: Hidden impacts and vulnerabilities in Kwandu Conservancy, Namibia. *Conservation and Society, 13*(3), 232–243.
30. Mason, T. H. E., et al. (2018). Wicked conflict: Using wicked problem thinking for holistic management of conservation conflict. *Conservation Letters, 11*(6).
31. Nair, R. D. (2009). Environmental refugees: Lessons from Africa. In S. B. Verma, A. B. Sharan, & S. K. Verma (Eds.), *Environment and climate change* (pp. XX–XX). Pentagon Press.
32. Nair, R. D., et al. (2010). *Role of indigenous communities in forest conservation: Lessons from Africa*. Institute of Social Research and Action.
33. Nair, R. D. (2022). Counteracting climate change: A review on feasibility of the circular economy approach. *International Journal of Current Science, 12*(3).

34. Nair, R. D. (2024). Impact of climate change on developing countries: Case of least developed countries. *International Journal of Research in Education Humanities and Commerce, 5*(2).
35. Population Connection. (2023). *No place to hide: Climate change is worsening human-wildlife conflict.* Retrieved from https://populationconnection.org/blog/climate-change-is-worsening-human-wildlife-conflict/
36. Ravindranath, N. H., et al. (2010). *Impact of climate change on forests in India.* Centre for Ecological Sciences, Indian Institute of Science.
37. Redfern, J. V., et al. (2013). Assessing the risk of ships striking large whales in marine spatial planning. *Conservation Biology, 27*(2), 292–302.
38. Scoones, I. (1998). *Sustainable rural livelihoods: A framework for analysis* (IDS Working Paper No. 72).
39. Seppälä, R., Buck, A., & Katila, P. (Eds.). (2009). *Adaptation of forests and people to climate change: A global assessment report* (IUFRO World Series, Volume 22).
40. Shen Z & K. Ma (2014), 'Effects of Climate Change on Biodiversity,' *Chinese Science Bulletin*, pp.1-2.
41. Smit, B., et al. (2000). An anatomy of adaptation to climate change and variability. *Climatic Change, 45*, 223–251.
42. Sukumar, R. (1989). *The Asian elephant: Ecology and management.* Cambridge University Press.
43. Surovell, T. A., et al. (2016). Test of Martin's overkill hypothesis using radiocarbon dates on extinct megafauna. *Proceedings of the National Academy of Sciences, 113*, 886–891.
44. The Guardian. (2024). *Collapsing wildlife populations near 'points of no return.* Retrieved from https://www.theguardian.com/environment/2024/oct/10/collapsing-wildlife-populations-points-no-return-living-planet-report-wwf-zsl-warns

45. World Bank. (2023*). Human-Wildlife Conflict: Global Policy and Perception Insights*. Retrieved from https://www.worldbank.org/en/programs/global-wildlife-program/brief/human-wildlife-conflict-global-policy-and-perception-insights
46. WWF. (2023). *Living Planet Report 2023.*
47. WWF. (2025). *C2C—conflict to coexistence: A global approach to manage HWC.*

CHAPTER: 4
IMPLICATIONS OF HUMAN WILDLIFE CONFLICT

4.1 Introduction

Globally, HWC is worsening and the repercussions are severe, disrupting agriculture, endangering human lives, undermining wildlife conservation, and destabilizing socio-economic conditions. Deforestation, farming, and urban development shrink wildlife habitats, pushing animals into human-occupied areas (WWF, 2023). Additionally, shifting weather patterns influence animal movements, increasing human-wildlife encounters (IPCC, 2022). Meanwhile, expanding human settlements further invade wildlife territories, escalating tensions (UNEP, 2023). This chapter explores the ecological and socio-economic effects, direct and hidden costs, and emphasizes different types of wildlife damage.

Table:4.1 Gravity of HWC around the world, 2020

Country	*Type of Implication*	*Units*	*Implication*
Sri Lanka - 2019	People killed by wild elephants	Number	121
	Elephants killed due to HWC	Number	405
Tanzania	People killed by lions per year	Number	60
	Lions killed due to HWC per year	Number	150
Bardia, Nepal	Average per-species cost of crop damage per household and incident	$	20
	Average cost of property damage by elephant per household and incident	$	73
Europe - 2005-2012	Average annual compensation for all livestock damage by carnivores	$ - million	41.38
	Average cost per year per wolf	$	3500
	Average cost per year per bear	$	2,600
	Average cost per year per lynx	$	1,000

Source: Gross E, et. al, 2021

HWC has serious consequences for human health, safety, and well-being, as well as ecosystem stability and biodiversity. These effects can be direct or indirect. Direct impacts include physical attacks causing injury or death, vehicle collisions, the spread of zoonotic diseases, and economic losses from crop, property, and livestock damage (Woodroffe et al., 2005). Indirect effects include lost income for farmers, reduced mental well-being, disrupted livelihoods, and food insecurity.

Often, the hidden costs of HWC—such as psychological distress, individual hardships, and opportunity losses—are overlooked in assessments because they are non-monetary (Barua et al., 2013). Research indicates that women and female-headed households bear a disproportionate share of HWC burdens compared to men (DeMotts & Hoon, 2012). Emotional tolls include fears for safety, livelihood instability, and resentment toward external stakeholders. Table 4.1 highlights the severity of global HWC incidents in the recent past.

Table:4.2 Costs of HWC

Type of cost	*Continuous events*	*Discrete events*
i. Direct costs	• Physical risk • Time lost from chasing animals away as they try to enter fields	• Crop loss • Livestock predation • Human injury • Infrastructure damage • Death
ii. Indirect costs	• Additional time investment • Fear of what will happen if one encounters a dangerous animal; fear of what will happen if crop is lost; anger at the conservancy; uncertainty about being able to provide for one's household • Lost sleep staying on the lookout for animals	• Fear/stress during animal encounters • Food loss, hunger • Income loss • Opportunity cost • Lost labour investment • Lost financial investment

Source: Khumalo K E & L A Young (2015)

HWC creates ongoing hardship and sudden crises that threaten the way forest-adjacent communities earn a living and access food. Various costs of HWC are detailed in Table 4.2. Treating ongoing hardship as a slow burn, gradually making life more difficult, while sudden crises are like a punch, hitting hard and fast (Scoones, 1998). People living on the edge of forests in developing nations, particularly women, are often ill-equipped to handle either of these. These difficulties disproportionately affect women for a couple of key reasons. Firstly, factors like poverty, being unmarried, having little or no farmland, and limited rights make women more susceptible to both immediate crises and long-term stresses. Secondly, when crops are destroyed, livestock are killed, or family members are hurt or killed by wildlife, women bear a heavier burden (Khumalo & Young, 2015). These losses worsen their already disadvantaged situation, making them even more vulnerable to future problems.

Causes and impact of HWC in a model format is shown in Figure 4.1. Eleven drivers and eight pressures of HWC are segregated and elven impacts are briefed.

Figure: 4.1
Causes & Impact of HWC – A Model

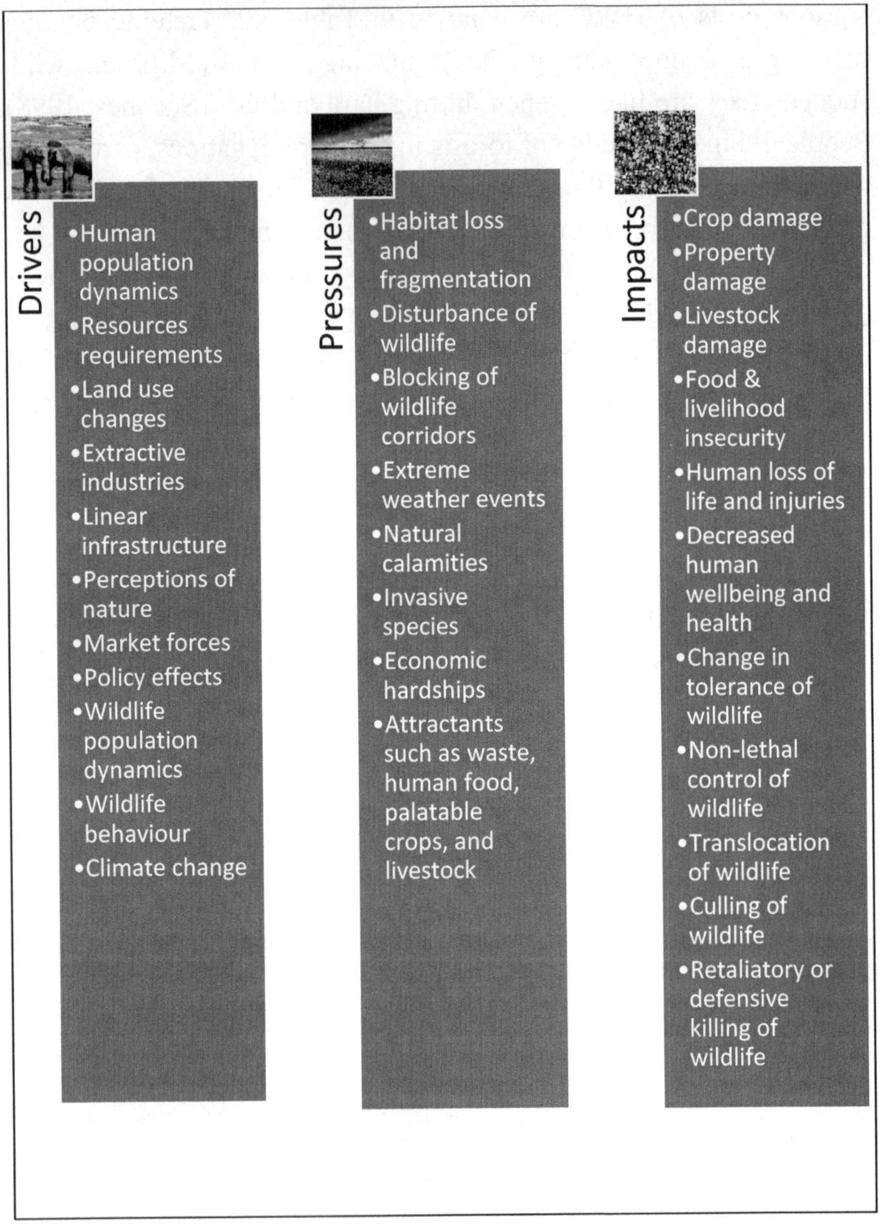

Source: Gross E (2019)

4.2 Ecological and Socio-economic Impacts

HWC often leads to disagreements within communities. Because different groups of people view wildlife issues from their own unique standpoints, these situations can spark complicated arguments across all levels of society. One of the most serious dangers of encountering wildlife is the risk of death or injury to local people. While attacks by top predators are rare, they can be deadly. Historically, venomous snakes have been responsible for the most human deaths caused by animals in Asia and Africa (Williams, et al., 2019). In Africa, crocodiles, elephants, and hippos are also significant causes of wildlife-related human fatalities (Chomba, et. al., 2012). It's important to note that most of these deaths happen during chance encounters with wildlife.

Research indicates that worldwide, 24 types of land-based meat-eating animals prey on farm animals (Boitani, et.al., 2012). In Asia and Africa, elephants are known for causing considerable damage to crops like maize, rice, oil palms, and fruit trees. Deer, antelopes, and monkeys can also inflict widespread damage on newly planted fields (Wiafe, 2019). Wild boars are a globally recognized species that cause extensive damage to farms located near forests or wooded areas (Pandey, et. al. 2016). When local communities are empowered, trained, and well-equipped to manage HWC themselves, it can be more beneficial for them. This approach can create lasting ways for them to earn income and support their livelihoods. Furthermore, reconnecting with their traditions, stories, and beliefs about their history can help communities feel a sense of pride in coexisting with wildlife.

Major ecological and socio-economic impacts of HWC can be summarized as follows.

i. *Wildlife population decline*: Retaliatory killings and habitat destruction threaten endangered species. Major species affected by HWC are summarized in Table-4.3

Table: 4.3 Species Affected by HWC, 2023

Species	*Region*	*Threat Level*	*Annual Mortality*
African Elephant	Sub-Saharan Africa	Endangered	500+
Bengal Tiger	India, Bangladesh	Vulnerable	100+
Snow Leopard	Central Asia	Endangered	50+
Gray Wolf	North America, Europe	Least Concern	200+

Sources: IUCN (2023), WWF (2023)

ii. *Economic losses:* Farmers suffer crop damage and livestock predation, leading to financial instability (FAO, 2022).

iii. *Human casualties:* Attacks by large carnivores (lions, tigers, elephants) result in hundreds of deaths annually (Figure-4.2). Direct encounters with wildlife have led to injuries and fatalities. For example, in Malawi, the relocation of 263 elephants resulted in at least 10 human fatalities and extensive damage to crops and property (UNEP, 2023).

Figure: 4.2 Annual Deaths due to HWC, 2022-23

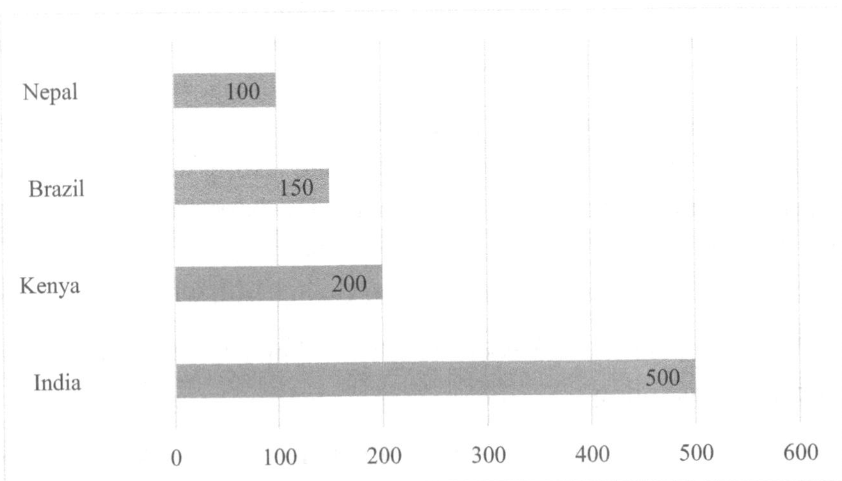

Sources: FAO (2023), WHO (2023)

iv. *Agriculture damage:* Crop destruction is the most frequently reported impact of HWC, and is reported to be 79% of people in affected villages. In Africa, 90% of affected people identified crop damage as a primary concern, while in Asia and the Pacific, the figure stands at 80% (FAO, 2023b).

v. *Livestock predation:* Livestock depredation is another major issue, with 60% of governments highlighting it as a significant concern. In Latin America and the Caribbean, 91% of affected people reported livestock predation as a primary impact, and in Europe, the figure is 87% (WWF, 2023b).

Detailed account of the impact of HWC is briefed in Table-4.4.

Table: 4.4 Nature of Impact of HWC

Nature of impact	*Impact*	*Quantification of loss*
Economic Impacts	Annual global crop losses due to wildlife	$5 billion
	Livestock predation costs African farmers	$1 billion yearly
Ecological Impacts	Retaliatory killings of threatened endangered species	Killing of lions, tigers, and elephants
	Disruption of ecosystem balance due to declining predator populations.	
Social Impacts	Human fatalities	e.g., 500+ deaths annually from elephant attacks in Asia and Africa
	Psychological trauma and reduced support for conservation efforts.	

Sources: FAO, 2023; WWF, 2023; IUCN Red List, 2023; National Geographic, 2023

Wildlife-related socio-economic problems can generally be grouped into three main areas of impact on society as detailed below.

i. *Economic Impacts:* These occur when wildlife damage reduces people's earnings, primarily affecting those who depend on the land like farmers, orchard owners, forestry professionals, and plant nursery operators.
ii. *Health and Safety Impacts:* These can be broken down into three types such as the spread of diseases from wildlife, accidents involving vehicles and animals, and direct physical harm caused by wildlife.
iii. *Psychological Impacts:* These arise when wildlife disrupts people's usual routines or their surroundings. While many of these issues also have financial costs, the emotional and mental effects can often be more significant than the purely economic ones.

The way wildlife damage affects society over time through a series of stages, as outlined in Table *4.5*.

Table: 4.5 Stages in the evolution of wildlife damage

Stage	*Damage issue*
1. Concern	Individuals or groups recognize unfavourable effects of wildlife at this level.
2. Involvement	At this stage, some sections in the society begin to turn to one another for support and to approach decision-makers with their issues. Some stakeholders believe that there are many problem animals in the area, while others believe that lack of tolerance has prevented people from adjusting to wildlife and nature.
3. Issue	At this stage, major effects are generally acknowledged. To move toward a solution, it is imperative that everyone agrees about the existence and nature of the issue.
4. Alternatives	During the stage, people provide alternative solutions for resolving the effects of the problem.
5. Consequences	Upon alternative actions are proposed, the consequences are evaluated from diverse perspectives. Stakeholders used to reach different conclusions about major concerns.
6. Choice	Stakeholders deliberate on the alternative options with variety of possibilities. The stakeholders will resolve differences and settle acceptable actions.

7. Implementation.	In this stage, a set of management actions are placed into effect.
8. Evaluation	The impacts of management actions are assessed and society develops judgment about the actions taken.

Source: Daniel J. Decker, et.al (2002)

4.3 Hidden Costs

The impacts of HWC on communities are primarily psychological, physical, and social. The destruction of crops, livestock, or human life brings not only financial hardship but also long-term emotional and societal consequences, particularly for vulnerable groups. HWC disrupts traditional workloads and gender roles, often leaving affected communities stigmatized by their losses. Additionally, people may have to modify their daily routines and livelihood activities to mitigate conflicts, leading to opportunity costs.

The burden on communities intensifies as they must replant damaged crops, rebuild infrastructure, and guard fields day and night against wildlife—increasing labor demands and causing sleep deprivation (Jadhav & Barua, 2012). Other hidden costs include food insecurity, financial strain from repairing damages, and health-related expenses, all of which strain household budgets.

Living near wildlife also generates chronic fear and stress among residents. This anxiety limits social interactions, prevents children from attending school, and contributes to lasting psychological trauma. When fatalities occur, families endure profound grief and mental distress. For example, studies in India revealed that more than 50% of widows who lost spouses to tiger or crocodile attacks faced severe physical and mental health challenges (Barua, 2013).

If a family's primary earner is killed or injured due to HWC, surviving members—often women—must shoulder additional responsibilities to sustain their livelihoods. In regions with frequent conflicts, women disproportionately bear these hardships (Jadhav & Barua, 2012).

4.4 Impact on Commodity Production & Zoonosis

In South Asia and Southern Africa, pests including insects, weeds, and pathogens cause severe damage to crops, resulting in annual yield losses of up to 40% (Oerke, 2006). Such significant production declines often force farming communities to abandon traditional crops or even relocate entirely. The situation becomes even more dire in cases of human-elephant conflict, where farmers can lose their entire harvest—up to 100% of crops—threatening food security (Graham et al., 2010). Subsistence farmers with limited crop diversity face particularly severe hardships. For instance, near India's Bhadra Tiger Reserve, households lost 11% of their annual grain production to elephant raids between 1996 and 1999 (Madhusudan, 2003).

HWC often disrupts fundamental components of agricultural supply chains, creating ripple effects throughout entire value chains. In Sabah, Malaysia, for example, Bornean elephants frequently damage oil palm plantations, leading to retaliatory killings—30 elephants were reportedly killed due to such conflicts in 2018 alone (Othman et al., 2019).

The financial toll extends globally. In Europe, annual compensation payments for livestock losses from HWC averaged $41.38 million between 2005 and 2012, highlighting the substantial economic burden of these conflicts (Bautista et al., 2019).

Many new diseases, like Ebola, Zika, Nipah encephalitis, and almost all major global disease outbreaks, including bird flu, HIV/AIDS, and COVID-19, have originated from contact between wildlife, farm animals, and people (Jones K.E., et al., 2008). The danger of pandemics is growing quickly, with more than five new diseases appearing in humans each year. The increasing spread of animal-borne diseases is linked to human-caused changes, particularly in how we use land. While wild animals can carry various diseases, it's primarily human actions that alter the environment and lead to these outbreaks.

4.5 Conclusion

HWC creates major risks for both the variety of life on earth and the well-being of people. Finding lasting answers demands teamwork among governments, conservation groups, and local communities. Taking preventative steps, such as restoring natural habitats and using technologies to reduce conflict, is vital for people and wildlife to live alongside each other.

Human activities and changes in land use have pushed many animal species close to extinction. In fact, some of the very species involved in HWC are endangered and protected by law. Out of 260 land-based vertebrate species known to have negative interactions with humans, 53 are classified as threatened (Torres D.F., et. al., 2018). Currently, significant portions of the natural habitats of tigers in India (35%), African lions (40%), and African and Asian elephants (70%) lie outside of designated protected areas (Gross E, et. al., 2021).

The clash between human needs and wildlife survival presents serious difficulties for protecting nature and for people's ways of life. To encourage coexistence, it's critical to understand why these conflicts happen and to put effective strategies in place to lessen them. Working together – involving governments, local people, and conservation organizations – is key to tackling and minimizing these conflicts.

References

1. Barua, et. al. (2013), 'THe Hidden Dimensions of HWC: Health Impacts, Opportunity and Transaction Costs,' *Biological Conservation*, Vol. 157, pp. 309-316.
2. Bautista C., et al. (2019), 'Large carnivore damage in Europe: Analysis of compensation and prevention programs,' *Biological Conservation*, No. 235, pp. 308-316.
3. Boitani L., Powell R.A. (2012), *Carnivore Ecology and Conservation: A Handbook of Techniques*, Oxford University Press, New York, USA.

4. Chomba C, et. al. (2012), 'Pattern of HWCs in Zambia, Causes, Consequences and Management Responses,' *Journal of Ecology and the Natural Environment*, Vol. 4, No. 12, pp. 303-313.
5. Cromsigt, Joris P.G.M, et. al. (2013), 'Hunting for fear: Innovating management of HWCs,' *Journal of applied ecology*, No. 50, pp.544-549, British Ecological Society.
6. Daniel J. Decker, et. al. (2002), *HWC Management: A Practitioners Guide,* Human Dimensions Research Unit, Cornell University, Ithaca, New York.
7. DeMotts, R and P. Hoon (2012), 'Whose Elephants? Conserving, Compensating, and Competing in Northern Botswana,' *Society and Natural Resources*, Vol. 25, No. 9, pp.837-851.
8. FAO. (2023a). *HWC and Food Security*.
9. FAO. (2023b). *Global Assessment of HWC Impacts on Agriculture*.
10. Graham M.D., et. (2010), 'Patterns of crop-raiding by elephants, Loxodonta africana, in Laikipia, Kenya, and the management of human-elephant conflict,' *Systematics and Biodiversity*, Vol. 8, No. 4, pp. 435-445.
11. Gross, E. M. (2019). *Tackling routes to coexistence: Human-elephant conflict in sub-Saharan Africa.* GIZ Partnership against Poaching and Illegal Wildlife Trade.
12. Gross E, et.al. (2021), *A Future for All: The Need for Human-Wildlife Coexistence*, WWF, Gland, Switzerland.
13. Hillman G, et. al. (2016), 'New evidence of Late Glacial cereal cultivation at Abu Hureyra on the Euphrates,' *The Holocene,* Vol. 11, No. 4, pp. 383-393.
14. IUCN. (2023). *Red List of Threatened Species*.
15. Jadhav S., Barua M (2012), 'The Elephant Vanishes: impact of human-elephant conflict on people's wellbeing,' *Health Place*, Vol. 18, No. 6, pp. 1356-1365.

16. Jones K.E., et al. (2008), 'Global trends in emerging infectious diseases', *Nature* Vol. 451, No. 7181, pp. 990-993.
17. Khumalo K E & Young L A (2015), 'Women, HWC, and CBNRM: Hidden Impacts and Vulnerabilities in Kwandu Conservancy, Namibia,' *Conservation and Society*, Vol. 13, No.3, pp. 232-243.
18. Knight et al., (2009), 'Deer facilitate invasive plant success in a Pennsylvania forest under-story', Natural Areas Journal, No. 29, pp. 110-116.
19. Leong, K.M (2009), 'The tragedy of becoming common: landscape change and perceptions of wildlife,' *Society and Natural resources*, No. 23, pp. 111-127.
20. Madhusadan, M.D. (2003), 'Living amidst large wildlife: Livestock and crop depredation by large mammals in the interior villages of Bhadra Tiger reserve, South India,' *Environmental Management,* Vol. 31, No. 4, pp. 466–475.
21. Oerke E.C (2006), 'Crop losses to pests,' *The Journal of Agricultural Science*, Vol. 144, No. 1, pp. 31-43.
22. Othman N., et. al. (2019), 'Shift of paradigm needed towards improving human-elephant coexistence in monoculture landscapes in Sabah,' *International Zoo Yearbook*, Vol. 53, No. 1, pp.161-173.
23. Pandey P., Shaner P.J., Sharma H.P (2016), 'The wild boar as a driver of HWC in the protected park lands of Nepal,' *European Journal of Wildlife Research,* Vol. 62, No. 1, pp. 103-108.
24. Panthera. (2023). *Lion Guardians Program Report.*
25. Scoones, I (1998), Sustianble Rural Livelihoods: A Framework for Analysis,' *IDS Working Paper*: 72.
26. Torres D.F., et. al. (2018), 'Conflicts Between Humans and Terrestrial Vertebrates: A Global Review' *Tropical Conservation Science*, No. 11.
27. UNEP. (2023). *Global Environment Outlook.*
28. UNEP. (2023). *Climate Change and HWC.*

29. White, P C. L. & Alastair I. Ward (2010), 'Interdisciplinary approaches for the management of existing and emerging human–wildlife conflicts,' *Wildlife Research*, Vol. 37, No.8, pp. 623-629.
30. Wiafe E.D. (2019), 'Primates crop raiding situation on farmlands adjacent to South-West of Mole National Park, Ghana,' *Ghana Journal of Agricultural Science,* Vol. 54, No. 2, pp. 58-67.
31. Williams D.J, et al. (2019), 'Strategy for a globally coordinated response to a priority neglected tropical disease: Snakebite envenoming,' *PLoS Neglected Tropical Diseases,* Vol. 13, No. 2.
32. Woodroffe, RT, et.al. (2005), *People and Wildlife: Conflict or Coexistence*, Cambridge University Press, Cambridge.
33. WWF. (2023a). *Living Planet Report.*
34. WWF. (2023b). *Living with Wildlife: Mitigation Strategies.*

CHAPTER: 5
HUMAN WILDLIFE CONFLICT AND MANAGEMENT

5.1 Introduction

HWC arises when humans and animals compete for the same resources, resulting in harmful encounters such as crop destruction, attacks on livestock, and even human injuries or deaths. The World-Wide Fund for Nature (WWF, 2023) reports that millions of people, especially in Africa, South America and Asia, are impacted by HWC each year as farming activities increasingly intrude on wildlife territories.

With the growth of human settlements into natural areas, interactions—and often conflicts—between people and wildlife have become more frequent. These clashes lead to economic damage, injuries, and loss of life for both humans and animals. To create effective solutions, it is essential to understand the underlying causes of HWC. This issue presents major obstacles to preserving biodiversity, ensuring human safety, and sustaining livelihoods globally. The chapter stresses the need for collaborative efforts among local communities, governments, and conservation groups to promote peaceful coexistence. This chapter also explores various HWC management approaches, focusing on mitigation and adaptation strategies, and relevance of co-management and participatory planning. Effective solutions involve blending traditional knowledge, modern technology, and community-led initiatives. Additionally, the chapter outlines policy suggestions to support long-term harmony between humans and wildlife.

5.2 Management Strategies

Managing HWC demands a comprehensive approach that combines preventing problems, involving local communities, and implementing supportive policies. Physical barriers like electric fences, trenches, and beehive fences have shown promise, with electric fences achieving an 85% success rate in Africa and Asia (WWF, 2023). Early warning systems, such as drone monitoring and SMS alerts, help communities prepare for wildlife movements, thereby minimizing surprise encounters (KWS, 2023). Creating habitat corridors and agroforestry buffer zones helps reduce conflict by maintaining natural animal migration routes and limiting their need to enter farmlands (UNEP, 2023).

Community involvement through strategies like compensation for losses has been tried in countries like India under Project Elephant, though its effectiveness varies (IUCN, 2023). Offering alternative ways for people to earn a living, such as beekeeping and eco-tourism, can lessen their reliance on activities that lead to conflict (WWF, 2023). Policy measures, including integrated land-use planning and international wildlife agreements, further aid in reducing conflict (CBD, 2023). Successful examples include Botswana's lion guardian program, which significantly reduced livestock predation (Panthera, 2023), and Nepal's use of chilli fences and predator-proof enclosures to reduce leopard attacks (NTNC, 2023).

Despite these efforts, challenges like insufficient funding, cultural resistance, and inconsistent data collection remain. Improving early warning technologies, expanding insurance programs, and strengthening international cooperation through frameworks are crucial for the long-term management of HWC.

Various methods, both traditional and modern, are employed to mitigate HWC. Physical barriers like fences, sometimes natural features such as rivers or dense vegetation, are commonly used to keep wildlife out of human settlements. These barriers also help control invasive species, disease spread, and protect endangered wildlife. While fencing can be effective, its high construction and maintenance costs can be prohibitive. Some studies show that natural deterrents like chillies and lemon plants have shown limited success in Asia and

Africa (Hedges & Gunaryadi, 2010). Habitat modification, such as altering water sources or changing crop types, can also reduce conflict. Interestingly, farmer-friendly species like honeybees have been successfully used to deter elephants in Kenya (King et al., 2011).

Traditional methods like guarding livestock, sometimes with trained animals like dogs, remain effective but are labour-intensive (Marker et al., 2005). Various technologies are used to repel wildlife through fear-inducing stimuli, and capture-and-release methods also help manage HWC. Modern technologies like radio telemetry are increasingly important. Sterilization is also used to control wildlife populations.

Economic incentives play a significant role in fostering tolerance and collaboration in HWC resolution. Compensation for losses (crops, livestock, injury, or death) is common, though damage assessment can be challenging. Insurance schemes, where participants pay premiums, offer a similar approach. Performance payments link financial rewards to conservation objectives, and sharing ecotourism revenue can incentivize local communities.

A major driver of increasing HWC is the growth of wildlife populations amidst shrinking habitats. Wildlife population control, particularly through non-lethal fertility control measures, is being explored globally (Lapidge et al., 2007). However, biological, economic, social, and legal hurdles need to be overcome for widespread implementation (Fagerstone et al., 2010).

HWC management strategies are broadly categorized under the following three categories.

Mitigation Strategies:

i. *Community-Based Approaches:* Engaging local people in conservation has proven effective. For example, the Sonitpur Model in Assam, India, trains locals to safely guide elephants away from crops and uses non-lethal electric fences to reduce conflicts (IUCN, 2023).

ii. *Technological Interventions:* Innovations offer new ways to reduce conflict. Beehive fences, which take advantage of elephants' natural fear of bees, have reduced crop raids by up to 85% (King, 2011). In Montana, drones have been used to successfully deter bears from human settlements as a non-lethal management tool (WWF, 2023).

iii. *Infrastructure Solutions:* Designing infrastructure with wildlife in mind helps minimize conflicts. Wildlife crossings, such as overpasses and underpasses, allow animals to safely cross roads, reducing vehicle collisions. Wildlife corridors that connect fragmented habitats support natural migration and reduce human-animal encounters.

Preventive Measures

i. *Physical Barriers:* Structures such as electric fences, trenches, and bee-based barriers help prevent elephants from entering human settlements.

ii. *Early Warning Systems:* Technologies like drones and text message alerts notify residents when wild animals are nearby, enhancing safety (KWS, 2023).

iii. *Habitat Corridors: Reestablishing natural migration pathways minimizes unnecessary wildlife displacement (UNEP, 2023).*

Incetive-Based Approaches

i. *Compensation Programs:* Initiatives like Project Elephant in India provide financial reimbursement to farmers for damages caused by wildlife, supported by governments and NGOs.

ii. *Income Diversification:* Encouraging activities such as beekeeping and eco-tourism helps communities shift away from agriculture, which often leads to human-wildlife conflicts (WWF, 2023).

A detailed account of direct and indirect interventions to HWC is provided in Appendix-4.

Various methods, many rooted in the traditional practices of indigenous communities worldwide, are employed to manage HWC. These measures vary based on the specific context, including the types and frequency of animal interactions, and can range from lethal to non-lethal approaches. A brief outline of overlap between wildlife and humans is provided in Figure-5.1. The goal of these interventions is either to prevent HWC incidents from happening or to reduce how often they occur. These measures can be implemented with or without formal regulation and may sometimes require significant infrastructure investment or government involvement.

Socio-economic and cultural shifts, along with technological advancements, have impacted human values and behaviors, including those of forest-fringe communities. Transforming human behavior to be more environmentally conscious is crucial for reducing HWC. Governments, NGOs, community-based organizations, and international conservation bodies have a vital role in promoting this change through education, co-management, participatory planning, and supportive policies. Factors influencing human-wildlife coexistence are complex and vary by region and species (Nyhus, 2016).

Some researchers suggest a shift from a purely conservation-focused approach to a management paradigm that includes regulating wildlife populations in certain contexts (Marchini & Crawshaw, 2015).

Generally, HWC management perceptions and approaches fall into three main categories:

i. *Technical:* These interventions focus on modifying the external environment at the human-animal interface. This includes physical barriers, changes in land use, and efforts to influence animal populations or behavior. These are often short-term solutions.
ii. *Cognitive:* These measures aim to shift negative human attitudes and behaviors towards wildlife and conservation by

increasing awareness and understanding through education programs or social media campaigns.

iii. *Structural:* These measures seek to address the underlying social, political, and economic factors that contribute to HWC. This includes financial tools to manage the economic costs of coexisting with wildlife, legislative changes to promote new rules and behaviors, and social transformation through mediation, stakeholder engagement, and inclusive decision-making processes.

Figure: 5.1 Areas of overlap between wildlife and people (%)

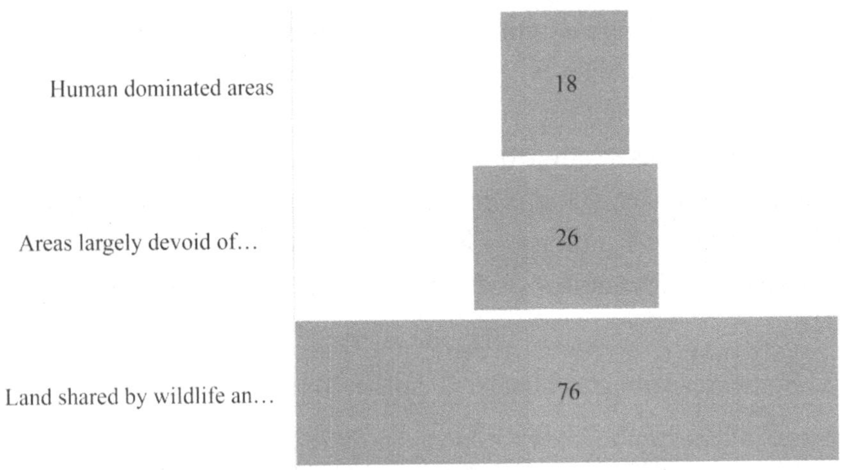

Source: Gross E, et. al, 2021

As apex predators, carnivores play a crucial role in maintaining the balance of ecosystems by regulating prey populations. Their presence, and even the fear they instill, influences herbivore behavior, preventing them from overgrazing in a single area. Large herbivores like elephants also significantly shape landscapes by creating pathways, aiding ecosystem regeneration, digging waterholes, and promoting plant diversity (Fritz H, 2017).

In the marine systems too conflicts frequently arise between marine megafauna, including sharks, sea turtles, whales, and seals, and fishing activities. The issue of HWC in marine environments tends to be underreported and lacks adequate regulation. Legal mechanisms like zoning and spatial planning are essential for mitigating conflicts involving marine mammals (Redfern J.V. et al., 2013). Effectiveness of mitigation strategies in selected countries to counter HWC is illustrated in Figure-5.2.

Figure: 5.2 Effectiveness of HWC Mitigation Strategies (%)

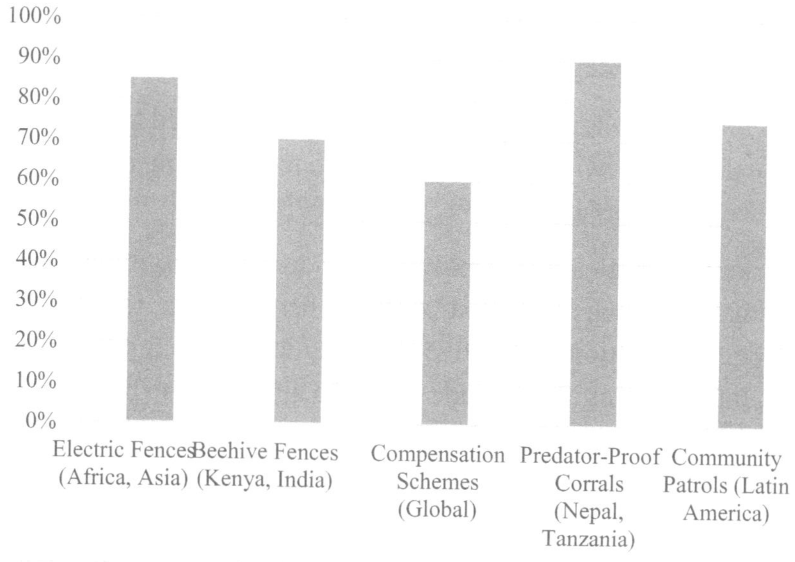

Source: FAO, 2023; IUCN, 2023; Panthera, 2023; UNEP, 2023

From the foregone discussions the six key stages of HWC management can be traced such as the following (KWS, 2000):

i. *Conflict Assessment:* Analyzing the conflict context through hotspot mapping, community perception studies, and evaluation of spatial and temporal patterns.
ii. *Impact Mitigation:* Minimizing negative consequences post-conflict via compensation schemes, insurance programs, and livelihood diversification.

iii. *Incident Response:* Managing active HWC situations by establishing rapid-response units, improving reporting systems, and implementing standardized protocols.
iv. *Conflict Prevention:* Proactively reducing HWC risks using barriers, early warning systems, and safety measures for high-risk areas.
v. *Policy Framework:* Developing legal and institutional guidelines, including international/national laws, management plans, and land-use policies to regulate HWC resolution.
vi. *Performance Evaluation:* Tracking intervention effectiveness through data monitoring, knowledge dissemination, and adaptive strategy refinement.

According to Riley et al. (2002), Adaptive Integrated Management (AIM) exhorts the wildlife manager to concentrate on impacts and view management as an adaptive, ever-evolving process.

Various strategies are employed to address HWC, ranging from educational outreach aimed at shifting perspectives to providing knowledge, instructions, incentives, and regulations to modify human actions. Interventions also include efforts to alter wildlife behavior and manage wildlife populations. Engaging stakeholders effectively involves a series of key steps including comprehending the existing situation, identifying all relevant stakeholders, establishing clear objectives, choosing an appropriate approach for stakeholder involvement, designing specific strategies, implementing these strategies, and conducting a thorough evaluation of their impact.

5.3 Co-Managing HWC and Participatory Planning

Co-management involves collaborative governance between local communities impacted by HWC and relevant government and non-governmental organizations (Treves et al., 2006). In principle, this approach enables communities to address HWC while preserving biodiversity. However, current HWC incidents predominantly occur in forest-edge zones, often impacting endangered species that fall under the mandate of wildlife authorities (KWS, 2000). Implementing effective co-management demands technical, logistical, and financial support—resources often scarce for conservation agencies in developing nations.

Community responses to HWC and their vulnerability are influenced by the intensity and recurrence of losses, alongside socio-economic and environmental factors (Carter, 1997). Personal coping strategies—such as securing land, labor, or capital—often reflect an individual's economic status and political connections. At the community level, resilience is built through kinship ties, collective resource-sharing traditions, and cooperative land stewardship, illustrating a spectrum between individual and collective adaptation strategies.

Research from the U.S. demonstrates that adaptive management strengthens HWC mitigation by improving institutional capabilities and pinpointing successful interventions, including sustainable financing models (Keith et al., 2011). Notably, effective HWC strategies must incorporate metrics of harmonious coexistence, such as fostering positive human-wildlife interactions and cultivating societal tolerance toward wildlife (Frank, 2016).

Participatory planning offers a powerful way to address HWC and also shape the strategies, projects, and results. This approach necessitates clearly defined shared goals, carefully designed interventions, and a monitoring system that considers potential challenges and opportunities (Gillingham, 2001). While improving community livelihoods and conserving wildlife might seem at odds, participatory planning should aim to achieve both, requiring an integrated link between development efforts and wildlife conservation.

Collaborative and inclusive strategies are vital for successful HWC management and promoting coexistence. Effective knowledge sharing and communication are crucial components. Strong governance and the exchange of best practices are essential for long-term HWC reduction. Interventions to reduce HWC encompass actions aimed at reducing the frequency of human-wildlife encounters, as well as activities that increase human tolerance in conflict situations (Treves, 2009). Reducing interaction frequency can involve building barriers, employing guards and deterrents, relocating wildlife or people, and modifying human behaviors like cropping patterns. In tragic cases involving human fatalities, lethal removal of the responsible animals may be deemed necessary. Often, a combination of strategies is needed for a lasting resolution. Enhancing tolerance among affected communities can be achieved through compensation programs, incentive schemes, environmental education, and regulated public harvesting. However, achieving permanent solutions to HWC in forest-adjacent areas often remains a distant goal, as mitigation efforts can be ineffective and may conflict with conservation objectives.

5.4 Financial Support and Livelihoods

Human-wildlife interactions lead to significant economic costs, including livestock predation and damage to crops and property (Dickman & Hazzah, 2016). These losses can severely impact livelihoods, particularly in impoverished communities living near wildlife. For instance, studies in Zimbabwe showed a 20% reduction in annual income for agricultural communities due to livestock predation (Butler, 2000), and in India's Bhadra Tiger Reserve, crop and livestock losses caused an 11% income decrease (Madhusadan, 2003). Predation and other wildlife damage also affect fisheries, commercial farms, and sporting activities (Soffker et al., 2015). A key strategy to manage these conflicts involves reducing the economic burden through compensation for losses and fostering greater tolerance.

Compensation is a widely used conflict management tool, often seen as a straightforward way to improve public perception of conservation efforts by directly addressing the financial costs of living with wildlife (Hemson et al., 2009). However, compensation schemes have several drawbacks. They primarily address the visible consequences of conflict rather than the underlying causes (Hoare, 2015). Furthermore, these schemes are susceptible to corruption, insufficient funding, lengthy processing times, unfair compensation rates, social opportunity costs, and limited ability to adapt to changing circumstances (Ravenelle & Nyhus, 2017). These issues can breed resentment among affected communities and increase opposition to conservation (e.g., Dickman et al., 2014). Challenges also arise in verifying claims, and individuals may attempt to fraudulently claim compensation when proving predation is difficult (Bulte & Rondeau, 2005). As a long-term solution, compensation schemes risk failure unless they are transparent, consistently monitored, adequately funded, and trusted by all stakeholders.

Research indicates that insurance schemes offer a practical solution for HWC management, as risk-adjusted premium pricing helps guarantee equitable compensation (Chen et al., 2013). However, the effectiveness of such programs can be enhanced through supplementary support from government bodies, NGOs, or community-based initiatives like eco-tourism revenue sharing (Nyhus, 2016). Pilot compensation programs, such as those implemented by the Big Life Foundation and Amboseli for Elephants in Kenya have demonstrated some success in offsetting losses caused by predators and large herbivores (Okello et al., 2014). Nevertheless, studies suggest these approaches require complementary strategies to foster lasting community acceptance of wildlife. While non-monetary assistance (e.g., food and water provisions) has been employed as a conflict mitigation tool, its efficacy remains understudied (Hoare, 2015).

For sustainable HWC resolution, experts recommend blending traditional and contemporary practices through interdisciplinary collaboration between natural and social sciences (White & Ward, 2010). Crucially, this approach demands consistent evaluation of community involvement and inclusive policy development to ensure long-term success.

5.5 Poaching, Translocation & Wildlife Utilization

Governments sometimes employ regulated lethal control as a seemingly inexpensive way to manage harmful human-wildlife interactions like predation (McManus et al., 2015). These methods include harvesting, culling, legalized hunting, and selectively killing 'problem' animals, particularly when they directly threaten human safety or property (Naughton-Treves et al., 2005). Removing aggressive individuals has been reported to prevent human fatalities in specific situations. However, the effectiveness of lethal control largely depends on the behavior of the targeted species (Swanepoel, et al., 2015).

Historically, lethal controls were a common HWC mitigation tactic in nearly all indigenous communities. However, the use of such measures has, in some instances, led to the eradication of entire populations or species. Firearms, poison, and traps like neck snares and rotating jaw traps are some of the methods historically and currently used (Boitani & Powell, 2012). While hunting and poaching are often illegal outside of game reserves, retaliatory killings, particularly in less developed countries in Asia and Africa, are also unlawful. Studies in South Africa indicate that more leopards die from retaliation than from regulated hunting (Swanepoel, et al., 2015). Nevertheless, in situations where human life is genuinely at risk, government intervention to lethally remove the threatening animal may be necessary.

In contrast, non-lethal measures prioritize wildlife conservation and protection by aiming to minimize human-wildlife interactions. These include translocating wildlife and creating barriers like fences, walls, trenches, mechanical tools, chemicals, and electronic devices to separate humans and animals. Translocation, while a potential solution in severe cases, is often costly and can have a low success rate, sometimes even leading to the death of the animal due to the stress of a new environment and competition from existing species (Fontorbel & Simoetti, 2011). Studies have shown particularly high mortality rates among translocated carnivores. The process negatively impacts animal welfare through multiple pathways: stress during capture, nutritional deficiencies, dehydration, compromised immune function, and increased predation vulnerability (Massei, 2010). Additional complications include animals straying beyond designated release zones or causing similar conflicts in new locations.

While costly, mitigation strategies like using acclimatization enclosures and providing supplemental food/water can substantially improve outcomes by reducing post-release mortality and dispersal. Of particular concern are documented cases where translocated animals introduced zoonotic diseases to local human populations near release sites.

Across the globe, the rising numbers of hoofed mammals (ungulates) are causing growing problems for the environment and human society. These include damage to forests and farms, crop destruction in Africa and Asia, a greater chance of diseases spread by vectors, more wildlife-vehicle accidents, and issues with wild animals that have become used to suburban areas and private land in North America and Europe (Leong, 2009). In some instances, too many ungulates can disrupt natural ecosystems and even lead to the local disappearance of endangered species, which can then make it easier for non-native plants to invade (Knight et al., 2009). In this context, Cromsigt Joris's (2013) research discusses how hunting can be used in various ways to manage HWC. Conflicts in managed areas like timber forests or farmland are having a disproportionately large effect on more natural ecosystems.

It's been suggested that inconsistent actions and problems with figuring out the root causes, especially when personal opinions come into play, are key reasons why HWC are on the rise (White & Alastair Ward, 2010). A crucial first step in wildlife management plans should be to create hunting strategies that are specific to locations and times. This would focus hunting efforts in areas where wildlife damage needs to be reduced and ensure that there's enough variation in the levels of risk across different places and times. The increasing conflicts with ungulates worldwide present a chance to explore fundamentally new approaches to managing these large plant-eating animals.

When governments and responsible organizations fail to adequately address the challenges posed by wildlife, they unintentionally foster an environment where poaching can thrive. Local communities, frustrated by the lack of official response to the problems caused by wildlife, may collaborate with poachers to eliminate the problematic animals themselves. This lack of effective government action is a fundamental factor contributing to the extinction of certain species.

Wildlife utilization is an important means to control HWC and can be treated in the following ways.

i. Eco-tourism

Instead of solely relying on external compensation for damage, some HWC management strategies focus on using wildlife to create alternative income sources (Waylen et al., 2015). Ecotourism is a prominent example, proving effective by incentivizing the conservation of species that attract tourists through the revenue generated (Vannelli et al., 2019). In countries like South Africa, tourism initiatives have significantly contributed to wildlife population recovery and reintroductions (Trinkel & Angelici, 2016). Furthermore, residents involved in tourism schemes often report a greater sense of responsibility or ownership towards wildlife (Vannelli et al., 2019), and tourism revenue can fund other conflict management efforts like compensation or additional conservation projects (Cisneros-Montemayor et al., 2013).

However, using tourism for conflict management is not without its criticisms, including issues like poor governance, imposed restrictions, unequal benefit distribution, and challenges in revenue sharing with local communities (Trinkel & Angelici, 2016). Community-based tourism, such as homestays, offers a way to give local communities more control over tourism practices and the resulting income (Vannelli et al., 2019). These schemes are often considered more sustainable, culturally appropriate, and provide a stronger motivation for conservation (Caro & Riggio, 2013).

Nevertheless, studies also highlight problems like corruption, exclusion, and coercion within community-based tourism (Bluwstein, et al, 2016). Areas with higher wildlife concentrations, such as villages bordering nature reserves, tend to receive more benefits than others, potentially increasing existing resentment towards conservation efforts in less privileged communities (Hanley, 2015).

ii. Conservation-related employment

Employing local people in conservation-related jobs offers another avenue for managing HWC, moving beyond external compensation for damages. This includes roles in site maintenance, monitoring, and surveillance. The Lion Guardians initiative, which hires Maasai warriors in Kenya to conserve lions and protect local communities, exemplifies this approach (Hazzah, 2006). By respecting Maasai culture and beliefs, this initiative, unlike traditional monetary compensation in the same region, reinforces their spiritual connection to lions while providing income and contributing to the cessation of lion killings (Hemson et al., 2009). However, it's important to recognize that the value and significance of wild animals vary across different cultures and societies.

5. 6 Investment & Innovations

Integrated HWC management, which considers the needs of both wildlife and people, presents a compelling investment opportunity for international organizations, governments, and local communities. It not only safeguards wild species and maintains healthy ecosystems but also improves community safety. Furthermore, effective HWC strategies contribute to sustainable regional development, economic growth, public health, education, and broader positive change.

Wildlife Credits is a performance-based payment system that rewards landowners, farmers, and wildlife custodians for achieving successful conservation outcomes. This model empowers community-led conservation efforts and has the potential to transform HWC situations into human-wildlife coexistence through direct and measurable payments, increasing efficiency. The goal of Wildlife Credits is to foster human-wildlife coexistence by highlighting the inherent value of wildlife as a valuable global asset (Hanley, 2015). This requires governments to grant rights and benefits to landholding communities, allowing them to envision a wildlife-based economy where increased wildlife populations translate to greater rewards.

Wildlife Credits directly connects those willing to pay for conservation with landholding communities, offering a cost-effective way to achieve conservation goals and incentivize human-wildlife coexistence. The initiative is expanding to encompass larger wildlife areas, offering communities the opportunity to dedicate farmland to conservation in exchange for performance-based payments (Cisneros-Montemayor, et al. 2013). These schemes operate with the consent of local communities, ensuring a 'no performance, no payment' risk structure.

While human-wildlife coexistence has spurred global innovation, technological solutions like early warning systems alone are insufficient for effective conflict management. Achieving sustainable solutions requires novel, interdisciplinary approaches that integrate community engagement, social and biological sciences, engineering, private sector involvement, and policy development. Success depends on building trust, mutual respect, and inclusive decision-making that balances human and wildlife needs. Rigorous monitoring of interventions—both successful and unsuccessful—is critical for assessing their long-term viability.

Persistent underfunding in HWC mitigation necessitates mobilizing international resources through multilateral banks, development agencies, government budgets, and private investments. A deeper understanding of conflict drivers, ecological processes, and socio-economic impacts is essential for developing innovative management strategies. Interdisciplinary research—spanning social sciences, psychology, and environmental law—can provide valuable insights into human-wildlife interactions (White, at al. 2010).

Additionally, studies must account for emerging global trends, including climate change, urban expansion, industrial growth, and agricultural intensification, to identify new opportunities for coexistence.

The Wildlife Friendly Enterprise Network (WFEN) is a global network uniting farmers, ranchers, artisans, indigenous communities, and conservationists. It has a certification program to promote conservation and connect local and international efforts (Gillingham, 2001). To receive certification, businesses must demonstrate production methods that lessen threats to wildlife survival, involve local communities in their operations, and establish long-term monitoring practices.

WFEN certification specifically targets businesses operating in areas where wildlife and human activities overlap, often critical buffer zones experiencing high levels of HWC. These certified enterprises generate sustainable income for communities that depend on wildlife. Examples include predator-friendly beef and goat cheese from Namibia, Jaguar Friendly Coffee from Colombia, cashmere wool from Italy, and Certified Elephant Friendly tea from India (Marker L, 2019). These initiatives aim to reduce conflict with elephants, decrease elephant mortality, and minimize barriers to their movement.

Wildlife Friendly certified products appeal to a significant portion (40%) of global consumers who believe companies should address environmental issues and seek out responsible products (Treves, at al. 2009). These certified items are available through retailers worldwide and have received numerous awards for their environmental leadership and product excellence.

There are generally two main ways to approach governance in this context: a normative approach that evaluates the quality of governance, and a diagnostic approach that empirically investigates why governance sometimes fails (Peters, 2011). Governance is defined as the process by which decisions are put into action and should be fair, inclusive, participatory, consensus-oriented, accountable, transparent, responsive, effective, efficient, and law-abiding (United Nations, 2009).

The effectiveness of HWC interventions needs to be assessed by monitoring several factors (Curtin. C.G, 2002):

i. Whether the implemented interventions followed the planned activities.
ii. Whether the identified threat has been reduced or eliminated.
iii. Whether the project's goals, encompassing both conservation and human well-being, have been achieved.

5. 7 Conclusion

Managing HWC demands a comprehensive, multidisciplinary strategy that integrates technology, policy, and community involvement. Long-term solutions must prioritize both the well-being of people and the conservation of wildlife, recognizing HWC as a complex issue requiring multifaceted answers. By synergistically combining community participation, technological innovation, and strong policy frameworks, we can lessen conflicts and foster harmonious coexistence between humans and wildlife.

In this context, HWC management generally faces the following challenges.

i. *Limited Funding*: Many HWC programs lack consistent and reliable financial resources.
ii. *Human-Wildlife Coexistence Mindset*: Prevailing cultural beliefs and attitudes can make conflict resolution difficult.
iii. *Data Gaps*: Inconsistent and incomplete data collection hinders effective policy development and implementation.

Effective HWC management hinges on strong policies. The IUCN Guidelines offer frameworks for analyzing and addressing HWC, emphasizing strategies that promote coexistence. Similarly, the WWF's Conflict to Coexistence (C2C) Approach champions participatory frameworks that involve all stakeholders in achieving coexistence.

Policy and legal frameworks are essential in several key areas such as:

i. *Integrated Land-Use Planning*: Strategically balancing areas for agriculture and conservation (CBD, 2023).
ii. *International Collaboration:* Establishing agreements across borders for the protection of migratory species (Convention on Migratory Species, 2023).

To effectively reduce HWC, integrated planning is necessary, incorporating wildlife considerations into how land is used. Community engagement is crucial, empowering local populations through education and active participation in conservation efforts. Adopting appropriate technologies, such as beehive fences and drones, can also play a significant role. Robust policy implementation involves adopting and enforcing guidelines from organizations like the IUCN and WWF. Finally, effective data management requires developing comprehensive databases to track and analyze HWC trends. In this regard, the following areas require urgent action.

i. *Strengthen Early Warning Systems:* Utilizing advanced technologies like artificial intelligence and satellite tracking.
ii. *Expand Insurance Schemes:* Providing financial safety nets for farmers and herders affected by HWC.
iii. *Enhance Global Cooperation*: Strengthening collaboration through international platforms.

References

1. Bluwstein, J., Moyo, F., Kicheleri, R (2016), 'Austere conservation: Understanding conflicts over resource governance in Tanzanian wildlife management areas,' Conservation and Society, Vol. 14 No. 3, p. 218.

2. Boitani L., Powell R.A. (2012), *Carnivore Ecology and Conservation: A Handbook of Techniques*, Oxford University Press, New York, USA.
3. Bulte, E.H., Rondeau, D (2005), 'Why compensating wildlife damages may be bad for conservation,' *Journal of Wildlife Management*, Vol. 69, pp. 14–19.
4. Butler, J.R., 2000, 'The economic costs of wildlife predation on livestock in Gokwe communal land, Zimbabwe', *African Journal of Ecology*, Vol. 38, No. 1, pp.23–30.
5. Caro, T., Riggio, J (2013), 'The Big 5 and conservation,' *Animal Conservation*, Vol. 16, pp. 261–262.
6. Carter, M (1997), 'Environment, Technology and Social articulation of Risk in West African Agriculture,' *Economic Development and Cultural Change*, Vo.45, pp. 557-590.
7. Chen, S., Yi, Z-F., Campos-Arceiz, A., Chen, M-Y.,Webb, E.L (2013), 'Developing a spatially-explicit, sustainable and risk-based insurance scheme to mitigate human–wildlife conflict,' *Biological Conservation*, Vol. 168, pp. 31–39.
8. Cisneros-Montemayor, A., Barnes-Mauthe, M., Al-Abdulrazzak, D., Navarro-Holm, E., Sumaila, U (2013), 'Global economic value of shark ecotourism: Implications for conservation,' *Oryx*, Vol. 47, No. 3, pp. 381–388
9. Curtin. C.G (2002), 'Integration of Science and Community based Conservation in Mexico, US borderland, *Conservation Biology*, Vo. 16, No.4, pp.880-886.
10. Dickman et al. (2014), 'Carnivores, culture and 'contagious conflict: Multiple factors influence perceived problems with carnivores in Tanzania's Ruaha landscape', *Biological Conservation,* Vol. 178, pp.19-27.
11. Dickman, A.J., Hazzah, L. (2016). 'Money, myths and man-eaters : Complexities of human–wildlife conflict,' In: Angelici, F.M. (editor), *Problematic wildlife*, Cham: Springer, pp. 339–356.

12. Fagerstone , K A (2010), 'Review of Issues Concerning the Use of Reproductive Inhibitors with Particular Emphasis on Resolving HWC in North America,' *Integrative Zoology*, Vol.1, pp.15-30.
13. FAO. (2023). *Global Assessment of HWC Impacts on Agriculture.*
14. Fontorbel FE & Simoetti JA (2011), 'Translocations and Human-carnivore Conflicts: Problem Solving or Problem Creating?,' *Wildlife Biology*, Vol. 17, pp.217-224.
15. Frank, Beatrice (2016), 'Human–Wildlife Conflicts and the Need to Include Tolerance and Coexistence: An Introductory Comment,' *Society and Natural Resources*, Vol. 29, No. 6, pp. 738-743.
16. Fritz H (2017), 'Long-term field studies of elephants: understanding the ecology and conservation of a long-lived ecosystem engineer,' *Journal of Mammalogy*, Vol. 98, No. 3, pp.603-611.
17. Gillingham, S (2001), 'Social Organization and Participatory Resources Management in Brazilian Ribeirinho Communities: A Case Study of the Mamiraua Sustainable Development Reserve, Amazonas,' *Society and Natural Resources,* Vol. 14, PP.803-814.
18. Gross E, et.al. (2021), *A Future for All: The Need for Human-Wildlife Coexistence*, WWF, Gland, Switzerland.
19. Hanley, N. (2015). 'Understanding conservation conflicts: An economic perspective', In: Redpath, S. M., Gutiérrez, R.J., Wood, K.A., Young, J.C. (editors*), Conflicts in conservation: Navigating towards solutions*, Cambridge: Cambridge University Press, pp. 79–93.
20. Hazzah, L.N (2006), *Living among Lions: Coexistence or Killing? Community Attitude towards Conservation Initiatives and the Motivations behind Lion Killing in Kenyan Maasailand*, University of Wisconsin-Madison .

21. Hedges, S & Gunaryadi D (2010), 'Reducing Human-elephant Conflict: Do Chillies Help Deter Elephants from Entering Crop Fields?,' *Oryx*, Vol. 44, pp.139-146.
22. Hemson, G., Maclennanan, S., Mills, G., Johnson, P., Macdonald, D (2009), 'Community, lions, livestock and money: A spatial and social analysis of attitudes to wildlife and the conservation value of tourism in a human–carnivore conflict in Botswana,' *Biological Conservation,* Vol. 142, No. 11, pp. 2718–2725.
23. Hoare, R. (2015), 'Lessons from 20 years of human–elephant conflict mitigation in Africa,' *Human Dimensions of Wildlife,* Vol. 20, No. 4, pp. 289–295.
24. IUCN. (2023). *Red List of Threatened Species*.
25. Keith, D. A, et. al. (2011), 'Uncertainty and adaptive management for biodiversity conservation,' *Biological conservation*, Vol. 144, No. 4, pp. 1175-1178.
26. King, L E, et. al. (2011), 'Beehive Fences as Effective Deterrents for Crop-raiding Elephants: Field trials in Northern Kenya,' *African Journal of Ecology*, Vol. 49,pp. 431-439.
27. KWS (2000), *Wildlife-Human Conflicts: Sources, Solutions and Issues*, Wildlife Service, Nairobi.
28. Lapidge S, et. al. (2007), 'Global Harmonisation in the field of invasive species management product development,' *Proceeding of the International Symposiums* on Managing Vertebrate Invasive Species, Vol. 7-9, August, Fort Collins, Co, USA, pp. 34-41.
29. Madhusadan, M.D. (2003), 'Living amidst large wildlife: Livestock and crop depredation by large mammals in the interior villages of Bhadra Tiger reserve, South India,' *Environmental Management,* Vol. 31, No. 4, pp. 466–475.
30. Marchini S & P. G Crawshaw (2015), 'HWCs in Brazil: A Fast-growing Issue,' *Human Dimensions of Wildlife*, Vol. 20, pp. 323-328.

31. Marker, L (2005), *Aspects of Cheetah – Biology, Ecology and Conservation Strategies on Namibian Farmlands*, University of Oxford, Oxford.
32. Marker L (2019), 'Cheetahs Race for Survival: Ecology and Conservation' *IntechOpen.*
33. Massei, Giovanna (2010), 'Can translocations be used to mitigate human–wildlife conflicts?' *Wildlife Research*, Vol. 37, No. 5, pp. 428-439.
34. McManus etal. (2015), 'Dead or alive? Comparing the costs and benefits of lethal and non-lethal human–wildlife conflict mitigation on livestock farms,' *Oryx*, Vol. 49, No. 4, pp. 687–695.
35. Naughton-Treves, Holland and Brandon (2005), 'The role of protected areas in conserving biodiversity and sustaining local livelihoods.,' *Annual Review of Environment and Resources,* Vol. 30, No. 1, pp. 219–252
36. Nyhus, Philip, J, (2016), HWC and Coexistence, *Annual Review of Environment and Resources,* Vol.41, pp.143-171.
37. Okello, Kiringe and Warinwa (2014), 'Human–carnivore conflicts in private conservancy lands of Elerai and Oltiyiani in Amboseli area, Kenya,' *Natural Resources*, Vol. 5, pp. 375–391.
38. Panthera. (2023). *Lion Guardians Program Report.*
39. Peters, B. G (2011), 'Governance as political theory,' *Critical Policy Studies*, Vol. 5, No. 1, pp. 63–72.
40. Ravenelle, J., Nyhus, P. J (2017), 'Global patterns and trends in human–wildlife conflict compensation,' *Conservation Biology,* Vol. 31, No. 6, pp. 1247–1256.
41. Redfern J.V., et al. (2013), 'Assessing the risk of ships striking large whales in marine spatial planning,' *Conservation Biology*, Vol. 27, No. 2, pp. 292-302.
42. Riley et al. (2002), 'The essence of wildlife management,' *Wildlife Society Bulletin*, Vol. 30, pp. 585-593.

43. Soffker et al., (2015), The impact of predation by marine mammals on Patagonian tooth -fish longline fisheries', *PLoS ONE*, Vol. 10, No. 3.
44. Swanepoel LH, et. al. (2015), 'Functional Responses of Retaliatory Killing verses Recreational Sport-Hunting of Leopards in South Africa,' *PLOS One*, Vol10, No. 4, e0125539.
45. Treves, Adrian, et.al. (2006), 'Co-managing HWCs: A Review,' *Human Dimensions of Wildlife,* Vol.11, pp.383-396.
46. Treves, Adrian, et. al. (2009), 'Participatory Planning of Interventions to Mitigate HWCs,' *Conservation Biology*, pp. 1-11.
47. Trinkel, M., Angelici, F.M (2016), 'The decline in the lion population in Africa and possible mitigation measures', in: Angelici, F.M. (editor), *Problematic wildlife*, Cham: Springer, pp. 45–68.
48. United Nations (2009), *What is good governance?*, Economic and Social Commission for Asia and the Pacific, Bangkok, p.3.
49. UNEP. (2023). *Climate Change and HWC.*
50. Vannelli et al. (2019), Community participation in ecotourism and its effect on local perceptions of snow leopard (Panthera uncia) conservation.,' *Human Dimensions of Wildlife*, Vol. 24, No. 2, pp. 180–193.
51. Waylen et al. (2015), 'Can scenario-planning support community-based natural resource management? Experiences from three countries in Latin America,' *Ecology and Society*, Vol. 20, No. 4.
52. White, P C. L. & Alastair I. Ward (2010), 'Interdisciplinary approaches for the management of existing and emerging human–wildlife conflicts,' *Wildlife Research*, Vol. 37, No.8, pp. 623-629.
53. WWF. (2023). *Living with Wildlife: Mitigation Strategies.*

CHAPTER: 6
WILDLIFE AND CO-EXISTENCE

6.1 Introduction

Wildlife is essential for healthy ecosystems, contributing to processes like pollination, seed dispersal, and sustaining food chains. Yet, as human development encroaches on natural habitats, interactions between people and wildlife have risen, frequently leading to conflict. The World Wildlife Fund reports that over 75% of wild species are impacted by HWC (WWF, 2023). To safeguard both biodiversity and human well-being, effective coexistence strategies are crucial.

Promoting peaceful human-wildlife relations is key to preserving biodiversity and ecological stability. However, factors such as population growth, habitat degradation, and climate change have worsened these conflicts. This chapter examines the dynamics of human-wildlife co-existence, its dimensions and explores sustainable approaches to fostering coexistence. The chapter also discusses key success factors and major challenges to co-existence. As human activity and environmental shifts increase encounters between people and wildlife, species decline become more common. Nevertheless, conservation initiatives worldwide show that coexistence is possible through targeted actions, community involvement, and technological advancements.

Even though HWC is escalating, innovative coexistence programs in various regions prove that sustainable sharing of landscapes is achievable. Wildlife coexistence involves methods that minimize conflict while allowing humans and animals to inhabit the same spaces. With natural habitats diminishing, proactive approaches—such as community collaboration, habitat rehabilitation, and tech-based solutions—are proving successful.

Just as HWC varies by context, so does coexistence, requiring human decisions to sustainably share resources and landscapes with wildlife. Achieving this often depends on consensus or cooperation among different stakeholders of wildlife management.

6.2 Concept of Wildlife Co-existence

Wildlife coexistence involves humans and wild animals sustainably sharing landscapes while reducing conflict, preserving biodiversity, and supporting both ecological and human well-being. Unlike conventional conservation methods that often segregate humans and wildlife, coexistence focuses on flexible approaches that enable both to flourish in shared environments. Key initiatives and their outcomes in this regard are summarized in Table 6.1.

As human expansion increasingly invades wildlife habitats, conflicts between people and animals have intensified. While past strategies mainly addressed conflict mitigation, contemporary research underscores the need for coexistence approaches that foster mutual understanding and tolerance. This shift has made human-wildlife coexistence a central theme in wildlife management, moving beyond mere conflict resolution to cultivating acceptance. Recent studies reveal a changing attitude toward human-wildlife interactions, showing that communities become more receptive to wildlife when effective coexistence measures are applied (Nyhus, 2016). A crucial factor in successful coexistence is the active participation of local communities in wildlife conservation efforts.

Table: 6.1 Global Wildlife Co-existence Initiatives

Co-existence Model	*Project*	*Initiative*	*Impact*
Africa: Community-Based Conservation	Namibia's Conservancy Program	Local communities manage wildlife resources and benefit from eco-tourism.	i. Lion populations increased by 90% since 1995. ii. Retaliatory killings reduced by 60% in conservancy areas.
	Kenya's Beehive Fences	Beehives installed around farms deter elephants (who fear bees).	i. 80% reduction in crop raids. ii. Additional income from honey production.
Asia: Conflict Mitigation and Habitat Corridors	India's Project Elephant & Tiger Corridors	Early warning systems, habitat corridors, and compensation schemes.	i. 30% decline in human-elephant fatalities. ii. Tiger populations increased by 33% since 2014.
	Bhutan's Compensation and Insurance Schemes	Government compensates farmers for livestock lost to snow leopards.	i. Retaliatory killings dropped by 50%. ii. Improved local support for conservation.
North America: Coexistence Through Technology	USA & Canada: Range Rider Programs	Riders monitor wolves and bears to prevent livestock predation.	60-70% reduction in livestock losses.
	Mexico's Jaguar-Friendly Beef Certification	Ranchers adopt jaguar-friendly practices in exchange for premium beef prices.	Reduced jaguar killings by 40%.
	Brazil's Onçafari Program	Eco-tourism and jaguar habituation to	Increased jaguar sightings, boosting

South America: Agroforestry and Eco-Tourism		reduce fear-based killings.	local tourism revenue.
	Peru's Coffee Corridors for Wildlife	Shade-grown coffee plantations provide habitats for birds and small mammals.	Biodiversity increased by 25% in coffee-growing regions.

Source: Defenders of Wildlife (2023); IUCN (2022); NTCA (2023); Panthera (2023); Rainforest Alliance (2023); Save the Elephants (2022); WWF (2023)

Key features of coexistence, as defined by the IUCN (2023), include the following.

i. *Coexistence is more than just the absence of conflict*: Coexistence is best understood as an active process rather than simply a point opposite conflict on a spectrum. A coexistence state doesn't mean conflict or negative interactions are absent; rather, it refers to how these challenges are perceived and handled. In fact, even in generally coexistence-oriented settings, conflicts still occur but are effectively managed or tolerated.

ii. *Coexistence values all types of human-wildlife interactions:* When examining human relationships with wildlife, it's important to include positive and neutral interactions, not just negative ones. Using positive framing and language can help address conflicts constructively, provided it does not dismiss genuine community concerns.

iii. *Coexistence focuses on human-wildlife relationships across shared landscapes:* Wildlife of all types—including common, less charismatic, and non-native species—can significantly affect people's lives and conservation attitudes. A coexistence approach acknowledges and includes all such interactions within multi-use landscapes.

iv. *Coexistence needs to operate at both local and landscape levels:* The goal is to shift conflict situations toward sustainable coexistence not just in isolated areas but across broader landscapes (WWF, 2022). This involves considering multiple species (including those less prioritized by conservationists), diverse stakeholder perspectives, large-scale ecological and social patterns, various management strategies suited to different contexts, and differing resource capacities.

v. *Coexistence is complex and depends heavily on context:* Current research shows that human-wildlife and human-human interactions are highly complex and vary greatly depending on the local setting (NTCA, 2023). Ongoing efforts aim to build a broad and diverse body of knowledge across different environments.

vi. *Coexistence demands self-awareness from conservationists:* While conservationists may seek coexistence with wildlife, those directly affected by wildlife may have different priorities. Recognizing and respecting these differing views requires conservationists to reflect on their own positions and be open to alternative perspectives, especially those of local and indigenous communities.

vii. *Coexistence must address power dynamics, fairness, and justice:* Effectively understanding and managing human-wildlife relations means accounting for historical conservation practices and current inequalities in influence among different groups. Efforts to promote coexistence should be inclusive, ensuring that all affected parties—human and animal alike—participate in fair, transparent decision-making processes and retain a degree of autonomy in shared landscapes (IUCN, 2022b).

HWC has long been a major issue, often resulting in animals being killed to safeguard crops, livestock, or human lives. Yet, with growing recognition of ecological balance and animal rights, there is an increasing push for non-lethal approaches to living alongside wildlife. Wildlife coexistence emphasizes living in harmony, promoting sustainable practices, and adopting innovative methods to manage conflicts while conserving biodiversity.

The core principles of wildlife coexistence focus on prevention, education, and innovation. By protecting natural habitats, involving local communities, employing humane deterrents, and utilizing modern technology, it is possible for humans and wildlife to coexist peacefully. Killing should be viewed as a last resort, not the first reaction. Achieving true coexistence requires a commitment to compassion, sustainability, and smart conflict resolution strategies. The key principles supporting wildlife coexistence include (WWF, 2022):

i. *Non-lethal conflict management:* Implementing humane methods to prevent wildlife-related damage without resorting to killing, such as using safe deterrents to keep animals away from human areas.
ii. *Shared benefits:* Ensuring that local communities benefit directly from conservation initiatives, encouraging their support and participation.
iii. *Ecological balance*: Protecting and restoring ecosystems to ensure long-term survival for both humans and wildlife. Since habitat loss from deforestation, urban development, and farming drives animals into human areas, maintaining natural habitats is crucial to minimizing conflict.
iv. *Adaptive management:* Continuously refining and improving conflict mitigation strategies based on current data and changing conditions.

The primary aim of managing HWC is to ensure the safety of both people and wildlife while fostering mutual benefits through coexistence. In communities with low tolerance for HWC incidents, retaliatory actions against wildlife can escalate conflicts, often leading to the complete removal of problematic animals—a measure that may ultimately drive species to extinction (Gillingham, 2001). However, in economically disadvantaged regions, communities often exhibit greater tolerance toward wildlife, even in high-conflict situations, enabling wildlife populations to persist in human-dominated areas.

While eliminating HWC is rarely feasible, a well-structured and integrated approach can significantly reduce conflicts by promoting coexistence. The shift from conflict to coexistence is a fluid process, with neither state being permanent. Human attitudes toward wildlife can evolve over time and vary across different regions and contexts. When coexistence is achieved, ongoing negative interactions between humans and wildlife diminish significantly.

The IUCN SSC Human-Wildlife Conflict & Coexistence Specialist Group (HWCCSG)—previously known as the IUCN SSC HWC Task Force—serves as an interdisciplinary advisory body and think tank, supporting professionals in HWC management and coexistence strategies (Marker, 2019). It offers expert guidance, resources, and capacity-building initiatives, bridging the gap between policy, science, and local communities while consolidating knowledge for effective conflict resolution.

The HWCCSG's key objectives include (IUCN, 2023):

i. Advising on best practices for HWC and coexistence management.

ii. Promoting interdisciplinary approaches to conflict mitigation.

iii. Strengthening capacity through technical guidance, training workshops, and digital learning platforms, including an online resource library.

This approach ensures a balanced and sustainable framework for human-wildlife interactions.

6.3 Dimensions of Wildlife Co-existence

Wildlife co-existence describes how people and wild animals can live together in shared environments, ensuring that both thrive. This idea is more important than ever as cities and industries expand, increasingly mixing human and natural spaces. To build lasting connections with nature and protect the variety of life on Earth, it's crucial to grasp the different aspects of this co-existence.

Ecological Dimension

One key part of wildlife co-existence is the ecological dimension, which involves maintaining healthy ecosystems that support both wildlife and human needs. This requires conserving or restoring forests, wetlands, grasslands, and marine areas to provide food, shelter, and breeding grounds for animals. This ecological balance also provides essential services for humans like pollination, climate regulation, and clean water. Recognizing the link between humans and nature emphasizes the importance of biodiversity conservation. The ecological dimension is characterized by (IUCN, 2023):

i. *Habitat Connectivity:* Wildlife corridors, such as those for elephants in India which decrease HWC, allow safe movement between separated habitats.
ii. *Biodiversity Conservation:* Protecting key species like wolves and elephants to ensure ecosystem stability.
iii. *Climate Resilience:* Healthy wildlife populations helping ecosystems adapt to climate change.

Socio-Economic Dimension

A critical socio-economic aspect of wildlife co-existence recognizes that many communities near wildlife areas depend on natural resources for their survival. For successful co-existence, their needs and rights must be acknowledged. Approaches like eco-tourism, sustainable use of forest products, and community-led conservation can create mutual benefits for both wildlife and people. By incentivizing local responsibility, we not only empower communities but also achieve better conservation outcomes. The socio-economic dimension is characterized by:

i. *Livelihood Integration*: Generating income through eco-tourism, sustainable agriculture, and beekeeping while simultaneously protecting wildlife, as seen with Namibia's $10 million annual earnings from wildlife tourism in conservancies (WWF, 2023).

ii. *Compensation Schemes:* Providing financial support to farmers for losses caused by wildlife, such as Bhutan's compensation for snow leopard attacks on livestock (Defender of Wildlife, 2023).
iii. *Community Stewardship:* Enhancing conservation success through the involvement of local communities and the application of indigenous knowledge.

Technological Dimension

In today's world, technological related aspects are also crucial for wildlife co-existence. Modern technologies like GPS tracking, camera traps, and drones have transformed wildlife conservation by enabling better data collection and management. Simultaneously, strong laws and policies—such as protected areas, wildlife corridors, and anti-poaching rules—create the necessary legal structure for co-existence. These policies must be supported by robust governance and community involvement to ensure they are followed and fair. Key features of the technological dimension include:

i. *Early Warning Systems:* Using AI, drones, and SMS alerts to predict animal movements. For example, Kenya's Lion Guardians use GPS to track lions near villages (WWF, 2022).
ii. *Non-Lethal Deterrents:* Employing methods like beehive fences for elephants, flashing lights for predators, and chili fences for elephants to prevent conflict without harming animals.
iii. *Genetic and Population Monitoring*: Using DNA tracking to help manage populations of overabundant species.

Policy & Governance Dimension

The policy and governance dimensions establish the necessary framework for wildlife co-existence. International agreements, including Convention on International Trade in Endangered Species of Wild Fauna and Flora (CITES), Convention on Biological Diversity (CBD), and UNEP, offer guidelines for managing co-existence across countries. Within nations, laws such as anti-poaching measures, land-use zoning, and incentives like wildlife-friendly farming subsidies are essential, as seen in Mexico's 2020 Jaguar Conservation Plan (Defender of Wildlife, 2023). Furthermore, local governance structures, such as village committees, are often responsible for addressing and resolving HWC at the community level.

Cultural & Ethical Dimension

Cultural and ethical aspects are also vital for wildlife co-existence. Many cultures globally have traditionally respected animals and nature through their beliefs and practices, often promoting harmony that aids conservation. Ethically, we are urged to see wildlife as sentient beings with their own value, fostering a moral basis for co-existence. This includes traditional knowledge like Maasai lion rituals, a shift in conservation thinking towards shared landscapes, and the importance of education and awareness through schools and media to reduce fear of wildlife (WWF, 2023a). Education and awareness are fundamental to building a culture of co-existence, helping individuals understand the value of wildlife and conservation. Schools, media, and local campaigns are key to spreading knowledge and shaping attitudes, encouraging practices that reduce conflict and support conservation (Madhusudan, 2003).

In essence, wildlife co-existence is a multidimensional idea involving ecological, socio-economic, cultural, technological, and educational elements. It requires a comprehensive approach balancing human development with the needs of nature. As global environmental issues worsen, embracing these dimensions is crucial for a sustainable future for all life.

6.4 Strategies for Co-existence

In our increasingly crowded world, where human expansion constantly encroaches on natural habitats, learning to co-exist with wildlife is no longer optional but a growing necessity. Achieving a balanced relationship between people and animals demands thoughtful and inclusive strategies that tackle the fundamental causes of HWC, actively promote conservation, and cultivate mutual respect between communities and the ecosystems they share.

Crucially, education and public awareness play an equally vital role. By informing people about wildlife behavior and the ecological importance of different species, we can diminish fear and foster positive attitudes (IUCN, 2022). Schools, the media, and community workshops are all essential avenues for building a culture of co-existence. When people understand how the presence of wildlife contributes to a healthy environment—through processes like pollination, pest control, and maintaining soil fertility—they are more likely to adopt practices that minimize conflict and support conservation efforts.

The Wildlife Stakeholder Acceptance Capacity (WSAC) refers to the range of wildlife impacts that a given stakeholder—whether an individual, group, or community considers tolerable (Carpenter et al., 2000). The lower boundary of WSAC represents a stakeholder's willingness to accept the absence of positive wildlife effects, while the upper boundary reflects their threshold for enduring negative wildlife impacts. Contemporary wildlife management challenges largely revolve around WSAC, which encompasses both tolerance for wildlife-related difficulties and expectations of benefits from wildlife. This capacity is shaped by human attitudes, beliefs, and values, making the understanding and management of these human dimensions a central focus of wildlife conservation efforts. Unlike economic valuation approaches that calculate wildlife's net value by subtracting negative impacts from positive ones, the WSAC framework adopts a more comprehensive perspective that integrates social, cultural, and psychological factors alongside economic considerations (Conover, 1997).

Effective co-existence strategies are multifaceted, incorporating technological innovations, community involvement, policy reforms, and habitat restoration.

Technological Innovations

Technology is playing an increasingly significant role in facilitating wildlife co-existence. Tools such as GPS collars, motion-sensor cameras, and drones enable conservationists to monitor animal movements and proactively prevent potential conflicts. Early warning systems can alert communities to the proximity of large animals like elephants or predators, allowing them to take necessary precautions (Frank, 2016). Furthermore, employing non-lethal barriers such as solar-powered electric fences, bio-fencing using thorny vegetation, or beehive fences can effectively deter animals from entering farmlands without causing them harm. Example includes:

i. *Early Warning Systems:* As seen in Assam, India, the 'Haati App' provides communities with alerts about nearby elephant movements, thereby reducing unexpected and potentially dangerous encounters (IUCN, 2022).
ii. *Surveillance Technologies*: In Bermuda, modified infrared GoPro cameras are used to monitor the elusive cahow seabird, providing valuable data for its conservation (WWF, 2022).

Community Engagement

Engaging local communities in conservation efforts is another vital approach. These communities are often the first to experience both the challenges and the benefits of living near wildlife. By involving them directly in conservation, we ensure that strategies are rooted in practical knowledge and cultural understanding. Training and empowering local people to protect wildlife through initiatives like eco-tourism, sustainable resource management, or employment in park services transforms them into conservation allies (Curtin, 2002). Revenue-sharing programs that benefit local economies can further enhance community support and reduce incentives for illegal activities such as poaching. Example includes:

i. *Community-Based Sanctuaries:* Belize's Community Baboon Sanctuary, where local landowners are involved in protecting the Yucatán black howler monkey, has successfully increased its population from 800 to over 3,500 (Nyhus, 2016).

ii. *Women's Conservation Groups:* The Community Baboon Sanctuary Women's Conservation Group in Belize exemplifies the empowerment of women in conservation efforts, linking biodiversity protection with sustainable development (White, el al.2010).

Policy and Legislative Measures

Policy and governance form a critical foundation for successful co-existence strategies. Laws that regulate land use, protect endangered species, and penalize illegal hunting are essential, but their implementation must be fair and transparent. Wildlife management policies should be evidence-based and incorporate input from local stakeholders. Governments must also invest in conflict mitigation programs, including compensation schemes for losses caused by wildlife, which can reduce retaliatory actions against animals and build trust with affected communities (Riley, 2002). Example includes:

i. *Protected Areas and Reserves*: The establishment of protected areas, such as China's 67 panda reserves, has proven instrumental in the recovery of species (WWF, 2022).

ii. *International Cooperation*: Collaborative efforts, such as the reintroduction of the Arabian oryx across Oman, Saudi Arabia, and the UAE, highlight the importance of cross-border conservation initiatives (IUCN, 2022b).

iii. *Compensation Schemes*: Governments and NGOs provide financial assistance for losses of crops or livestock caused by wildlife.

iv. *Early Warning Systems*: The use of SMS alerts and drone surveillance in Africa has been effective in reducing conflicts with elephants (WWF, 2023).

Habitat Restoration

Preserving and restoring natural habitats is one of the most effective long-term strategies for wildlife co-existence. Wildlife requires safe and healthy environments to thrive, making the conservation of natural landscapes such as forests, wetlands, and grasslands crucial. Governments and conservation organizations must prioritize the protection of biodiversity hotspots and implement reforestation or habitat rehabilitation in degraded areas. Furthermore, creating wildlife corridors—connected stretches of natural habitat that link isolated ecosystems—enables animals to migrate, find food, and reproduce without encountering human populations (Frank, 2016). Example includes:

i. *Corridor Creation:* Wildlife corridors in India have been shown to reduce tiger-human conflicts by 40% (NTCA, 2022).

ii. *Agroforestry:* Integrating trees into farming practices helps reduce habitat fragmentation, providing pathways for wildlife.

A brief account of co-existence strategies is given in Table-6.2. Despite challenges, concerted conservation efforts have led to remarkable recoveries of several species, demonstrating the potential for positive outcomes through targeted actions.

Harmonious coexistence between humans and wildlife can be achieved by integrating habitat conservation, local community engagement, technological solutions, public awareness programs, and strong policy frameworks. These approaches are mutually reinforcing and should be adapted to local ecological and social contexts. In the face of accelerating biodiversity decline and climate disruption, implementing such holistic and participatory strategies becomes essential for creating sustainable shared spaces where both wildlife and human communities can flourish.

Table: 6.2 Review of Coexistence Strategies

Strategy	*Description*	*Success Rate (%)*
Community Engagement	Involving locals in wildlife management	75
Compensation Programs	Financial compensation for losses	60
Education and Outreach	Raising awareness about wildlife	70

Source: Nyhus, 2016

6.5 Key Success Factors

True wildlife coexistence means humans and animals sharing spaces peacefully, without lethal interventions. This delicate balance demands ecological awareness, community collaboration, and creative problem-solving (Ravenelle, et al. 2017). Several vital components make this possible, ensuring both biodiversity and communities thrive together.

As human settlements expand, wildlife habitats shrink—pushing animals into closer contact with people. Protecting forests, wetlands, and grasslands, along with rehabilitating degraded areas, provides essential space and resources for wildlife. Establishing wildlife corridors—safe pathways linking fragmented habitats—allows animals to roam freely without encroaching on human areas. When animals have access to their natural environments, conflicts diminish.

Local communities near wildlife habitats often face the greatest challenges—crop destruction, livestock losses, and safety risks. Educating residents about animal behavior, ecosystem benefits, and conflict prevention fosters tolerance. Involving them in conservation efforts—such as wildlife monitoring or eco-tourism—creates economic incentives to protect rather than harm animals (Hoare, 2015). When communities benefit from coexistence, they become conservation allies rather than adversaries. Best practices of wildlife restoration through co-existence is provided in Table 6.3.

Instead of harmful measures like poisons or hunting, modern coexistence relies on humane deterrents such as physical barriers (electric fencing, chili-based repellents), guard animals (dogs, donkeys to protect livestock), and behavioral conditioning (lights, noise deterrents) (Panthera, 2023).

These methods prevent harm while fostering a culture of peaceful cohabitation. Innovations like camera traps, drones, and real-time alerts help communities anticipate and prevent conflicts. For example, in Africa and Asia, SMS warnings notify farmers of approaching elephants, allowing safe redirection (Save the Elephant, 2022). Such tools reduce surprise encounters and eliminate the need for violent responses. When wildlife causes damage, compensation schemes and community insurance prevent resentment and retaliatory killings (Frank, 2016). Government or community-run programs help offset losses, encouraging long-term coexistence strategies instead of viewing wildlife as threats.

Table: 6.3 Successful wildlife restoration through co-existence

Species	*Region*	*Lessons*
Elephant	India	Reduced human-elephant fatalities by 30% through early warning systems and habitat corridors.
Lions	Namibia	Local communities benefit from eco-tourism, reducing retaliatory killings of lions.
Giant Panda	China	Wild population increased to over 1,800; status downgraded from 'Endangered' to 'Vulnerable'.
Bald Eagle	United States	Population rebounded to over 316,000; removed from endangered species list in 2007.
Arabian Oryx	Middle East	Reintroduced into the wild after extinction; current wild population exceeds 1,000.
Mountain Gorilla	Central Africa	Population increased from 620 in 2008 to over 1,000 by 2018 due to anti-poaching and habitat restoration.
Partula Snail	French Polynesia	Reintroduced into the wild after being declared extinct; now classified as 'Critically Endangered'.

Source: IUCN, 2023

Changing perceptions is crucial. Media, education, and indigenous knowledge can reshape attitudes—portraying wildlife not as pests but as vital to healthy ecosystems. When societies value nature, they support policies that promote harmony. Key success factors include the following (NTCA, 2023).

i. *Community Benefits*: Eco-tourism, compensation, and shared ownership of conservation efforts.
ii. *Habitat Connectivity*: Wildlife corridors prevent isolation and reduce human-wildlife encounters.
iii. *Innovative Solutions*: AI monitoring, beehive fences, and other non-lethal deterrents.
iv. *Policy & Governance*: Strong legal frameworks ensure long-term, sustainable coexistence.

Achieving true harmony requires habitat protection, community partnership, technology, fair policies, and cultural change. It's not just about avoiding conflict—it's about creating a world where both humans and nature thrive together. The journey demands collaboration, patience, and deep respect for the natural world—ensuring a sustainable future for all species.

6.6 Challenges to Co-existence

While striving for wildlife coexistence is a vital and commendable goal, it faces significant hurdles in today's rapidly changing world. Expanding human populations and accelerating economic development are shrinking the boundaries between communities and wildlife habitats. This growing overlap has intensified HWC, making peaceful coexistence increasingly complicated. Recognizing these challenges is crucial for creating effective, and sustainable solutions.

One of the most urgent issues is habitat loss and fragmentation. As forests are cleared for farming, infrastructure, and urban growth, wildlife is left with smaller, isolated habitat patches. This forces animals into human areas in search of food and shelter, often resulting in conflict, injuries, and fatalities for both people and wildlife.

Fragmentation also disrupts migration and breeding patterns, threatening the genetic health and long-term survival of species.

Increasing HWC is another major challenge, particularly in rural and farming communities. Animals like elephants, leopards, and wild boars often damage crops and livestock, leading to significant financial losses for farmers and triggering retaliatory killings (WWF, 2022). Such conflicts deepen negative attitudes toward wildlife and weaken conservation efforts. A lack of timely compensation or support from authorities often makes local communities feel neglected and fuels resentment.

Poaching and illegal wildlife trade also threaten coexistence. Driven by high global demand and profit, poaching has severely reduced populations of species such as rhinos, tigers, and pangolins (Othman, et al. 2019). Beyond the loss of individual animals, poaching destabilizes ecosystems and strengthens criminal networks, creating unsafe environments for local communities and conservation workers.

Climate change is an emerging and intensifying threat. Changing weather patterns, rising temperatures, and shifting ecosystems are forcing animals to migrate into new areas, often clashing with human activities (FAO, 2023). Water shortages, for example, can drive wildlife closer to human settlements, while habitat changes can reduce food and breeding opportunities, putting additional pressure on vulnerable species.

Lack of public awareness and education also impedes coexistence efforts. Many people, even in rural areas, may not fully understand the ecological importance of wildlife. Fear and misunderstanding can lead to hostility, while limited access to information and resources prevents the adoption of wildlife-friendly practices (Woodroffe, 2005). Conservation policies that ignore local cultures and perspectives often meet resistance and fail to succeed.

Finally, poor policy implementation and governance further complicate coexistence efforts. Despite the existence of wildlife protection laws, enforcement is often weak due to corruption, limited funding, or political disinterest in Less Developed Countries (White, et al. 2010). When conservation efforts are seen to favor wildlife over human needs, they can foster resentment and alienation among local communities.

From the foregone discussion the key challenges can be summarized as follows (IUCN, 2022a):

i. *Urban Encroachment*: Expanding cities and agriculture are breaking up natural habitats.
ii. *Climate Change*: Shifts in animal behavior and migration patterns lead to more conflicts.
iii. *Funding Gaps*: Many conservation initiatives lack sustainable financial support.
iv. *Policy Enforcement:* Weak legal frameworks allow illegal activities and habitat loss.

Achieving true wildlife coexistence requires tackling these intertwined challenges through a comprehensive approach that addresses ecological, economic, social, and political dimensions. With collaboration, innovation, and mutual respect for human and animal needs, coexistence can move from aspiration to reality.

6.7 Conclusion

Human-wildlife interactions around the world are highly complex, shaped by both ongoing conflicts and notable conservation successes. Positive examples from different regions highlight the value of comprehensive strategies that blend technology, community engagement, and policy improvements. Sustained dedication to these integrated efforts is crucial for achieving lasting coexistence between humans and wildlife.

Global coexistence projects show that reducing conflict is achievable through collaboration, innovation, and sustainable practices. Expanding these successes will require greater investment, stronger enforcement of conservation policies, and the sharing of knowledge and experiences across borders. Key actions needed to support sustainable coexistence include (IUCN, 2023):

i. Strengthening habitat protection policies.
ii. Increasing financial support for conflict mitigation efforts.
iii. Boosting community involvement in conservation initiatives.

Looking ahead, special focus should be placed on the following areas (WWF, 2022).

i. *Scaling up proven models*: Expand successful initiatives like Kenya's beehive fence projects and India's Project Elephant.
ii. *Building stronger international partnerships*: Encourage collaboration between organizations like IUCN, WWF, and grassroots NGOs.
iii. *Leveraging technology*: Utilize AI, satellite monitoring, and crowd-sourced data to better manage conflicts.
iv. *Empowering local communities*: Ensure that local population lead and benefit directly from coexistence strategies.

Achieving sustainable human-wildlife coexistence demands a holistic approach that places community participation and education at its core.

References

1. Curtin. C.G (2002), 'Integration of Science and Community based Conservation in Mexico, US borderland, *Conservation Biology*, Vo. 16, No.4, pp.880-886.
2. Defenders of Wildlife. (2023). *Range Rider Programs in North America.*
3. FAO. (2023). *Global Forest Resources Assessment.*
4. Frank, Beatrice (2016), 'Human–Wildlife Conflicts and the Need to Include Tolerance and Coexistence: An Introductory

Comment,' *Society and Natural Resources*, Vol. 29, No. 6, pp. 738-743.

5. Gillingham, S (2001), 'Social Organization and Participatory Resources Management in Brazilian Ribeirinho Communities: A Case Study of the Mamiraua Sustainable Development Reserve, Amazonas,' *Society and Natural Resources,* Vol. 14, PP.803-814.
6. Hoare, R. (2015), 'Lessons from 20 years of human–elephant conflict mitigation in Africa,' *Human Dimensions of Wildlife,* Vol. 20, No. 4, pp. 289–295.
7. IUCN. (2022a). *HWC Resolution Strategies.*
8. IUCN. (2022b). *HWC Solutions in Asia.*
9. IUCN (2023), *IUCN SSC guidelines on HWC and coexistence,* First Edition, Gland, Switzerland: IUCN.
10. Madhusadan, M.D. (2003), 'Living amidst large wildlife: Livestock and crop depredation by large mammals in the interior villages of Bhadra Tiger reserve, South India,' *Environmental Management,* Vol. 31, No. 4, pp. 466–475.
11. Marker L (2019), 'Cheetahs Race for Survival: Ecology and Conservation' *IntechOpen.*
12. NTCA. (2022). *Tiger Conservation in India.*
13. NTCA. (2023). *India's Tiger Conservation Success.*
14. Nyhus, P. J. (2016). *HWC: The Basics.*
15. Nyhus, Philip, J, (2016), HWC and Coexistence, *Annual Review of Environment and Resources,* Vol.41, pp.143-171.
16. Oerke E.C (2006), 'Crop losses to pests,' *The Journal of Agricultural Science*, Vol. 144, No. 1, pp. 31-43.
17. Panthera. (2023). *Jaguar-Friendly Beef Initiatives.*
18. Ravenelle, J., Nyhus, P. J (2017), 'Global patterns and trends in human–wildlife conflict compensation,' *Conservation Biology,* Vol. 31, No. 6, pp. 1247–1256.
19. Riley et al. (2002), 'The essence of wildlife management,' *Wildlife Society Bulletin*, Vol. 30, pp. 585-593.
20. Save the Elephants. (2022). *Beehive Fences in Kenya.*

21. White, P C. L. & Alastair I. Ward (2010), 'Interdisciplinary approaches for the management of existing and emerging human–wildlife conflicts,' *Wildlife Research*, Vol. 37, No.8, pp. 623-629.
22. Woodroffe, RT, et.al. (2005), *People and Wildlife: Conflict or Coexistence*, Cambridge University Press, Cambridge.
23. WWF (2022). *Living with Wildlife: Global Best Practices.*
24. WWF. (2023a). *Living Planet Report.*
25. WWF. (2023b). *Community-Based Conservation in Namibia.*

CHAPTER:7
GRAVITY OF HUMAN WILDLIFE CONFLICT

7.1 Introduction

HWC is becoming a major global issue, especially in areas where growing populations and development are increasingly overlapping with natural habitats. As human settlements expand into wildlife territories, these encounters are happening more often and with greater intensity. These conflicts endanger biodiversity, put food supplies at risk, and harm livelihood of local communities. This chapter examines the extent of HWC around the world, emphasizing Asia, South and North Americas. It also looks at specific problems in different regions, the economic costs involved, and the challenges for conservation, with the goal of framing suitable policies for humans and wildlife to live together peacefully.

Figure 7.1 illustrates a theoretical model of HWC, where the horizontal axis (X) represents the spectrum of interactions or results, ranging from negative impacts like crop damage to positive ones like tourism. The vertical axis (Y) measures the severity of the impact, from minor issues like nuisance from birds to severe outcomes like loss of human life. The depth axis (Z) indicates how often these interactions occur, from common to rare. By tracking HWC incidents on these dimensions helps to understand gravity of the issues and helps in developing suitable management strategies and policies.

Figure: 7.1 A Model of HWC

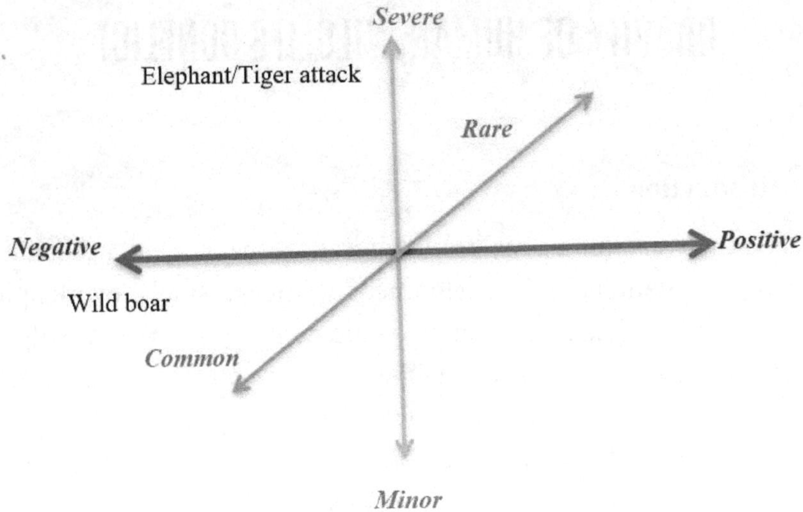

Source: Nyhus, Philip, J, (2016).

HWC arises when interactions between people and wild animals lead to negative outcomes, such as the destruction of crops, attacks on livestock, injuries, or fatalities. As human settlements expand into natural areas, conflicts with animals like elephants, large cats, and primates have become more severe (IUCN, 2021). The main factors contributing to HWC reported across the world are summarized as in Table 7.1.

Table: 7.1 Major Causes of HWC

Cause	*Description*
Habitat loss and fragmentation	Urbanization, agriculture, and infrastructure reduce and fragment natural habitats.
Competition for resources	Wildlife competes with humans for water, food, and space.
Climate change	Altered migration patterns and resource availability bring animals closer to humans.
Human encroachment	Settlements and farms near protected areas increase encounters.

Source: FAO (2023)

A detailed account of the gravity of HWC and major threatened species is provided in Appendix-2.

7.2 Global Trends in HWC

HWC is becoming a growing global concern, fueled by interconnected worldwide trends. As human populations grow and encroach into once-pristine natural habitats, interactions between people and wildlife have become more frequent and intense. These conflicts often result in damaged crops, livestock losses, property destruction, and even risks to human safety, which can trigger retaliatory actions against wildlife and intensify the struggle between conservation efforts and human survival needs.

Key factors like urbanization and agricultural expansion are major contributors to habitat destruction and fragmentation, forcing wildlife into closer contact with human communities. In regions such as Africa and Asia, elephants frequently invade farmland, while large carnivores like lions, leopards, and tigers attack livestock, causing severe financial strain for rural populations (NWF, 2023). Likewise, in North America and Europe, animals such as bears, coyotes, and wolves are increasingly entering suburban areas in search of food, often resulting in confrontations with residents and domestic animals (USDA, 2023).

Climate change further worsens HWC by disrupting weather patterns and altering ecosystems, compelling wildlife to migrate, adapt their feeding habits, or seek new habitats—sometimes bringing them into human-occupied areas. Droughts, for example, force animals like elephants in India and Africa or primates in Southeast Asia to raid farms and villages for water and food.

Moreover, successful conservation initiatives have helped some wildlife populations recover—a positive development for biodiversity. However, this also means more animals now share landscapes with humans, increasing the potential for conflict. The reintroduction and resurgence of wolves in parts of Europe and the U.S., for instance, have reignited tensions with farmers and ranchers concerned about livestock losses (UWI, 2023). Figure 7.2 illustrates the annual average economic losses attributed to HWC in selected countries from 2010 to 2023.

Figure: 7.2 Annual Economic Loss due to HWC, 2010-23 (million$)

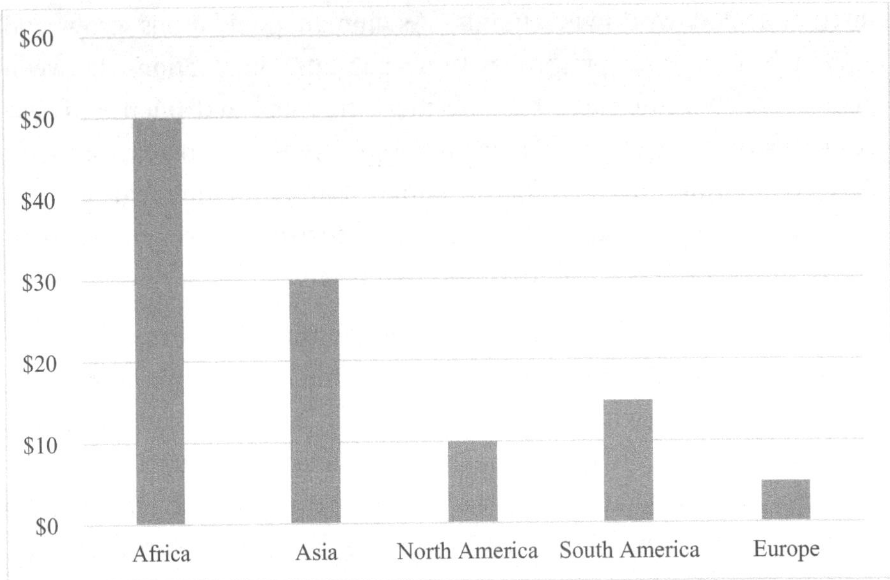

Sources: WWF (2022), IUCN (2021), FAO (2023)

Table: 7.2 Reported HWCs by Region, 2010-2023

Region	*Key Species Involved*	*Human Fatalities (Annual Avg.)*	*Wildlife Fatalities (Annual Avg.)*
Africa	Elephants, Lions	200	500+
Asia	Tigers, Leopards, Elephants	150	400+
North America	Wolves, Bears	5	100+
South America	Jaguars, Capybaras	20	200+
Europe	Wolves, Wild Boars	2	50+

Sources: WWF (2022), IUCN (2021), FAO (2023)

Addressing HWC requires tailored solutions that reflect the specific context, balancing conservation objectives with the needs of local communities. There is a growing emphasis on integrated strategies that engage local populations in wildlife management, incorporate technologies like early warning systems, and promote land-use planning that accommodates both people and wildlife (IUCN, 2021). Additionally, international collaboration and the exchange of knowledge are vital, as many HWC challenges and potential solutions are common across different regions and ecosystems.

HWC is a dynamic and multifaceted issue shaped by global factors such as habitat loss, climate change, urban expansion, and even successful conservation efforts. Tackling this conflict demands innovative, fair, and sustainable approaches that foster coexistence and ensure the long-term well-being of both human and wildlife populations. Table 7.2 presents reported HWCs across key regions between 2010 and 2023.

7.2.1 South America

HWC is an escalating issue in South America, driven by expanding agriculture, deforestation, and urban growth that increasingly disrupt natural habitats and bring wildlife into closer proximity with communities. The region's rich biodiversity—including jaguars, pumas, capybaras, and caimans—frequently leads to conflict, particularly in rural and even urban settings. In the Amazon basin, for instance, land cleared for cattle ranching and soybean cultivation has fragmented jaguar habitats, prompting these top predators to target livestock and triggering retaliatory actions by farmers (Michalski, 2006). Similarly, jaguar encounters in the Pantanal wetlands have intensified tensions with ranchers, complicating conservation efforts for this near-threatened species.

Agricultural development is a key driver of conflict in countries like Brazil, Argentina, and Colombia. Capybaras regularly damage crops, resulting in financial losses for farmers, while parrots and monkeys cause destruction in fruit orchards (FAO, 2023). In response, some farmers employ lethal control measures, further threatening vulnerable wildlife populations. Urban sprawl in cities such as São Paulo and Bogotá has also increased encounters with species like foxes, raccoons, and snakes, raising concerns for public safety (Marichini, et al. 2015). In the Andes, spectacled bears are often involved in conflicts when they venture into farmland in search of food, straining relations with local communities.

To reduce HWC, various mitigation strategies have been implemented across South America. These include conservation initiatives, educational outreach, and the use of non-lethal deterrents. Efforts to protect jaguars, for example, include compensation schemes for livestock losses and the promotion of coexistence tools such as guard animals and secure enclosures (Conover, 1995). Ecotourism has emerged as a viable alternative income source, encouraging communities to preserve rather than harm wildlife. Nevertheless, significant challenges remain, including weak enforcement of environmental regulations, inadequate conservation funding, and the ongoing expansion of industrial agriculture. Effective resolution of these conflicts requires a holistic approach that supports both biodiversity conservation and community livelihoods, ensuring that human development does not come at the cost of ecological integrity (White, et al. 2010). Without coordinated action, rising HWC could cause irreversible harm to the region's ecosystems and species.

A study by Michalski (2006) in the Amazon forest revealed that predation events were more likely to occur near riparian corridors connecting forest patches over 1,000 hectares, especially in areas with a high proportion of open and closed canopy forests within a 5 km radius. The study also found that livestock predation increased with larger cattle herds and greater forest cover nearby, while it decreased with greater distance from these riparian links. These findings suggest that the proximity of agricultural land to large, forested areas at the deforestation frontier heightens the risk of conflict, particularly involving large carnivores. Table 7.3 highlights the severity of HWC across South America.

Table: 7.3 Gravity of HWC in South America

Country	*Common Conflicts*
Brazil	Jaguar-livestock predation
Argentina	Puma attacks
Bolivia	Crop raids by monkeys, tapirs

Source: Michalski (2006)

7.2.2 North America

HWC in North America has emerged as a pressing issue as human settlements and wildlife increasingly occupy the same spaces. Urban sprawl, forest clearing, and land conversion have fragmented natural habitats, pushing animals into closer contact with people (Conover, 1997). As development encroaches on forests, grasslands, and wetlands, species like bears, coyotes, mountain lions, and deer are regularly seen in neighborhoods, creating situations that endanger both humans and animals.

A notable example is the growing number of black bears venturing into suburban areas in the U.S. and Canada (Conover, 1998). With shrinking natural food supplies due to habitat degradation and climate shifts, bears are drawn to human-provided food sources like trash, pet food, and birdseed. Such encounters sometimes result in property damage or, in rare instances, attacks—leading to the lethal removal of 'problem' bears. Coyotes, highly adaptable predators, have also become more common in urban and suburban settings, where they occasionally target pets and even pose risks to children, raising public alarm and management challenges.

Large herbivores, such as deer and moose also contribute to HWC through vehicle collisions causing injuries, deaths, and expensive repairs. In agricultural regions, deer also devastate crops, inflicting financial harm on farmers. Deer population control methods, including regulated hunting and sterilization, often trigger disputes among conservationists, hunters, and animal rights groups. Meanwhile, in the western U.S., the resurgence of wolves has renewed conflicts with ranchers over livestock losses, fueling calls for predator control (Conover, 2002).

Climate change has worsened HWC by altering animal behavior and movement patterns. Wildfires, droughts, and shifting weather conditions force wildlife into human-occupied areas in search of resources. For instance, extended droughts in the western U.S. have driven more animals into towns for water and food, while milder winters disrupt hibernation, keeping wildlife active longer and increasing human encounters (Gross, et al. 2021).

Mitigating HWC demands a comprehensive strategy, including public education, wildlife management, and thoughtful land-use policies. Measures like bear-resistant trash bins, protective fencing, and community outreach on coexistence can help reduce conflicts. Conservation efforts that preserve habitat corridors and wild spaces are also crucial to sustaining wildlife populations without increasing human-wildlife clashes (Mesmer, et al. 1999). Success hinges on balancing ecological health with human safety through informed policies and adaptive management.

The following studies highlight the severity of HWC in North America:

i. Mesmer (1999) found that more than 60% of U.S. suburban and urban households face wildlife-related issues.

ii. Western U.S. farmers report substantial economic losses from wildlife damage (Conover, 2002).

iii. Approximately 5,000 people are injured or sickened annually by wildlife, with 415 fatalities, and related damages nearing $3 billion per year (Conover et al., 1995).

iv. Interestingly, 51% of U.S. farmers have modified their land to support wildlife (Conover, 1998).

Deer, bears, and coyotes are the most common culprits in North American HWC incidents. Table 7.4 provides further insight into the scale of these conflicts.

Table: 7.4 Gravity of HWC in North America

Species	*Conflict Type*	*Reported Cases (2023)*
White-tailed deer	Vehicle collisions	1.5 million
Black bears	Garbage raids, home entry	35,000+
Coyotes	Pet predation, urban encounters	7,000+

Source: NWF (2023); State DOTs (2023)

7.2.3 Asia

HWC is an increasingly pressing concern in Asia. Rapid urbanization, agricultural expansion, and deforestation are shrinking natural habitats, forcing wildlife into closer proximity with human populations. The continent's high human density combined with its rich biodiversity creates a dangerous situation, leading to frequent clashes between people and animals like elephants, tigers, leopards, and monkeys. In South Asia, particularly India and Sri Lanka, elephants frequently raid crops, destroying farmland and sometimes causing human deaths, which tragically leads to retaliatory killings (WWF, 2023). Similarly, in Southeast Asia, tigers and leopards entering villages to hunt livestock—and occasionally people—generate fear and hostility among rural communities.

Box: 7.1 Human – Elephant Conflict Management in Kui Buri district of Thailand

In Thailand, human-elephant conflict is a growing issue, largely driven by habitat loss and degradation caused by the spread of mono-crop plantations. To address this, Bangkok Ecotourism & Sustainable Tourism and its partners are carrying out initiatives to foster coexistence between communities and elephants. These include community-led tree nurseries, conservation education programs, homestay tourism, and cultural events. These interventions are backed by scientific evaluations and behavioral monitoring of elephants to ensure effectiveness. In many elephant range countries, crop damage by elephants is a persistent challenge. Research indicates that elephants that frequently feed on crops tend to grow faster, become more dominant, and reproduce more successfully. To mitigate this, experts recommend altering cropping patterns to make fields less attractive to elephants, promoting alternative livelihoods such as honey production, and aligning agricultural practices and income strategies with local ecological and economic realities.

The Tom Yum project is a notable example of such a strategy, aiming to reduce conflict by moving away from pineapple cultivation—an elephant-attracting crop—and instead growing less appealing crops like lemongrass, Kaffir lime leaves, and galangal. Products made from these herbs are marketed to generate income for local communities, with the goal of doubling household earnings. A portion of the proceeds also supports reforestation efforts to restore elephant habitats.

Source: Chiyo P.I., et al., 2011b.

The fundamental causes of these conflicts are deeply rooted in the loss and fragmentation of natural habitats. Large infrastructure projects, such as roads, dams, and plantations, disrupt vital wildlife corridors, leaving animals with no alternative but to venture into human-dominated areas. In countries like Indonesia and Malaysia, the conversion of forests for palm oil cultivation has displaced species like orangutans and sun bears, leading to more frequent encounters with humans (WWF, 2021). Even in urban environments, especially in cities like Bangkok and Mumbai, conflicts with monkeys, snakes, and leopards have increased as these animals adapt to finding food in human settlements. Climate change further complicates the issue by altering ecosystems and driving wildlife beyond their traditional territories in search of food and water.

Efforts to reduce HWC in Asia involve a combination of traditional and modern methods. Electric fences, early warning systems, and community patrols are used to deter elephants in countries like India and Nepal, while compensation programs aim to reduce retaliatory killings of predators such as tigers and leopards (MoEFCC, 2023). Conservation initiatives also promote coexistence through education and alternative income sources, like ecotourism and beekeeping, which lessen reliance on forest resources. However, progress is hampered by challenges such as insufficient funding, weak governance, and conflicting priorities for land use. Long-term solutions require integrated landscape planning that balances conservation with sustainable development, ensuring that both Asia's wildlife and human populations can live alongside each other. Without decisive action, the increasing conflicts threaten both biodiversity and the livelihoods of millions, highlighting the urgent need for collaborative and region-specific strategies to tackle this growing crisis.

Asia's dense populations and expanding agriculture result in frequent HWC involving species like tigers, leopards, and elephants. Table 7.5 illustrates the seriousness of HWC in major Asian countries.

Table: 7.5 Gravity of HWC in Asia

Country	*Common Conflicts*	*Incidents/Year*
India	Elephant crop damage, tiger attacks	100,000+ crop raids
Nepal	Rhino-human encounters	~50 reported/year
Indonesia	Orangutan conflict and palm oil expansion	High

Source: MoEFCC (2023); WWF Nepal (2021)

Box: 7.2 Human – Elephant Conflict Management in Sabah, Malaysia

Oil palm plantations occupy 23% of Sabah's land area, creating significant financial challenges for agricultural companies like Sabah Softwoods Berhad (SSB) due to human-elephant conflicts. In 2012, WWF-Malaysia partnered with SSB to develop sustainable solutions, including designating 1,067 hectares as a dedicated wildlife corridor. Using movement data from satellite-collared elephants, WWF provided technical guidance and helped install strategically placed electric fencing.

The innovative approach allowed controlled elephant access to specific plantation areas while minimizing crop damage. SSB covered most implementation costs, and the investment paid off through improved land management strategies and long-term reductions in agricultural losses. The conservation initiative expanded through collaboration with NGO 1StopBorneo Wildlife, creating an ecotourism program. Visitors participate in tree-planting activities and elephant observation, and with generated funds supported corridor maintenance and community safety education programs.

This multi-faceted approach has yielded significant benefits:

i. Reduced operational costs for SSB,

ii. Fewer elephant-related incidents,

iii. Effective electric fencing minimizing human-wildlife conflicts,

iv. Enhanced biodiversity in the corridor area, and

v. Improved corporate reputation through demonstrated conservation leadership.

The project demonstrates how agricultural operations can successfully integrate wildlife conservation while maintaining economic viability, serving as a model for sustainable plantation management in biodiverse regions.

Source: WWF, 2022

7.3 Consequences of HWC

HWC has far-reaching effects worldwide, disrupting ecological balance, endangering communities, and threatening animal species in severe and interconnected ways. The ongoing expansion of human settlements into natural areas has intensified encounters with wildlife, creating consequences that jeopardize both conservation goals and human welfare. These conflicts frequently lead to fatalities, economic damage, and entrenched hostility toward animals—factors that often hinder global wildlife protection initiatives.

Table: 7.6 Implications of HWC

Type	*Impact*
Economic	Crop loss, livestock depredation, infrastructure damage
Human Safety	Injuries and fatalities due to wildlife attacks
Wildlife Mortality	Retaliatory killings, habitat loss, road accidents
Conservation	Reduced tolerance for conservation efforts, poaching

Source: KWS, 2023

A critical consequence of HWC is its toll on human survival and economic stability. Rural populations, particularly in Africa and Asia, regularly endure crop raids by elephants, wild boars, and primates, as well as livestock attacks by predators like lions, tigers, wolves, and leopards (WWF, 2021). For subsistence farmers and herders, such losses can be catastrophic, pushing affected communities toward retaliatory killings. Poisoning, snaring, and shooting of problem animals frequently result, sometimes wiping out threatened species and causing collateral harm to other wildlife. The broader implications of HWC are summarized in Table 7.6.

Box: 7.3 Integrated approach to HWC in Nepal

In Nepal's Chitwan National Park, an integrated management approach has significantly reduced tiger predation on livestock by 75% over the past decade. This period also saw a substantial increase in the tiger population, rising from 38 in 2000 to 92 in 2018. A key factor in this successful coexistence has been the government's policy of allocating 30% of the Chitwan National Park's entry fee revenue to neighboring communities. National buffer zone management guidelines continue to support such investments in community development to lessen the reliance on forest resources and promote better human-wildlife coexistence. Furthermore, the government's national relief guidelines of 2009 include compensation for communities affected by wildlife-related damage, including payments for losses caused by wild animals.

A thorough system involving both governmental and non-governmental organizations is in place to monitor HWC. Trained response teams, working alongside national park staff actively track and manage these conflicts. HWC management in Chitwan is a flexible and ongoing process that adapts to evolving situations.

Source: Lamichhane B.R., et al., 2019

In India between 2019 and 2023, elephant encounters tragically resulted in over 500 human deaths each year, and retaliatory actions led to the deaths of more than 100 elephants annually (MoEFCC, 2023). HWC also significantly hinders conservation efforts. When local communities view wildlife as a danger to their safety and financial well-being, their support for conservation policies and protected areas diminishes. This conflict is particularly pronounced in areas bordering national parks or wildlife reserves, where local people bear the burden of coexisting with potentially dangerous or destructive animals but may not see any advantages from conservation or tourism. Consequently, poaching, illegal wildlife trade, and encroachment on habitats can increase, jeopardizing biodiversity and undoing years of conservation work.

In urban environments, conflicts manifest differently but remain significant. Across North America and Europe, animals like bears, coyotes, deer, and foxes are increasingly venturing into suburban areas in search of food, sometimes causing vehicle accidents, property damage, or even attacks (SANParks, 2022). These incidents can create public fear and pressure governments to manage or remove wildlife, often through lethal methods, which can be controversial and harmful to the ecosystem. Furthermore, climate change is exacerbating these interactions globally by disrupting ecosystems, changing animal behavior, and forcing species to move into new areas where they may come into conflict with human populations. Table 7.7 outlines the major impacts of HWC by continent.

Table: 7.7 Major Impacts of HWC by Continent

Continent	*Primary Impact*	*Affected Livelihoods*
Africa	Crop raiding, livestock predation	Smallholder farmers
|Asia	Human fatalities, infrastructure damage	Rural communities
North America	Livestock losses, pet attacks	Ranchers, suburban residents
South America	Deforestation conflicts, cattle predation	Farmers, indigenous groups
Europe	Agricultural damage, fear of predators	Farmers, hunters

Source: WWF, 2022

Beyond immediate human-wildlife encounters, HWC disrupts fundamental ecological processes. The loss of critical species—particularly apex predators and ecosystem engineers—through retaliatory killings or habitat displacement can trigger domino effects across entire food webs (Nyhus, 2016). This destabilization compromises natural systems that regulate everything from water purification to soil fertility. Furthermore, persistent conflicts often redirect conservation resources from proactive research and habitat protection to reactive measures, undermining long-term environmental stewardship.

As a worldwide challenge, HWC jeopardizes multiple dimensions of sustainability: human safety, economic stability, species survival, and ecological health. Effective solutions demand integrated strategies that combine local knowledge with scientific innovation—empowering communities through education, fostering sustainable land-use practices, and implementing science-backed conservation measures. Achieving harmonious coexistence between human societies and wildlife isn't merely idealistic; it's an essential pathway toward preserving biodiversity while safeguarding human development. Only through such holistic, collaborative approaches can we secure mutually beneficial futures for both people and wildlife.

7.4 Management Strategies

HWC presents a major obstacle to both biodiversity conservation and the well-being of communities, making it essential to implement mitigation strategies that balance ecological integrity with socio-economic interests. One of the most commonly used approaches is habitat management, which aims to conserve and restore wildlife corridors. These corridors help prevent animals from straying into human-inhabited areas by allowing them to move freely between fragmented habitats. Species such as elephants, tigers, and bears benefit from these connected landscapes, reducing the likelihood of conflict. Strategic land-use planning, including the creation of buffer zones around protected areas, further reduces interactions between humans and wildlife. In Africa, for instance, community conservancies have effectively minimized conflicts by establishing shared-use areas where wildlife and livestock can coexist under managed grazing systems (IUCN, 2020).

Another vital approach is the use of deterrents and barriers to protect agricultural land and livestock. Tools such as electric fencing, trenches, and secure enclosures have successfully kept large herbivores like elephants and wild boars away from crops. In India, non-lethal techniques like chili-based repellents and beehive fences deter elephants, while flashing lights and sound alarms discourage nocturnal pests such as deer and primates (WWF, 2023). Carnivore attacks on livestock have been reduced using predator-resistant pens and guard animals like dogs and donkeys. These humane measures help safeguard rural livelihoods while encouraging communities to tolerate and coexist with wildlife.

Community involvement and education are central to long-term solutions. When residents are included in conservation efforts, they are more likely to take responsibility for wildlife protection. Financial tools like compensation and insurance for crop and livestock losses help ease economic burdens and reduce retaliatory killings. In Nepal, community-based anti-poaching teams and rapid response units have played a key role in reducing human-tiger incidents by quickly managing conflicts and relocating animals (WWF, 2021). Ecotourism has also proven to be a valuable alternative income source, motivating communities to protect wildlife rather than harm it. Public education initiatives that inform people about animal behavior and coexistence practices further strengthen local capacity to prevent conflict. Table 7.8 outlines successful mitigation strategies from various regions.

Table:7.8 Successful Mitigation Strategies around the world

Strategy	*Effectiveness*	*Country Cases*
Fencing and barriers	High for crops	Electric fences in Kenya and Bhutan
Compensation schemes	Moderate if timely	India's elephant crop loss compensation
Early warning systems	Increasingly effective	SMS alert systems in Sri Lanka and Nepal
Community-based conservation	High if participatory	Namibia's conservancy model
Wildlife corridors	Long-term solution	Terai Arc in India-Nepal, Yellowstone to Yukon (US-Canada)

Source: IUCN, 2021

Cutting-edge technologies are playing an increasingly vital role in HWC prevention. Advanced tracking systems like GPS collars and satellite monitoring provide real-time data on wildlife movements, enabling authorities to alert communities about approaching animals. Surveillance tools such as drones and camera traps, combined with mobile reporting applications, create comprehensive monitoring networks. Sri Lanka's successful SMS alert system demonstrates how simple technologies can effectively warn farmers of nearby elephant activity, preventing crop damage and dangerous encounters (WWF, 2023).

Effective governance plays an equally critical role in conflict resolution. Strong legal protections for wildlife habitats must be coupled with policies promoting sustainable land management. For migratory species crossing political boundaries, international cooperation is essential to develop unified conservation approaches. Support from global organizations can enhance local implementation through funding and technical expertise.

The most sustainable solutions emerge from integrated strategies has the following components (FAO, 2023).

i. Habitat preservation,
ii. Community engagement,
iii. Technological innovation, and
iv. Policy reinforcement.

This multifaceted approach shifts the paradigm from conflict to coexistence, protecting biodiversity while supporting human communities. As anthropogenic pressures intensify, such adaptive and inclusive measures will become increasingly crucial for achieving ecological balance and sustainable development.

7.5 Conclusion

HWC is a complicated and diverse problem that demands solutions involving many different fields of expertise. While efforts to reduce HWC are underway, their success depends on the participation of local communities, sufficient financial support, and careful long-term planning for land use. Sharing knowledge and working together globally are crucial for fostering coexistence. Finding a balance between protecting wildlife and supporting human livelihoods is essential for long-lasting coexistence. Governments, non-governmental organizations, and local communities must work together to put effective strategies in place to reduce conflict.

HWC has become a critical global issue because human settlements and wildlife habitats are increasingly overlapping. As human populations grow and natural areas are converted for farming, infrastructure, and urban development, wildlife is pushed into closer contact with people, leading to greater conflict. This conflict appears in various ways, including animals raiding crops, preying on livestock, damaging property, and even threatening human lives. For example, in Africa, elephants often raid farmlands, destroying livelihoods, while in South Asia, tigers and leopards sometimes attack villagers living near forests. Similarly, in North America, the expansion of cities has led to more frequent encounters between bears, coyotes, and people (WWF, 2022).

Table: 7.9 Major lessons from HWC around the World

Continent	*Country*	*Wildlife involved*	*Issue*	*Major Impact*	*Sustainable Solution*
Africa	Kenya	Elephant	Elephants raid crops, destroying livelihoods.	Over 60% of farmer income losses in Tsavo region linked to elephants	Beehive fences and community-based conservation programs.
Asia	India	Tiger	Tigers kill livestock and occasionally humans near reserves.	125 human deaths annually in Sundarbans	Early warning systems and compensation schemes.
North America	USA	Wolf	Wolves prey on cattle in Montana and Idaho.	300+ cattle killed annually	Non-lethal deterrents and rancher compensation.

Sources: Kenya Wildlife Service (2023); WWF India (2022); USDA (2023)

Climate change makes these conflicts even worse by changing how wildlife behaves and where they can live. Droughts and shrinking water sources drive animals into areas inhabited by humans in search of food and water, increasing the chances of confrontations. Additionally, the decline in natural prey due to habitat loss forces predators like lions and wolves to prey on livestock, leading to more retaliatory killings by affected communities. Marine environments are also affected, as overfishing and rising ocean temperatures push marine animals like sharks and seals closer to human coastal activities, sometimes resulting in dangerous interactions (IUCN, 2021). Table 7.9 summarizes lessons learned from HWC around the world.

Attempts to reduce HWC have had mixed results. While traditional methods like fences, guard animals, and deterrents are still common, newer strategies such as conservation led by communities, wildlife corridors, and compensation programs are becoming more popular. Technology also offers solutions, with early warning systems, GPS tracking, and drone surveillance helping to avoid encounters. However, lasting solutions depend on finding a balance between protecting the environment and meeting human development needs. Policymakers need to focus on protecting habitats, planning land use sustainably, and involving communities to encourage coexistence. If we don't act quickly, increasing conflicts will threaten both the variety of life on earth and human welfare, highlighting the need for a peaceful relationship between people and wildlife in an increasingly crowded world.

References

1. Chiyo P.I., et.al. (2011), 'No risk, no gain: effects of crop raiding and genetic diversity on body size in male elephants,' *Behavioral Ecology*, Vol. 22, No. 3, pp. 552-558.
2. Conover, et al. (1995), 'Review of human injuries, illness, and economic losses caused by Wildlife in the United States,' *Wildlife Society Bulletin*, Vol. 23,m pp.407-414.

3. Conover (1997), 'Monetary and intangible valuation of deer in the United States,' *Wildlife Society Bulletin,* Vol. 25, pp. 298–305.
4. Conover, M.R (1998), 'Perceptions of American Agricultural Producers about Wildlife on their Farms and Ranches,' *Wildlife Society Bulletin*, Vol. 26, pp.597-604.
5. Conover, M.R (2002), *Resolving HWCs: the Science of Wildlife Damage Management,* Lewis Publishers, Boc Raton, Florida, USA.
6. Food and Agriculture Organization (FAO). (2023). *Global Trends in HWC.*
7. Gross E, et.al. (2021), *A Future for All: The Need for Human-Wildlife Coexistence*, WWF, Gland, Switzerland.
8. IUCN. (2020). *Mitigating HWC in Africa.* International Union for Conservation of Nature.
9. International Union for Conservation of Nature (IUCN). (2021). *Guidelines for HWC Management.*
10. Kenya Wildlife Service. (2023). *Annual HWC Report.*
11. Lamichhane B.R., et al. (2019), 'Contribution of Buffer Zone Programs to Reduce Human-Wildlife Impacts: the Case of the Chitwan National Park, Nepal', *Human Ecology.*
12. Marchini S & P. G Crawshaw (2015), 'HWCs in Brazil: A Fast-growing Issue,' *Human Dimensions of Wildlife*, Vol. 20, pp. 323-328.
13. Mesmer, et al. (1999), 'United States Public Attitudes regarding Predators and their Management to Enhance Avian Recruitment,' *Wildlife Society Bulletin*, Vo. 27, pp.75-85.
14. Michalski, et.al. (2006), 'HWCs in a Fragmented Amazonian Forest Landscape: Determinants of Large Felid Depredation on Livestock,' *Animal Conservation*, Zoological Survey of India, Vo..9, pp.179-188.
15. Ministry of Environment, Forest and Climate Change (MoEFCC), Government of India. (2023). *Elephant Census Report.*

16. National Wildlife Federation (NWF). (2023). *Human-Wildlife Encounters in the U.S.*
17. Nyhus, Philip, J, (2016), HWC and Coexistence, *Annual Review of Environment and Resources,* Vol.41, pp.143-171.
18. SANParks. (2022). *HWC Management Report.*
19. USDA. (2023). *Wolf Depredation on Livestock Statistics.*
20. Urban Wildlife Institute. (2023). *Coyote Conflicts in Urban America.*
21. White, P C. L. & Alastair I. Ward (2010), 'Interdisciplinary approaches for the management of existing and emerging human–wildlife conflicts,' *Wildlife Research*, Vol. 37, No.8, pp. 623-629.
22. World Wide Fund for Nature (WWF). (2021). *HWC Overview in Kenya.*
23. WWF. (2022). *Living with Wildlife: Reducing HWC.*
24. WWF India. (2023). *Elephant Human Conflict in Northeast India.*
25. WWF Nepal. (2021). *Rhino-Human Encounters: A Conservation Challenge.*

CHAPTER: 8
AFRICAN LESSONS IN THE MANAGEMENT OF HUMAN WILDLIFE CONFLICT

8.1 Introduction

HWC in Africa poses a major threat to conservation efforts, rural development, and food security. As human populations increase and expand into previously untouched wildlife areas in Africa, encounters between people and animals are becoming more frequent and often destructive (Chomba, 2012). These conflicts lead to financial losses, endanger human lives, and trigger retaliatory actions against wildlife, further jeopardizing Africa's rich biodiversity. Interactions between humans and animals—especially large mammals like elephants, lions, and hippos—have intensified in Africa, resulting in crop destruction, livestock predation, human injuries, and deaths (Mukeka, 2019). This chapter examines the causes, impacts, and trends of HWC in Africa and explores ways to reduce conflict and promote coexistence. Chapter also explores major take aways of HWC management.

HWC in Africa arises from a complex interplay of socio-economic, ecological, and political factors and is common in rural and semi-urban areas. The involvement of multiple stakeholders complicate the understanding of its causes and the implementation of effective solutions, often leading to delays in managing and reducing conflict (Roe, 1998). The socio-ecological systems include resource users, resources such as crops, livestock, wildlife, and habitat, public infrastructure and policies, and infrastructure providers, including the government (Anderies, et al., 2004). In many African countries, population growth and encroachment, along with increasing wildlife populations due to conservation efforts, are the primary drivers of rising HWC. These regions are often wildlife-rich areas where communities heavily rely on subsistence farming and are vulnerable to crop and livestock losses for various reasons. The core of the problem lies in the social acceptance of resilience among impoverished local communities, who used to face increasing wildlife populations due to conservation efforts largely driven by government and international agencies.

In Namibia, where conserved areas cover 16.1% of the land area, where HWC is frequently reported. Using mind-mapping, Mosimane and colleagues (2013) identified three key solutions for better HWC management in Namibia: improved and participatory land-use planning, enhanced policies and wildlife management, and building community resilience and friendly attitudes. They proposed inter-departmental coordination, participatory consultation, understanding wildlife needs, best land-use practices for specific regions, and sharing land-use data for better planning. For improved policies and wildlife management, these researchers highlighted conservancy management, government management and wildlife policy, and compensation for damage caused by problem animals. To enhance livelihood resilience and community attitudes, they suggested understanding livelihoods, developing alternative income sources, aligning benefit distribution with livelihood needs, improving understanding of conservation values, preventing and mitigating resource competition, and providing training and capacity building. Reported wildlife conflicts in selected African countries between 2018 and 2023 are summarized in Table 8.1.

Table: 8.1 Reported Wildlife Conflicts in African Countries, 2018–2023

Country	*Key Conflict Species*	*Annual Crop Losses ($)*	*Annual Livestock Losses*	*Human Fatalities (Annual Avg.)*
Kenya	Elephants, Lions	2 million	3,000+	30
Tanzania	Elephants, Hippos	1.5 million	2,500+	60

Botswana	Elephants, Lions	3 million	1,200+	15
South Africa	Leopards, Baboons	500,000	800+	10
Namibia	Lions, Hyenas	700,000	1,500+	5

Sources: WWF (2022), IUCN (2023), African Wildlife Foundation (2021)

8.2 Extent of HWC in Africa

The main factors contributing to HWC in Africa include habitat encroachment, competition for resources, and climate change. The rise in agricultural practices, urban development, and infrastructure projects are leading to fragmented ecosystems, which increases the proximity of wildlife to human populations.

A study conducted in Zambia from 2002 to 2008 found that 347 people lost their lives due to wildlife encounters, with Nile crocodiles accounting for 53% of the fatalities, followed by hippos at 19% and elephants at 18% (Chomba et al., 2012). In comparison, livestock deaths during this time were 12% lower than human fatalities, with lions responsible for 51% of livestock predation. Additionally, there were 4,270 reported incidents of crop damage during the same period. The primary management strategy employed was lethal removal rather than translocation, especially in cases involving human fatalities and livestock losses. This approach is often taken to alleviate community distress, as there are no compensation programs in countries like Zambia.

Africa faces considerable challenges with HWC, particularly with species such as elephants, lions, and hippos. Crop raiding and predation on livestock are prevalent issues. The annual economic impact of HWC in 2023 is illustrated in Figure 8.1.

Figure: 8.1 Annual Economic Loss due to HWC, 2023 (USD)

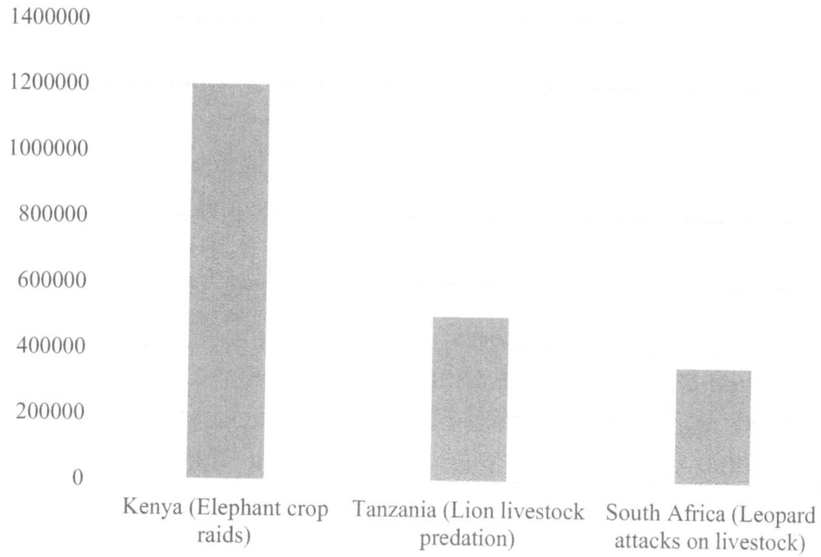

Source: IUCN (2020); SANParks (2022); WWF (2021)

HWC was severe and frequent in Africa's Game Management Areas, largely due to human encroachment. A major cause of HWC involving large predators like lions and leopards is the decline in their prey populations (Simukonda, 2008). This decline is attributed to increased poaching for wild meat and overfishing to feed growing urban populations (Chomba, et al., 2012). In many African countries, population growth and the rising demand for food, transportation, energy, and other urban needs lead to the encroachment of wildlife habitats and water sources. Major types of HWC include the following in Africa.

i. *Human-Crocodile Conflicts:* In many African nations, water bodies like rivers, streams, swamps, lagoons, dams, lakes, and floodplains provide ideal crocodile habitats. Simultaneously, rural populations depend on these same waters for their livelihoods, including fishing and transportation, often using canoes, rafts, or small boats in narrow channels, or even traveling by foot (Bourdillon, et al., 1985). Crocodiles can live undetected near human settlements for extended periods.

ii. *Human-Hippopotamus Conflicts:* Hippos typically graze at night in traditional pasture areas within 10 kilometers of their aquatic habitats. As previously mentioned, rural populations in Africa often farm in riverbeds and along the edges of water bodies. Crops like maize, rice, vegetables, and other cereals are ideal food for hippos (Chomba, et al., 2012). Sometimes, fishermen use crude homemade weapons to kill hippos in retaliation for their losses.

iii. *Human-Lion Conflicts:* Studies in Kenya have shown that lions are responsible for 86% of livestock attacks (Patterson, et al., 2004). Increased human encroachment due to population growth, along with cattle-keeping practices in Game Management Areas, is a primary driver of human-lion conflict in Africa.

The main factors fuelling HWC in Africa include (UNEP, 2021):

i. *Habitat Loss and Fragmentation*: The expansion of agriculture, logging, and infrastructure development shrinks wildlife habitats, forcing animals into areas dominated by humans.

ii. *Climate Change*: Droughts and changing rainfall patterns push wildlife closer to human settlements in search of water and food.

iii. *Human Population Growth*: Increasing settlements near protected areas lead to more frequent encounters with wildlife.

iv. *Livestock Encroachment:* Overgrazing in wildlife territories results in competition for resources and conflicts due to predation.

A detailed account of the causes of HWC in selected African countries is provided in Table 8.2.

Table: 8.2 Major Causes of HWC in African Countries

Country	*Wildlife Species Involved*	*Causes of Conflict*
Kenya	Elephants, lions, hyenas	Crop raiding, livestock predation
Tanzania	Elephants, buffalo, lions	Farmland encroachment, grazing competition
South Africa	Leopards, baboons, elephants	Urban expansion, garbage access
Zimbabwe	Elephants, crocodiles	Water access, fishing area conflicts
Uganda	Hippos, chimpanzees	Crop destruction, habitat overlap

Source: IUCN, African Wildlife Foundation, FAO Reports (2023)

8.3 Implications of HWC

HWC in Africa has extensive repercussions that impact ecosystems, economies, and communities throughout the continent. As human population grow and agricultural activities encroach on wildlife habitats, interactions between humans and animals have become more frequent, resulting in significant ecological and socio-economic issues. These effects are particularly pronounced in rural areas where communities rely on subsistence farming and livestock for their livelihoods. Elephants, lions, hippos, and other large mammals often raid crops, attack livestock, and, in some cases, injure or kill people, leading to retaliatory killings that threaten already endangered species (IUCN, 2023a). This ongoing cycle of conflict undermines conservation efforts and perpetuates poverty and food insecurity among affected communities.

One of the most immediate consequences of HWC is economic loss. Small-scale farmers, who are vital to many African economies, face severe crop damage from animals like elephants, baboons, and bush pigs. In Kenya alone, elephants cause millions of dollars in crop losses each year, pushing families further into poverty (IUCN, 2023a). Likewise, pastoralists lose livestock to predators such as lions, hyenas, and leopards, with some communities reporting the deaths of hundreds of cattle, sheep, and goats annually. These losses typically go uncompensated, forcing families to resort to extreme measures like poisoning or hunting problematic animals. The financial strain also impacts governments and conservation organizations, which allocate significant resources for mitigation efforts, compensation programs, and conflict resolution.

In addition to economic implications, HWC directly threatens human lives. Dangerous animals like elephants, hippos, and crocodiles result in numerous fatalities and injuries each year. For example, in Tanzania, hippopotamuses—often deemed the most dangerous mammal in Africa—cause more deaths annually than lions or elephants (Kaswamila & Songorwa, 2009). Crocodile attacks near water sources also claim lives, especially among communities that depend on these areas for fishing and domestic needs. The psychological trauma from such incidents breeds resentment toward wildlife, complicating conservation messaging. Fear and hostility often lead to increased poaching and habitat destruction as communities attempt to protect themselves, further intensifying the conflict.

The ecological impacts of HWC are equally concerning. Retaliatory killings contribute to the decline of endangered species, including lions, African wild dogs, and cheetahs. Large carnivores suffer significant population declines due to human persecution, with lion numbers halving in certain regions. Herbivores like elephants are also targeted when they damage crops, despite their essential role in maintaining ecosystem balance (MET/NACSO, 2018). Furthermore, habitat fragmentation caused by human expansion disrupts migration routes and diminishes genetic diversity among wildlife populations. The loss of key species can trigger cascading effects that destabilize entire ecosystems and reduce biodiversity, subsequently affecting tourism—a crucial revenue source for many African countries.

Efforts to address HWC have had mixed results, but sustainable solutions necessitate a comprehensive approach. Conservation strategies such as wildlife corridors, community-based natural resource management, and predator-proof livestock enclosures have shown potential in reducing conflicts (Simuconda, 2008). Technological advancements, including GPS tracking and early warning systems, can help prevent encounters before they occur. However, long-term solutions must also tackle underlying issues such as poverty, land-use planning, and climate change, which exacerbate conflicts. Education and awareness initiatives promoting coexistence are vital for changing attitudes toward wildlife, while equitable benefit-sharing from conservation projects can encourage communities to protect rather than harm animals.

Ultimately, HWC in Africa is not solely a conservation challenge but a complex socio-economic issue that requires urgent attention. Without effective intervention, the ongoing loss of wildlife and livelihoods will result in irreversible consequences for both people and ecosystems. Balancing the needs of growing human populations with the preservation of Africa's iconic wildlife calls for collaboration among governments, conservationists, and local communities (FAO, 2023). Only through inclusive and sustainable strategies can Africa aspire to achieve harmonious coexistence between humans and wildlife in the future. Data on human and wildlife casualties reported from 2020 to 2023 in African countries is given in Figure 8.2.

The impacts of HWC can be summarized as follows:

i. *Economic Impact:* Smallholder farmers and pastoralists experience significant economic losses due to crop destruction and livestock killings. In Kenya, over $3 million is lost annually because of wildlife-related crop damage (Kenya Wildlife Service, 2022). Farmers suffer from crop losses, while pastoralists lose livestock to predators. For instance, elephants are estimated to destroy around $2 million worth of crops annually in Kenya (WWF, 2022).

ii. *Human Casualties:* In Tanzania, wildlife attacks result in the deaths of over 200 people each year, primarily due to elephants and crocodiles (UNEP, 2021). The frequency of these incidents is increasing in areas where human settlements expand near protected regions. Large mammals like elephants, hippos, and crocodiles are responsible for fatalities, with reports indicating that wildlife causes 50-70 deaths annually in Tanzania (Tanzania Wildlife Research Institute, 2021).

Figure: 8.2 Human and wildlife causalities reported, 2020-23

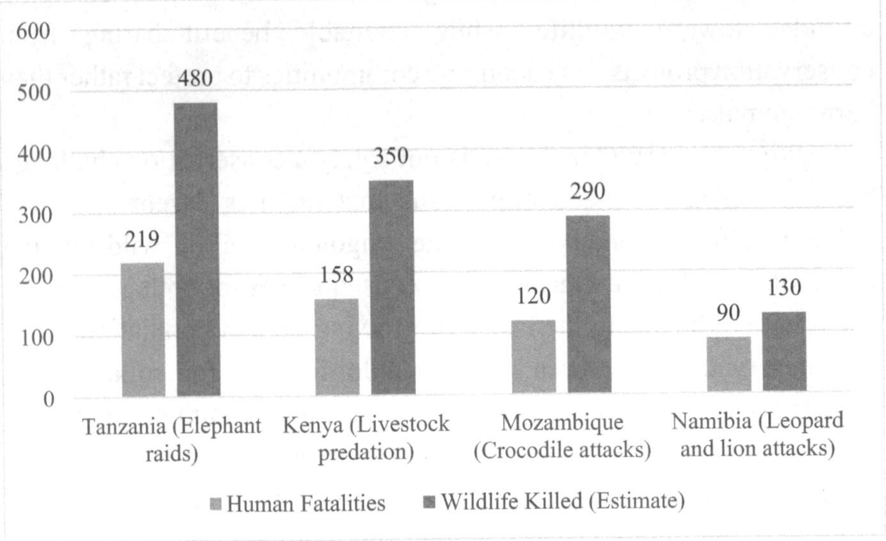

Source: UNEP (2023)

iii. *Wildlife Mortality:* Retaliatory killings are frequently employed as a reaction to wildlife attacks. For instance, the African lion population has decreased by over 40% in the last twenty years, with HWC playing a significant role in this decline (WWF, 2022). Such retaliatory actions pose a threat to endangered species. A summary of retaliatory wildlife killings in Africa from 2020 to 2022 is presented in Table 8.3.

Table: 8.3 Retaliatory Wildlife Killings in Africa (2020–2022)

Species	*Estimated Annual Retaliatory Killings*	*Primary Conflict Reason*
African Lion	200–300	Livestock predation
African Elephant	100–150	Crop raiding
Hyena	500+	Livestock attacks
Leopard	150–200	Livestock predation

Source: Panthera (2023)

In Africa, negative public perception of wildlife is also significantly influenced by biased media reporting, which often portrays wildlife as intruders in HWC incidents, despite human encroachment on their habitats. Participatory land-use planning models implemented in Tanzania to address HWC have been reported as ineffective due to insufficient involvement of stakeholders in the planning process and a lack of strong, transparent, and accountable implementation strategies (Kaswamila & Songorwa, 2009).

HWC undermines livelihoods, food security, and physical safety, leading people to believe that wildlife belongs to the government rather than the community (Ogra & Badola, 2008). This perception negatively impacts conservation efforts because the costs of living in these areas outweigh the perceived benefits of conservation. Studies in Namibia indicate that regions with higher HWC costs disproportionately burden vulnerable groups, particularly women, and affect their food security (Khumalo & Young, 2015). In Namibia, pigs cause the most crop damage, while elephants pose a dual threat to crops and human safety. Interestingly, while Namibian law allows people to own firearms (under regulations), their use against wildlife is monitored by conservancy game guards. Compensation for livestock predation began in Namibia in 2003 through a self-insurance scheme, and in 2007, a Conservancy and a local NGO initiated crop loss compensation. However, the Conservancy imposed strict conditions, such as the farmer's presence during crop loss, a minimum farm size of one hectare, and a loss of at least a quarter of the field, all of which disproportionately affected even local women.

Experiences with HWC in Kenya show that elephants were responsible for 46% of all HWC incidents, followed by buffalo (11%), zebras (8%), leopards (7%), hyenas (6%), lions (3%), and primates (12%) (Mukeka, et al., 2019). A study conducted between 2001 and 2017 in Narok County revealed that crop raiding (50%), attacks on humans (27%), and livestock predation (18%) were the most frequently reported wildlife attacks (IUCN, 2023b). Major drivers for increasing HWC included land conversion to farming and the growth of human and livestock populations. The high incidence of HWC in Kenya is also attributed to the fact that 65% of Kenyan wildlife resides on private and communal lands, outside protected areas (Western, et al., 2009). Although indigenous communities in Africa, such as the Maasai, are generally more tolerant of wildlife, they still engage in retaliatory killings (Mukeka J.M, 2018). Key strategies identified for reducing HWC included discouraging the conversion of wildlife habitats and controlling livestock density. Other suggested measures involve land-use zoning to minimize contact between people, livestock, and wildlife, effective livestock herding practices, predator-proof livestock enclosures, and fencing farms to protect crops.

8.4 Solution and Strategies

HWC in Africa presents a complex and pressing challenge that calls for innovative, sustainable solutions to ensure the harmonious coexistence of humans and wildlife. As human settlements and agricultural expansion continue to infringe on natural habitats, mitigation efforts must address both the immediate protection of livelihoods and the long-term conservation of biodiversity. Key among these efforts is the establishment of wildlife corridors and habitat restoration projects, which reconnect fragmented landscapes and enable animals to move along their traditional migratory paths without entering farms or villages. In Kenya, for example, elephant corridors have significantly lowered incidents of crop-raiding by providing safe passage between protected areas (Mukeka, et. al. 2019). Similarly, community-driven reforestation initiatives in Tanzania have restored critical habitats for primates and other species, reducing their reliance on human-modified environments.

Another important strategy involves non-lethal deterrents to protect farms and livestock from wildlife incursions. African farmers have employed inventive methods like chili-fortified fences and beehive barriers to safely repel elephants. In Botswana, flashing lights and sound devices have been successful in deterring nocturnal pests such as hyenas and jackals (AWF, 2021). For pastoralist communities, the use of predator-proof enclosures fortified with chain-link fencing has led to substantial reductions in livestock losses to lions and leopards. In addition, the deployment of specially trained guard dogs has proven highly effective in Namibia and South Africa in protecting livestock from carnivores (Khumalo, et al 2015). These techniques not only preserve livelihoods but also help foster a greater tolerance for wildlife by proving that conflicts can be managed without lethal measures.

Long-term conflict mitigation hinges on active community involvement and education. Empowering local communities through conservation education initiatives strengthens their role in protecting wildlife. Across Africa, programs that engage communities in wildlife monitoring and conflict management have nurtured a sense of ownership and accountability. In Zambia, for example, village scouts armed with GPS devices monitor lion movements and alert herders to imminent dangers, allowing them to take preventive action (Chomba, 2012). Compensation schemes and insurance programs for losses due to wildlife also help reduce retaliatory killings by easing financial burdens. Rwanda's government-supported compensation program for crop damage by elephants has notably improved community attitudes toward conservation, highlighting the importance of fair and accessible solutions (AWF, 2023).

Technological advances have further enhanced efforts to predict and prevent conflicts. Real-time tracking through GPS collars and satellite systems enables authorities to provide early warnings to at-risk communities. In Kenya, apps like 'M-Survey allow farmers to report wildlife sightings instantly, facilitating quick responses from conservation teams'(Mukeka, 2018). The use of drones and camera traps has expanded the ability to monitor wildlife and deter poaching activities, which often escalate during conflict periods. Combining indigenous knowledge with modern technology has shown promising results, as traditional practices often provide valuable insights into animal behavior that enhance conflict prevention strategies.

Effective policy and governance frameworks are crucial to the success of these mitigation measures. Strong collaboration between governments and conservation organizations is needed to enforce habitat protection laws and promote sustainable land-use practices. Cross-border cooperation is particularly vital for wide-ranging species like elephants and lions, necessitating coordinated management plans. Regional efforts such as the Kavango-Zambezi Transfrontier Conservation Area, which spans five southern African nations, have played a key role in harmonizing conservation policies and reducing HWC across national boundaries (AWF, 2023). International support in the form of funding and technical expertise also strengthens local capacities to maintain and scale up these initiatives.

Ultimately, mitigating HWC in Africa requires a holistic approach that integrates habitat conservation, community empowerment, technological innovation, and sound policy frameworks. By addressing root causes and encouraging collaboration among stakeholders, these strategies can secure a future where both wildlife and human communities thrive. Protecting Africa's rich biodiversity while supporting rural livelihoods is essential, and the lessons learned from current initiatives offer valuable guidance for building a more sustainable and peaceful coexistence between people and wildlife.

Some of the model case studies of current strategies to reduce HWC in Africa include:

i. *Physical Barriers*: Solutions such as electric fences and trenches, and projects like Kenya's Beehive Fences, effectively deter elephants from agricultural lands (KWS, 2022).
ii. *Community-Based Conservation*: Programs encourage wildlife-compatible farming and offer compensation for wildlife-related damages, reducing the drive for retaliatory killings.

iii. *Early Warning Systems:* Technologies like GPS-collared elephants and SMS alerts in Botswana help warn communities of approaching wildlife (AWF, 2021).
iv. *Predator-Proof Enclosures*: Reinforced bomas (livestock pens) help protect livestock from predators such as lions and hyenas (IUCN, 2023).
v. *Ecotourism and Alternative Livelihoods*: Wildlife tourism provides communities with income alternatives, lessening reliance on agriculture and promoting conservation.

From the foregone discussion current solutions and strategies used successfully in Africa can be summarized as follows:

i. *Community-Based Conservation:* Initiatives like the Maasai Mara Wildlife Conservancies Association in Kenya enable communities to benefit directly from wildlife through tourism (Patterson, 2004).
ii. *Compensation Programs*: Countries such as Botswana and Namibia have introduced compensation schemes for farmers, though issues around fairness and funding adequacy remain (AWF, 2021).
iii. *Technological Innovations*: New tools like geofencing, camera traps, and mobile alert systems are increasingly being used to keep wildlife away from farms and settlements.

8.5 African Take Aways in HWC Management

HWC in Africa has posed some of the most intricate and persistent challenges in the interaction between humans and nature. Nevertheless, it has also created a unique platform for learning and innovation. Throughout the continent, various experiences and strategies have emerged, providing important insights on managing and alleviating conflict while fostering coexistence between people and wildlife. These insights are not only significant for Africa but are also applicable to other regions facing similar issues.

Box: 8.1 Kavango-Zambezi (KAZA) Trans frontier Conservation Area (TFCA) in Angola, Botswana, Namibia, Zambia, and Zimbabwe

In the Kavango-Zambezi Transfrontier Conservation Area (KAZA), an integrated landscape development strategy links 20 national parks. At this large scale, land-use planning and zoning, guided by the distribution, movement patterns, and available habitat of wildlife, are employed to manage HWC. To foster coexistence between people and wildlife at a local level, the Eco-exist Trust, supported by the USAID Southern African Regional Environmental Programme (SAREP), implemented a micro-level land-use planning process in the Okavango Panhandle of Botswana.

Elephant-aware farming is practiced in this region, which involves avoiding cultivation in elephant corridors, using effective methods to deter elephants, and adapting farming practices. This includes incorporating conservation agriculture principles, using early-maturing and more resilient crop varieties. Conservation agriculture aims to increase the yields of various crops. These farmers are organized into cooperatives and are part of an "Elephant Aware" value chain.

The Eco-exist Trust is also working to develop an "Elephant Economy" to enhance the economic benefits for communities living with elephants, thereby promoting sustainable and environmentally friendly elephant-themed enterprise development. This initiative improves community-based access to tourism and related economic activities through diverse livelihood options that are compatible with living alongside elephants. Consequently, in the past three years, communities have seen an 80% increase in their income through elephant-related enterprises.

Source: AWF, 2023

A crucial takeaway from Africa is the significance of community-based conservation. In countries like Kenya, Namibia, and Zimbabwe, engaging local communities in wildlife management has proven effective in reducing conflict and enhancing conservation efforts (UNEP, 2021). These methods acknowledge that individuals living near wildlife are not merely passive victims but can become strong allies in preserving biodiversity—particularly when they receive concrete benefits such as tourism income, employment opportunities, or land rights. For instance, Namibia's communal conservancy model has been lauded for aiding in the recovery of wildlife populations while diminishing conflict incidents, as communities have a vested interest in safeguarding the animals that contribute to their livelihoods (MET/NACSO, 2019).

Box: 8.2 Community-based ecotourism in Bwindi, Uganda

Effective conservation initiatives must adopt an integrated approach that considers both socio- dynamic and HWC realities. Community-based ecotourism offers a viable model for equitable benefit-sharing, ensuring those coexisting with wildlife receive fair compensation for associated costs. This approach directly reinvests tourism revenues into affected communities, creating economic incentives for conservation.

Uganda's innovative funding model demonstrates this principle in action:

i. 20% of national park entry fees are allocated to local development projects.

ii. An additional $10 per gorilla trekking permit supports neighbouring communities.

iii. Revenue distribution prioritizes areas experiencing severe HWC and those adjacent to park boundaries.

These funds finance critical infrastructure including schools, medical facilities, and transportation networks. The Wildlife Act further strengthens this framework by mandating compensation for wildlife-related damages. The program also established certification standards for "Gorilla Friendly" community products through the Wildlife Friendly Enterprise Network. This enables local artisans and producers to create premium goods for tourist markets, generating alternative income streams while promoting conservation-compatible businesses. By aligning economic incentives with ecological protection, this comprehensive model demonstrates how conservation can deliver tangible benefits to both wildlife and human populations, fostering long-term coexistence.

Source: Franks & Twinamatsiko, 2017

Another vital lesson is the integration of traditional knowledge with contemporary conservation science. Many African communities have coexisted with wildlife for generations and possess valuable insights into animal behavior, seasonal migrations, and deterrent techniques. By weaving this indigenous knowledge into wildlife management approaches—such as utilizing chili fences to deter elephants or constructing kraals to shield livestock from predators—conflict can be mitigated in a culturally sensitive and economical manner (National Geographic, 2021). These low-tech, community-driven solutions often prove to be more sustainable and acceptable than externally imposed strategies.

Moreover, Africa illustrates that addressing HWC involves not only wildlife management but also addressing fundamental socio-economic challenges. Factors such as poverty, food insecurity, and limited access to essential services can exacerbate conflict, as vulnerable communities may exhibit less tolerance for wildlife-related damage. Insights from nations like Tanzania and Uganda indicate that initiatives aimed at reducing conflict should coincide with rural development and educational efforts (Frank, et al. 2017). When individuals have more stable incomes, access to compensation programs, and opportunities to gain from conservation, they are more inclined to support wildlife protection initiatives.

Additionally, the role of policy and governance is a key lesson. Effective conflict management necessitates clear regulations, robust institutions, and responsive wildlife authorities (Pillar, et al. 2020). In regions where wildlife laws are outdated or poorly enforced, individuals may resort to taking matters into their own hands, resulting in the killing of protected species. Conversely, in areas where governments collaborate with communities and conservation organizations, there tends to be increased transparency, trust, and success in mitigating conflict. Collaborative management plans and ongoing communication among stakeholders are essential for developing long-term solutions.

Box: 8.3 Community centred management of HWC: Success stories from Namibia

Namibia has been notably successful in creating an effective framework for managing HWC, supported by forward-thinking environmental and conservancy legislation. The country's Ministry of Environment and Tourism introduced a comprehensive policy known as Namibia's National Policy on HWC Management, which addresses multiple facets of conflict mitigation. This policy outlines the development of legal frameworks, best practices for management, financial support systems, public education initiatives, and rapid response procedures.

At the heart of Namibia's strategy is a community-based natural resource management approach that emphasizes decentralized governance of wildlife and tourism. Under this system, local conservancies are managed by elected committees responsible for protecting wildlife and ecosystems, while also generating revenue through the sustainable use of natural resources. This model empowers community members to act as custodians of wildlife and has been a key factor in Namibia's conservation success. Since the implementation of this model in the 1990s, the country has seen its elephant population triple, secured the survival of free-roaming black rhinos, and boosted national income by approximately US$86 million through conservation-related activities. In 2018 alone, tourism and trophy hunting generated around US$10 million in revenue

Instead of traditional compensation schemes for wildlife-related damages, Namibia adopted a HWC Self-Reliance Scheme, which applies to all communal areas. This initiative helps offset confirmed losses of livestock, crops, or human life—provided certain conditions are met—without relying solely on government payouts. Conservancies maintain a dedicated fund, sourced from tourism and hunting income, to cover these losses. The Ministry of Environment and Tourism also supports conservancies and individual landholders in accessing additional funding where needed.

Source: Source: MET/NACSO, 2019

African experiences underscore the necessity for adaptive, landscape-level planning. HWC does not occur in isolation; it is influenced by factors such as land use, climate change, migration routes, and ecosystem health. Countries like Botswana and South Africa have shown that planning land use to accommodate both human and wildlife needs—such as maintaining migration corridors or zoning areas for tourism, agriculture, and habitation—can significantly alleviate conflict (WWF, 2022a). This comprehensive approach promotes coexistence rather than separation as a foundational principle.

Africa's prolonged struggle with HWC has yielded valuable lessons rooted in community engagement, traditional knowledge, integrated development, and inclusive governance. While challenges persist, these lessons provide hope and direction for a future where humans and wildlife can share spaces more harmoniously. The African experience demonstrates that with the right strategies, coexistence is not only achievable but also advantageous for both biodiversity and human welfare.

8.6 Conclusion

HWC in Africa is a complex issue that has significant ecological and socio-economic impacts. Although efforts are underway to address these conflicts, there is a pressing need for more integrated, community-focused, and adequately funded strategies. Achieving protection for both people and wildlife requires a careful balance that takes into account the long-term sustainability of Africa's ecosystems and the communities reliant on them.

HWC in Africa continues to be a vital concern that necessitates comprehensive solutions that harmonize conservation efforts with human well-being. While mitigation tactics such as fencing, community involvement, and technological innovations have shown potential, lasting success hinges on habitat preservation, effective policy enforcement, and sustainable land-use planning. Collaborative initiatives among governments, conservation organizations, and local communities are crucial for fostering coexistence between humans and wildlife.

To effectively address HWC in Africa, the following areas need special attention.

- *i.* *Integrated Land-Use Planning*: Ensure that development initiatives account for wildlife migration corridors and buffer zones.
- *ii.* *Education and Awareness*: Enhance local understanding of wildlife behavior and promote safe coexistence practices.
- *iii.* *International Support:* Increase funding for conservation and conflict mitigation from global environmental and development organizations.
- *iv.* *Strengthen Legal Frameworks*: Improve policy enforcement to safeguard both human safety and wildlife conservation.

References

1. African Wildlife Foundation. (2021). *HWC in Africa: Trends and Solutions*.

2. African Wildlife Foundation (2023). *HWC Mitigation Strategies.*
3. Anderies, et. al. (2004), 'A Framework to Analyse the Robustness of Social-ecological Systems from an Institutional Perspective,' *Ecology and Society*, Vol. 19, p. 18.
4. Bourdillon, et. al. (1985), *Studies on the Fishing on Lake Kariba, Zimbabwe*, Mambo Press, Gweru, pp. 3-35.
5. Chomba C, et. al. (2012), 'Pattern of HWCs in Zambia, Causes, Consequences and Management Responses,' *Journal of Ecology and the Natural Environment*, Vol. 4, No. 12, pp. 303-313.
6. FAO (2023). *HWC: A Review of the Global Evidence with a Focus on Africa.*
7. Franks P., Twinamatsiko M (2017), *Lessons learnt from 20 years of revenue sharing at Bwindi Impenetrable National Park, Uganda*, International Institute for Environment and Development (IIED), London, UK.
8. IUCN (2023a). *Status of Wildlife in Africa.*
9. IUCN. (2023b). *Red List of Threatened Species: African Lion.*
10. Jones B.T.B., Diggle R.W., Thouless C (2015), 'From Exploitation to Ownership: Wildlife-Based Tourism and Communal Area Conservancies in Namibia,' in *Institutional Arrangements for Conservation, Development and Tourism in Eastern and Southern Africa: A Dynamic Perspective* (eds. R. van der Duim, M. Lamers, J. van Wijk), Springer Netherlands, Dordrecht, pp. 17-37.
11. Kaswamila A & A. N Songorwa (2009), 'Participatory Land-use Planning and Conservation in Northern Tanzania Rangelands,' *African Journal of Ecology*, Vol. 47, pp.128-134.
12. Kenya Wildlife Service (2022). *Annual Wildlife Report.*
13. Khumalo K E & Young L A (2015), 'Women, HWC, and CBNRM: Hidden Impacts and Vulnerabilities in Kwandu Conservancy, Namibia,' *Conservation and Society*, Vol. 13, No.3, pp. 232-243.

14. MET/NACSO (2018), 'The State of Community Conservation in Namibia,' *Annual Report 2018*, Windhoek, Namibia.
15. MET/NACSO (2019), 'The State of Community Conservation in Namibia,' *Annual Report 2019*, Windhoek, Namibia.
16. Mosimane, et. al. (2013), 'Using Mental Models in the Analysis of Humn-wildlife Conflict from the Perspective of a Social-ecological System in Namibia,' *Oryx*, Vol. 48, No. 1, pp.64-70.
17. Mukeka J.M, et. al. (2018), 'Characteristics of HWC in Kenya: Examples of Tsavo and Maasai Mara regions, *Environment and Natural Resources Research*, Vol. 8, No.3, pp.148-165.
18. Mukeka, J M, et. al. (2019), 'HWCs and their Correlates in Narok County, Kenya,' *Global Ecology and Conservation*, Vol. 18, pp.1-22.
19. National Geographic (2021). *Elephants on the Move: Climate and Conflict in Africa.*
20. Ogra M & R. Badola (2008), 'Compensating HWC in Protected Area Communities: Ground level Perspectives from Uttarakhand, India,' *Human Ecology*, Vol. 36, No. 5, pp.717-729.
21. Panthera. (2023). *Retaliatory Killings of Big Cats in Africa.*
22. Patterson B D, et. al. (2004), 'Livestock Predation by Lions and Other Carnivores on Ranches Neighbouring Tsavo National Park, Kenya,' *Biological Conservation*, Vol. 119, pp. 507-516.
23. Pillai, Nair, Jacob. (2010). *Role of Indigenous communities in Forest Conservation: Lessons from Africa.* Institute of Social Research and Action. Thiruvananthapuram.
24. Roe, E (1998), *Taking Complexity Seriously: Policy Analysis, Triangulation, and Sustainable Development,* Kluwer Academic Publishers, Boston, USA.
25. Simukonda C (2008), *Aerial Survey Report for Large Mammals: A Report submitted to Zambia Wildlife Authority*, Chilanga.
26. Tanzania Wildlife Research Institute. (2021). *HWC Statistics.*
27. UNEP (2021). *Wildlife and People: Living Together in Africa.*

28. UNEP. (2023). *African elephant database.* National Wildlife Authorities.

29. Western, et. al. (2009), The Status of Wildlife in Protected Areas Compared to Non-protected Areas of Kenya, *PLoS One*, Vol. 4, No. 7 https://doi.org/10.1371/journal.pone.0006140.

30. WWF (2022a). *Living with Lions: Reducing Conflict and Promoting Coexistence.*

31. WWF. (2022b). *Economic Impacts of Elephant Crop Raiding in Kenya.*

CHAPTER: 9
HUMAN WILDLIFE CONFLICT IN INDIA

9.1 Introduction

HWC is a pressing issue in India, largely due to the country's diverse ecosystems and the growing encroachment of human activities into wildlife habitats. In India, where rich biodiversity coexists with expanding human populations, conflicts often emerge over land use, farming practices, and competition for resources. The escalation of HWC in India can be attributed to habitat fragmentation, agricultural growth, and rising populations of both humans and wildlife. This chapter delves into the extent of HWC across India by focusing on fatalities, injuries, and crop losses. It also investigates strategies for mitigation and policy measures designed to promote coexistence between humans and wildlife. In regions where human settlements infringe upon wildlife areas, these interactions frequently lead to conflicts.

Figure: 9.1 Human death due to wildlife attack, 2018-23

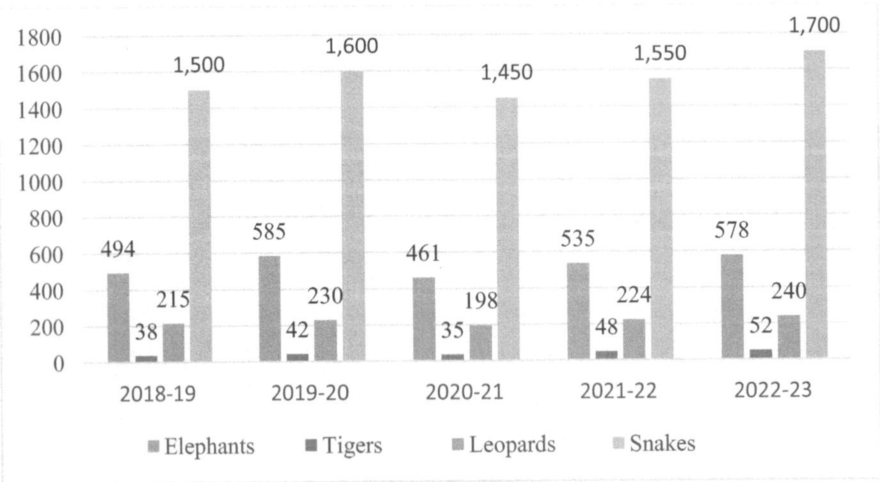

Source: MoEFCC, 2023

HWC continues to be an increasing concern in India due to habitat disruption, agricultural development, and population growth. The discussion in the chapter emphasizes the need for sustainable approaches that reconcile conservation efforts with human livelihoods. Rapid urbanization and deforestation have exacerbated HWC, especially in areas adjacent to forests. Species such as elephants, tigers, leopards, and wild boars are commonly involved in India in these conflicts (MoEFCC, 2017). A representation of human casualties resulting from wildlife attacks in India from 2018 to 2023 is illustrated in Figure 9.1.

9.2 Overview of HWC in India

In recent years, HWC has emerged as a critical issue in India. Factors such as rapid development, rising population, and competition for land and resources have led to the destruction, fragmentation, and deterioration of forests and wildlife habitats. As a result, humans and wildlife increasingly interact as they occupy the same space for survival. Nearly every Indian state has its own HWC management strategies, guided by policies from the central and state governments, as well as forest departments (Rai R.P., et al, 2014). These efforts reflect widespread initiatives to tackle conflicts. Certain states have effectively incorporated HWC mitigation into national programs like the Mahatma Gandhi National Rural Employment Guarantee Scheme.

A significant driver of HWC in India is the growing livestock population (Mishra, 1997). At the same time the country is home to more than 60% of Asia's wild elephants, and agricultural expansion has heightened conflicts. For instance, in Assam, elephants caused over 400 human deaths between 2015 and 2022, with retaliatory elephant killings also increasing (WWF India, 2023). Mitigation strategies such as fencing, compensation schemes, and awareness campaigns have been implemented, though their effectiveness differs across regions. Figure-9.2 outlines the primary causes of HWC in India.

Figure: 9.2 Causes of HWC in India (%)

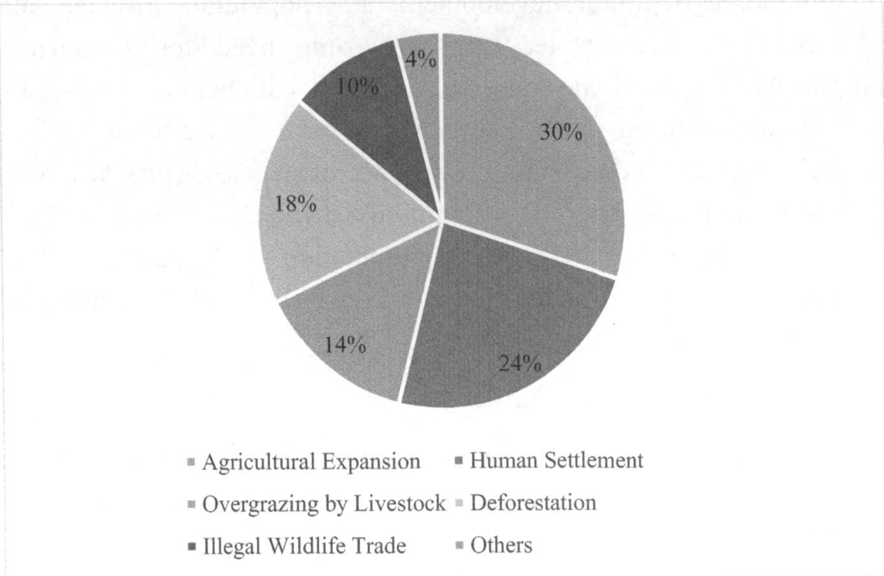

Source: WII, 2022

Major factors that trigger HWC in India included the following as we discussed in the previous chapters (Dasgupta, 2021):

i. *Habitat Loss and Fragmentation*: Agricultural and infrastructure growth has degraded wildlife habitats, reduced forest cover and driving animals into human-populated areas.
ii. *Agricultural Practices*: Growing crops like banana and sugarcane near forests lures wildlife, particularly herbivores such as elephants and wild boars, escalating conflicts.
iii. *Population Growth*: Rising human and wildlife numbers heighten competition for space and resources, leading to further encroachment into wildlife habitats.
iv. *Climate Change*: Shifts in rainfall patterns and prolonged droughts force wildlife to seek water and food near human settlements.

9.3 Effects of HWC

HWC in India has become a pressing ecological and societal issue, highlighting the growing friction between expanding human populations and diminishing wildlife habitats. With ongoing urban development, deforestation, and agricultural encroachment into forests and natural ecosystems, wildlife such as elephants, leopards, tigers, and wild boars are increasingly encountering human settlements. These interactions often lead to harmful outcomes for both people and animals. States like Kerala, Assam, Jharkhand, and Odisha frequently report incidents of crop destruction, livestock attacks, property damage, and even human fatalities due to wildlife encounters (WII, 2022). Such conflicts not only endanger biodiversity but also breed resentment within local communities toward conservation initiatives.

The impacts of HWC are wide-ranging and severe, affecting both people and wildlife. Major consequences include (MoEFCC, 2023):

i. *Economic Losses*: Farmers suffer considerable financial damage due to destruction of crops and loss of livestock.
ii. *Human Casualties*: Encounters with large animals like elephants and tigers can lead to injuries and deaths.
iii. *Wildlife Mortality*: Retaliation, illegal hunting, and accidents such as electrocution or roadkill pose significant threats to endangered species.

For many rural families, the economic toll is devastating. Sudden loss of crops or the death of livestock—key sources of livelihood—can push households into financial hardship. In states like Assam and West Bengal, elephants often raid paddy fields and village homes, inflicting serious economic damage. In response, retaliatory killings of wildlife have surged, reversing years of conservation progress (Indian Express, 2025). When leopards or other big cats wander into human settlements, violent encounters often result in casualties on both sides. This ongoing cycle fuels fear and hostility, making it increasingly difficult for conservation authorities to implement successful interventions.

Various studies highlight the complexities of HWC in India. For example, increased agricultural activity in Assam has led to more frequent interactions between elephants and farmers, causing property damage and human deaths. Similarly, the expansion of human settlements into tiger habitats in Rajasthan has intensified conflicts, prompting conservationists to seek solutions that accommodate both human and tiger needs.

Beyond the physical and economic damage, HWC also causes deep psychological and social distress. In many tribal and forest-fringe communities, fear of wildlife leads to school absenteeism and work disruptions. Constant anxiety, coupled with insufficient governmental support or compensation, takes a heavy mental toll (The Hindu, 2022). Although measures like solar fencing, wildlife corridors, and early-warning systems have been introduced by state governments and the Ministry of Environment, Forest and Climate Change (MoEFCC), these initiatives are often fragmented and under-resourced. According to Table 9.1, Odisha recorded the highest number of HWC-related deaths in 2023–24, followed by West Bengal, Jharkhand, Kerala, and Assam.

Table: 9.1 HWC fatalities by State, 2023

State	*Human Deaths*	*Key Wildlife Involved*	*Remarks*
Odisha	154	Elephants	Highest number of HWC-related deaths in India during this period.
West Bengal	99	Elephants	Significant fatalities due to elephant encounters.
Jharkhand	87	Elephants	Ranked third in HWC-related human deaths.
Assam	74	Elephants	High incidence of human-elephant conflicts; 383 human deaths over the past five years.
Kerala	82	Elephants, Tigers, Snakes	4,527 injuries reported between 2020–2024

Source: MoEFCC, 2023

Tackling HWC in India necessitates a comprehensive strategy that encompasses habitat restoration, community education, enhanced compensation programs, and the use of advanced technologies such as GPS tracking and AI-based monitoring. It is crucial to engage local communities in conservation efforts, positioning them as stakeholders rather than mere victims (Times, 2024). Only through cohesive and inclusive approaches can India effectively reduce the effects of HWC, paving the way for a sustainable coexistence between humans and wildlife. Table 9.2 outlines the crop damage caused by wildlife attacks in key states, with Karnataka experiencing the highest loss at Rs 260 crore, followed by West Bengal, Maharashtra, and Uttarakhand.

Table: 9.2 Crop Damage by Wildlife in Selected States, 2022 (₹ Crores)

State	*Elephants*	*Wild Boars*	*Monkeys*	*Nilgai*	*Total*
Karnataka	120	85	30	25	260
West Bengal	95	40	20	15	170
Maharashtra	60	70	45	50	225
Uttarakhand	80	30	25	10	145

Source: Wildlife Institute of India (WII), 2022

9.4 Mitigation Strategies

India has made significant strides in addressing coexistence and HWC through its national legislation. The Wildlife Protection Act empowers the Forest Department to implement measures that promote peaceful coexistence between humans and wildlife in protected areas (GoI, 2008).

Box: 9.1 Human – Elephant Conflict Management in Valparai and Hassan areas in Karnataka State, India

The Hassan region, characterized by its extensive coffee plantations and paddy fields, is home to over 100,000 people and about 45 elephants. The area's landscape also features tea plantations, riverside vegetation, and small patches of rainforest that serve as safe havens for elephants. HWC in this region leads to fear, trauma, and a sense of powerlessness among the local population. In response to 47 and 40 human deaths recorded in Valparai and Hassan respectively, the Nature

Conservation Foundation (NCF) implemented early warning systems. These included mobile phone alerts and digital display boards to keep local residents informed about elephant movements and potential risks.

The successful implementation of these systems, in collaboration with local communities and the state forest departments, empowered people to manage human-elephant conflict more effectively. Plantation companies also adopted a 'no drive policy' to avoid direct confrontation with elephants and improved communication and safety protocols. Consequently, conflict-related human fatalities decreased from three to one in both Valparai and Hassan. The companies acknowledged the positive impact of NCF's awareness programs in educating workers about safety measures and elephant behavior. The core strategy employed in this predominantly agricultural area involved a change in focus from targeting individual 'problem elephants' to addressing 'problem locations' where conflicts frequently occurred. The active involvement of local communities and plantation companies was crucial in ensuring the safety of workers and fostering a more harmonious coexistence.

Source: MoEFCC, 2017

The National Wildlife Action Plan 2017- '35, launched in 2017, places a strong emphasis on managing HWC (MoEFCC, 2017). The Ministry of Environment, Forests, and Climate Change, with support from non-governmental organizations and scientific institutions, has been tasked with developing national and regional conflict management plans, improving post-conflict relief processes, and creating local action plans. This action plan advocates for an inclusive approach to managing human-wildlife interactions by engaging local communities in the process. Such involvement ensures that community members receive training, education, and compensation, thereby empowering them in the management and protection of their own lands.

HWC occur frequently in India's rural regions, particularly in villages bordering forests. Most large carnivore species in India are known to attack human settlements, including people and livestock, with leopard attacks posing the most significant threat to human habitation (Goyal et al., 2000). Current policies to mitigate carnivore-related conflicts primarily involve compensating victims and capturing and relocating animals (Athreya et al., 2010). Lethal control has been banned since 1972, except in rare circumstances. India's Wildlife Protection Act, 1972 imposes stringent restrictions on the killing of wild animals. Key provisions include (Ramakumar, 2025):

i. *Section 11:* Only the State Chief Wildlife Warden can authorize the killing of a wild animal if it poses a threat to human life or is severely injured/incurably diseased.
ii. *Section 62:* Permits culling if an animal is declared vermin (a threat to crops/livelihoods).
iii. *Section 12:* Allows killing for approved scientific research.

Schedule I and II animals (including tigers and elephants) benefit from stronger legal protections. The 1991 amendments to wildlife Act further strengthened these conservation measures. Before 1947, individual princely states maintained their own hunting regulations. The Wild Birds and Animals Protection Act (1912), while imposing some restrictions, still permitted hunting activities. During British rule, hunting was legally recognized as a sport, allowing regulated killing of wild animals. Recent Supreme Court rulings have significantly tightened wildlife protections (Ramakuamr, 2025). Presently, killing wild animals is strictly prohibited except under the specific circumstances outlined in the Wildlife Protection Act (such as threats to human life or vermin declarations).

Translocation, used globally as a non-lethal alternative for managing HWC involving carnivores and large herbivores like elephants is mainly categorized into short-distance, long-distance, and reciprocal translocations between problem areas (Brown et al., 2009). However, studies on leopard translocations in India indicate limited effectiveness, with animals often returning after short-distance relocations or encroaching on human settlements in new areas (Athreya et al., 2010). Translocation can also alter carnivore behavior due to stressors like capture, captivity, transport, potential injury, and territorial competition in new habitats (Letty et al., 2007). Consequently, permanent captivity is suggested as an alternative to translocation or lethal control, though it presents economic, logistical, and animal welfare challenges.

Currently, efforts are underway to prepare a national HWC management strategy and action plan (HWC-NAP), involving collaboration between the Central government, the German Agency for International Development (GIZ), state forest departments, the Wildlife Institute of India, and local partners. The HWC-NAP aligns with national objectives related to sustainable development goals (SDGs), climate change, and biodiversity, and is integrated with plans from relevant sectors. Successful implementation of the HWC-NAP requires support from the forest department, stakeholders, and research institutions. This country-level framework will guide state-specific strategies and HWC management plans while allowing flexibility to address local issues.

Measures to mitigate HWC in India include the following.

i. *Habitat Restoration*: Reforestation and the creation of wildlife corridors to minimize animal incursions into human areas (Tribune, 2023). Protecting and restoring natural habitats can help reduce wildlife encroachment into settlements.

ii. *Early Warning Systems*: The 'Haati App' in Assam warns villagers of nearby elephant movements, while drones, SMS alerts, and sensor-based fences provide additional warnings to communities (Dasgupta, 2021).

iii. *Physical Barriers*: The installation of solar-powered fences in conflict-prone regions to deter wildlife from entering human spaces.

iv. *Community Engagement*: Involving local communities in conservation initiatives and decision-making through awareness programs and eco-development committees.

v. *Compensation Schemes:* Offering financial assistance to victims of wildlife attacks and crop damage, such as government compensation for losses under schemes like Pradhan Mantri Fasal Bima Yojana (MoEFCC, 2022).

vi. *Technological Solutions:* Utilizing AI-based monitoring and GPS collars to track animal movements. Implementing early warning systems and employing drones for surveillance can help prevent conflicts between humans and wildlife.

9.5 Conclusion

HWC in India is a complex issue that requires a blend of scientific, community-oriented, and policy-based approaches. By adopting comprehensive strategies, it is feasible to mitigate conflicts and encourage peaceful coexistence between humans and wildlife. Addressing HWC effectively involves a multi-faceted approach; while government policies and technological solutions play a role, sustainable outcomes hinge on habitat conservation and community involvement. Achieving sustainable coexistence is vital for both the protection of biodiversity and the well-being of humans.

HWC continues to be a significant challenge in India, necessitating collaborative efforts that prioritize the welfare of both humans and wildlife. By identifying the root causes and implementing specific mitigation strategies, it is possible to promote a harmonious relationship between these two groups.

To effectively tackle HWC in India following policy recommendations should be considered.

i. *Integrated Land-Use Planning*: Formulate land-use strategies that address the needs of both humans and wildlife.
ii. *Strengthening Legal Frameworks*: Revise wildlife protection laws to create a balance between conservation efforts and human safety.
iii. *Research and Monitoring*: Allocate resources for research aimed at understanding wildlife behavior and patterns of conflict.

References

1. Athreya V, et. al. (2010), 'Translocation as Tool of Mitigating Conflict with Leopards in Human-dominated Landscapes of India,' *Conservation Biology*, pp.1-10.
2. Brown, J, R, et. al (2009), 'Effectiveness of Short-distance Translocation and its Effects on Western Rattlesnakes,' *Journal of Wildlife Management*, Vol. 73, pp. 419-425.
3. Dasgupta, S. (2021). "Human-Elephant Conflict in India: Trends and Mitigation." *Journal of Wildlife Management*, 85(3), 456-470.
4. Government of India (2008), *The Wild Life (Protection) Act, 1972: (53 of 1972) as amended by the Wild Life (Protection) Amendment Act, 2006 (39 of 2006),* Universal Law Publishing Co., Delhi, India.
5. Government of India. (2022). *Compensation Schemes for Wildlife-Induced Damages*.
6. Goyal, S P, eta. al (2000), 'A Study on Distribution, Relative Abundance and Food Habits of Leopard (Panthera pardus) in Garhwal Himalayas,' *Technical Report*, Wildlife Life Institute of India, Dehradun.
7. Jhala, Y. V., Qureshi, Q., & Nayak, A. K. (2020). *Status of Tigers, Co-predators, and Prey in India.* NTCA.
8. Letty J, et. al. (2007), 'Problems Encountered by Individuals in Animal Translocations: Lessons from Field Studies, *Eco science*, Vol. 14, pp. 420 -431.
9. Mishra C (1997), Livestock depredation by Large Carnivores in the Indian trans-Himalaya: Conflict Perceptions and Conservation Prospects, *Environmental Conservation*, Vol. 24, No. 4, pp. 338-343.
10. MoEFCC (2017), *India's National Wildlife Action Plan 2017-2031.*, Ministry of Environment, Forests and Climate Change, New Delhi, India.
11. Ministry of Environment, Forest and Climate Change (MoEFCC). (2023). *Annual Report on HWC in India.*

12. Rai R.P., Ghose P.S., Shresta P (2014), 'Shifting perspectives in HWC: Unheard voices from the Sikkim and Darjeeling Himalaya,' in *HWC in the Mountains of SAARC Region: Compilation of Successful Management Strategies and Practices,* SAARC Forestry Centre Office, Thimphu, Bhutan, pp. 72-82.
13. Ramakumar R. (2025). Human Wildlife Conflict: The Central Government Viewpoints to be Corrected. *Mathrubhumi.com.* June 14.
14. The Indian Express. (2025, February 14). *HWC claimed 460 lives in Kerala in past 5 years*. https://indianexpress.com.
15. The Tribune. (2023, July 27). *2,950 killed in HWC in India in 5 years*. https://tribuneindia.com
16. The Hindu. (2022, February 13). *1000+ HWC-prone areas identified in Kerala*. https://thehindu.com
17. The Times. (2024, August). *Elephant warning app to protect villagers from being trampled.* https://thetimes.co.uk
18. Wildlife Institute of India (WII). (2022). *Economic Impacts of Wildlife Damage on Agriculture.*
19. Wikipedia contributors. (2025, March). *Human-elephant conflict in Kerala.* In *Wikipedia.* https://en.wikipedia.org/wiki/Human-elephant_conflict_in_Kerala
20. WWF India. (2023). Elephant Human Conflict in North East India.

CHAPTER:10
HUMAN WILDLIFE INTERFACE IN KERALA

10.1 Introduction

Kerala, known for its rich biodiversity, is increasingly facing conflicts between humans and wildlife. The state's high population density and development activities have resulted in habitat loss and fragmentation, bringing humans and wild animals into closer proximity and leading to more frequent conflicts. With approximately 11,531.9 sq. km of forest cover, which makes up 29.7% of Kerala's total area, the rising human population and anthropogenic pressures have heightened interactions and conflicts with wildlife (SPB, 2024). With forests covering a third of Kerala's land area, frequent encounters between wild animals and communities are inevitable (Ramakumar, 2025). Contrary to the belief that these conflicts are recent, historical records from the 1890s and an 1818 proclamation show that they have existed for a long time, with efforts made to deter wildlife from agricultural areas (Mahanti, & Kumar, 2018). Recently, tensions surrounding wildlife management have increased, particularly among communities near reserve forests and sanctuaries, due to habitat loss, changes in farming practices, and growing wildlife populations (SPB, 2022). Reported HWC cases surged from 2,292 in 2009-10 to 8,438 by 2023-24, indicating a sharp increase over the years (Ramakumar, 2025). Analysis indicates that HWC poses a significant threat across various forest divisions, especially in Wayanad, Palakkad and Idukki.

A new trend in Kerala reveals that conflict issues are arising even in regions far from forest edges, driven by factors such as abandoned farmland, waste accumulation, and the thriving populations of generalist species like wild boars and bonnet macaques. These species have begun to inhabit areas outside their traditional ranges, suggesting that HWC should not be viewed solely as an issue in forest fringes

(KFD, 2023). Over the past decade, HWC in Kerala has escalated due to habitat fragmentation, urban growth, human encroachment and climate change. This chapter reviews the extent, causes, and effects of HWC in the state and discusses mitigation strategies, including technological solutions and community-based approaches, aimed at promoting coexistence between humans and wildlife.

10.2 Scale of the Conflict

HWC has become a significant environmental and socio-economic challenge in Kerala. Rapid urbanization, habitat fragmentation, and agricultural expansion have increased encounters between humans and wildlife, resulting in crop damage, livestock predation, and human fatalities. Experts in the field advices the importance of sustainable land-use planning, community involvement, and advanced technological measures to mitigate conflicts. Figure-10.1 illustrates reported incidents during 2017-18 and 2022-23 in the state.

Kerala, known for its abundant biodiversity and dense forest cover is experiencing a rise in HWC and key species involved in these conflicts include elephants, wild boars, tigers, and leopards. In recent years, the state has reported more than 8,000 HWC incidents each year, impacting rural livelihoods and conservation initiatives (KFD, 2023). Gravity of HWC in Kerala is depicted in Table 10.1.

Figure: 10.1 Causality and reported incidents due to HWC in Kerala, 2017-18 & 2022-23

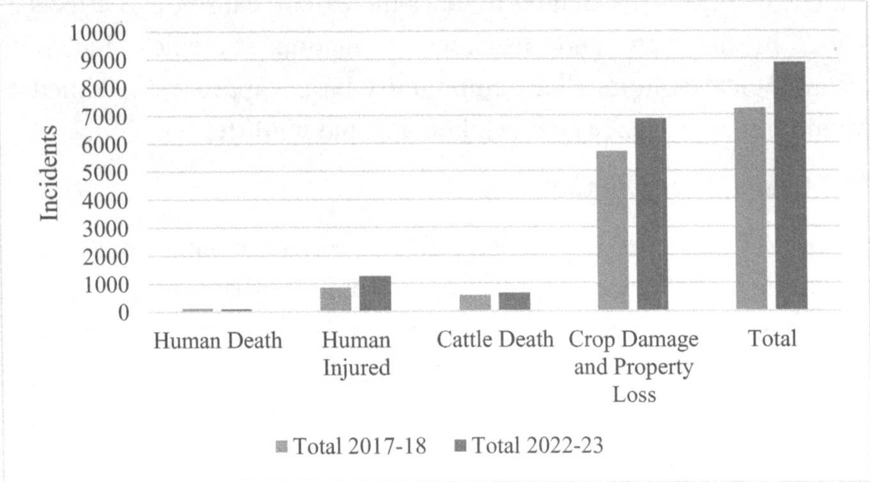

Source: Kerala Forest Department, 2023

Table: 10.1 Gravity of HWC in Kerala, 2022 & 2023

Parameter	*2022*	*2023*	*Change (%)*
Crop Damage Cases	6,542	7,891	+20.6
Human Deaths	38	45	+18.4
Elephant Deaths	28	32	+14.3
Compensation Paid (₹Cr)	85	112	+31.8

Source: KFD (2023)

Elephant attacks are the leading cause of harm to both lives and crops in forest fringe areas, though other animals such as tigers, leopards, wild pigs, and peacocks also contribute to conflicts (SPB, 2022). Notably, the frequency of such conflicts has increased, as reflected by a 25% rise in compensation claims in 2021–22, totalling ₹13.1 crore, as shown in Figure 10.2. The primary drivers of HWC include rising wildlife populations, habitat degradation and fragmentation, shifting agricultural practices, and climate change. Addressing HWC requires a comprehensive strategy that combines both immediate and long-term solutions focused on prevention and mitigation.

From 2016 to 2024, Kerala recorded a total of 7,917 injuries resulting from wildlife conflicts. The peak occurred in 2018–19, with 146 fatalities. In just the first six months of 2024, 22 deaths were reported, caused by snakebites, elephant attacks, and wild boar encounters. While HWC-related deaths have risen, over 60% are due to snakebites. Elephants are the leading contributors to HWC in Kerala, accounting for 2,518 incidents between April and September 2024, which resulted in 31 injuries. Despite media hype around elephant attacks, fatalities from them have actually declined—from 35 in 2021-22 to 19 in 2024-25, thanks to government measures (Ramakumar, 2025). Other problematic species include leopards (141 incidents), tigers (49 incidents), wild boars, and porcupines (Indian Express, 2025).

Figure: 10.2 Compensation paid in HWC in Kerala, 2017-18 & 2022-23 (Rs Crore)

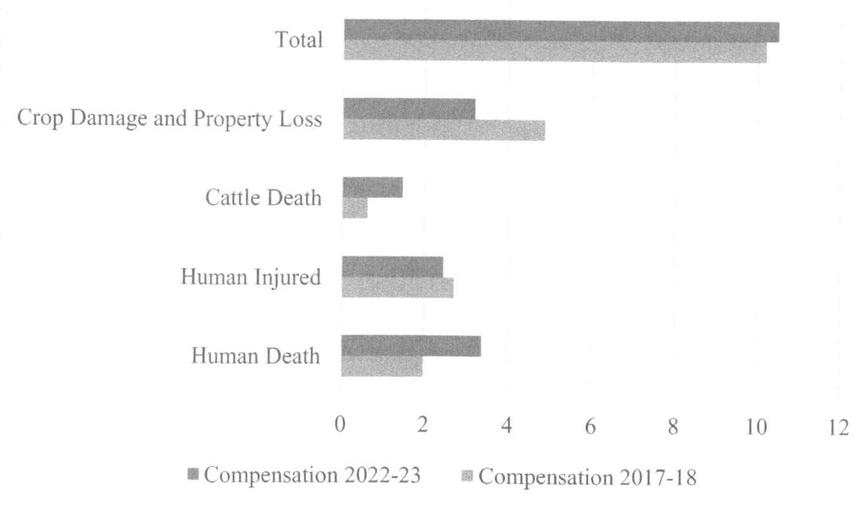

Source: KFD, 2023

A Kerala Forest Department study identified 273 local bodies as high-risk HWC zones, including 30 major hotspots and nine severely affected areas—mostly in Wayanad district. Palakkad reported the highest number of wildlife-related deaths, followed by Thrissur, Malappuram, and Wayanad (KFD, 2023). Table 10.2 provides detailed fatality details during 2020–23 period.

Table: 10.2 Human Fatalities in HWC in Kerala (2020–2024)

Year	*Human Fatalities*	*Injuries*	*Notable Districts Affected*
2020	74	800	Palakkad, Wayanad
2021	104	900	Thrissur, Malappuram
2022	100	850	Idukki, Kozhikode
2023	100	950	Kannur, Ernakulam

Source: Indian Express, 2025

From 2013–14 to 2018–19, the state recorded over 48,000 incidents of crop damage caused by wildlife, with elephants accounting for around 14,611 of these cases (NIE, 2024). To tackle these issues, Kerala has introduced the 'Safe Habitat Hack,' a hackathon designed to generate innovative solutions for reducing HWCs. Additionally, the state has launched 'Mission Fencing 2024,' which aims to repair and upgrade 1,400 km of solar-powered fences to keep wildlife from entering human settlements (Mathubhumi, 2024).

Seven types of HWCs have been reported in Kerala, including Human-Leopard Conflict, Human-Tiger Conflict, Human-Elephant Conflict, Human-Wild Boar Conflict, Human-Monkey Conflict, Human-Sloth Bear Conflict, and Human-Snake Conflict (Mahanti & Kumar, 2018). Most of these species are threatened and are experiencing habitat loss due to human encroachment.

The growing incursion of wild boars into farmlands and homesteads has severely impacted small-scale agriculture across many villages in the state. While the Wildlife Protection Act permits culling under Section 62 if the animal is declared vermin (as wild boars have been in Kerala), the Standard Operating Procedures (SOP) make the process cumbersome and often ineffective. Key challenges in this regard include (Ramakumar, 2025):

- *Procedural Complexities:* Even after vermin declaration, the killing protocols remain overly complicated, hindering timely action.
- *Documentation Burden:* States must submit detailed reports to the MoEFCC, including the extent and nature of agricultural losses, before seeking approval.
- *Exhaustion of Alternatives:* Authorities must prove that all non-lethal mitigation measures (e.g., fencing, deterrents) have failed, supported by evidence.
- *Restrictive Permissions:* Culling approvals are granted only for specific areas and limited periods, reducing operational flexibility.
- *Bureaucratic Delays:* The MoEFCC issues a formal notification only after reviewing the state's request, further prolonging the process.
- *Centralized Authority:* As per the 1991 amendment, only the Chief Wildlife Warden can authorize killings, adding another layer of oversight.

The Kerala lesson, especially with wild boars shows that these constraints often render the vermin declaration provision theoretical rather than practical, leaving farmers vulnerable to escalating crop raids. The policy makers in the State are of the opinion that the current legal framework under the Wildlife Protection Act has proven inadequate in addressing the rising human and economic toll of HWC (Ramakumar, 2025). State governments, including Kerala, have repeatedly highlighted this limitation to the MoEFCC. A key solution suggested by policy makers would be to decentralize authority by empowering state governments to declare problematic wildlife as vermin—even temporarily—to enable swift action during crises. This would help mitigate both immediate threats and public unrest.

In states like Kerala, where elephant attacks pose a recurring danger to forest-adjacent communities, the Act's failure to classify such species as vermin exacerbates the problem. Without streamlined procedures, HWC-related losses will continue escalating. Urgent intervention are requested by the concerned to revise the Act, simplifying its conditions and making it more responsive to ground realities (Ramakumar, 2025).

HWC, especially with elephants, is a complex problem. Habitat loss, poaching, and increasing elephant numbers in protected areas are pushing them into nearby farms to eat crops because traditional defenses are weakening. Human activities like farming, settlements, and building roads disrupt elephant movement and worsen this conflict (Sukumar, 2003). Changes in the environment, such as more secondary vegetation and artificial water sources, also draw wildlife closer to people.

This conflict has serious consequences for communities, including damage to crops, injuries or deaths, limited movement, reduced access to education and jobs, and psychological stress (WWF, 2023). These problems can create negative feelings towards wildlife, which hurts conservation efforts. To effectively manage wildlife damage, we need to focus on minimizing the most harmful impacts to improve people's lives and gain support for conservation.

In Kerala, HWC has become a major concern recently, with more animals entering human areas and causing damage to crops, property, and even leading to loss of life. The main reasons for this conflict in Kerala can be summarised as follows (Ramakumar, 2025):

i. *Habitat loss and fragmentation:* Forests are being cleared for farming, infrastructure, and settlements, shrinking wildlife habitats.

ii. *Agricultural encroachment*: Plantations near forests attract wildlife. Wild boars and elephants are responsible for most of the reported crop damages. Research indicates that elephants and other wild animals are drawn to cultivated crops due to their higher protein, calcium, sodium, and energy content compared to natural forest vegetation. This nutritional advantage drives them into farmlands, worsening conflicts.

iii. *Climate change and resource scarcity*: Changes in rainfall and droughts are forcing animals to look for food in human settlements. Recent shifts in climate and unpredictable rainfall have disrupted forest ecosystems, pushing wildlife closer to human settlements. Unlike neighboring states, Kerala's highlands—part of the Western Ghats—receive heavy rainfall, even during summer (January-May). This attracts animals from adjacent regions, intensifying HWC incidents.

iv. *Genetic and hormonal changes:* Genetic and hormonal changes, influenced by climate variations, are making male animals more aggressive. Increased territorial fights force some to migrate to forest fringes and human-inhabited areas, further fueling HWC.

In general, the main reason for HWC in Kerala is the destruction of habitats due to rapid urbanization and the expansion of agriculture. As forests are cleared for development, plantations, and housing, wildlife loses its natural home, forcing animals like elephants, wild boars, and tigers to venture into human areas to find food and shelter (SPB, 2022). The splitting of forests into smaller, isolated areas makes the problem worse by disrupting animal migration routes, leaving them no choice but to encroach villages and farmlands.

Another major factor is the changing way land is used. Converting natural forests into single-crop plantations like rubber, teak, and eucalyptus reduces the variety of plants and limits the food available for plant-eating animals. As a result, animals like elephants and deer are forced to raid crops, leading to conflicts with farmers (Onmanorama, 2024). Additionally, the decline in the number of prey animals due to hunting and habitat loss pushes predators like leopards and tigers to attack livestock, increasing tensions between people and wildlife.

Unpredictable rainfall, long periods of drought, and rising temperatures affect the availability of water and plants in forests, pushing animals towards human settlements in search of resources. For example, during dry seasons, elephants often enter villages to find water in wells and ponds, causing damage to property and sometimes harming people (SPB, 2022). Similarly, the lack of natural water sources force other wildlife to rely on agricultural fields, increasing the chances of conflict.

Poor waste management in rural and urban areas also attracts wild animals, especially monkeys and wild boars, into human habitats. Open garbage dumps and easily accessible food waste provide a readily available food source, making wildlife used to human presence and less afraid of people (Armstrong, 1991). This leads to frequent encounters, which can become aggressive, especially if the animals feel threatened. Furthermore, lack of proper fences and other protective measures around farms and residential areas makes it easier for wild animals to enter and cause damage.

Ineffective wildlife management policies and slow compensation processes also worsen the conflict. While the government has programs to compensate farmers for damage to crops or loss of livestock, the process is often slow and doesn't provide enough support, leaving affected communities feeling frustrated (KAD, 2023). Without better strategies to reduce conflict, such as early warning systems, animal-friendly barriers, and community-based conservation programs, the problem will continue to grow. Addressing the root causes through careful land-use planning, restoring habitats, and finding better ways for humans and wildlife to coexist is essential to reducing HWC in Kerala.

10.3 Impacts and Mitigation

As natural habitats diminish and deteriorate, wild animals such as elephants, wild boars, leopards, and monkeys are forced to venture closer to human settlements in search of food and shelter. These interactions often result in crop damage, livestock losses, property destruction, and, in severe cases, injuries or fatalities for both humans and animals, with the intensity of HWC in various regions as illustrated in Figure-10.3. Kerala's farm sector faces significant damage from wildlife, with around 45 crop varieties affected, including paddy, coconut, rubber, coffee, spices like ginger and cardamom, and fruits such as mango, jackfruit, and pineapple (Ramakumar, 2025).

In Kerala, elephants are the species most frequently involved in these conflicts, especially in districts like Wayanad, Palakkad, and Idukki. The raiding of crops by elephants leads to substantial economic losses for farmers and fosters fear and resentment within local communities. Likewise, wild boars pose a significant threat to agriculture, wreaking havoc on fields and resulting in repeated confrontations with farmers. These conflicts contribute to social unrest, heighten tensions between forest department and local residents, and can lead to retaliatory killings of animals, further disturbing the ecological balance. The impact of HWC can be summarized as follows:

i. *Economic Losses*: Annual crop losses are estimated at ₹200–300 crores (Kerala Agriculture Department, 2023). Compensation claims increased by 40% from 2020 to 2023 (KFD, 2023). The economic impact of HWC is considerable, with the Kerala government distributing ₹27.21 crore in compensation for fatalities and ₹24.07 crore for injuries between 2016 and 2024. Additionally, ₹8.77 crore was allocated for livestock losses, and ₹38.23 crore for crop damage.

ii. *Human Casualties:* In 2022, there were 45 reported human deaths due to elephant attacks (KFD, 2023). Incidents of leopard attacks in Wayanad and Idukki districts rose by 25% in 2023.

iii. *Wildlife Mortality*: In 2021-22 alone, 4 elephants, 20 deer, and one leopard got killed because of electrocution, poisoning, and in road accidents (KFD, 2023).

The effects of HWC go far beyond immediate physical harm and economic losses. It weakens conservation initiatives by diminishing public support, especially among communities living in conflict-affected areas. These communities often come to view wildlife as threats rather than essential parts of the ecosystem, making it harder to implement cooperative conservation efforts and policies for sustainable coexistence.

To effectively address HWC in Kerala, a comprehensive strategy is needed—one that includes restoring habitats, establishing buffer zones, offering fair and timely compensation, and involving local communities. Technological tools such as early warning systems, fencing, and surveillance can significantly reduce conflict incidents. Most critically, promoting coexistence through education and awareness initiatives can help reconcile human needs with wildlife protection. Without such an integrated approach, HWC may worsen, threatening both biodiversity and the livelihoods of local populations.

One major consequence of HWC has been a shift in land ownership along forest fringes. Many farmers, unable to cope with repeated crop losses, have sold their land to real estate developers who convert it to informal eco-tourism sites, often replacing productive farms with luxury resorts (Munster & Munster, 2012b). Farmers who remain tend to adapt through a 'resigned coexistence' with wildlife, modifying their farming practices and crop choices based on animal behavior (Sukumar, 2003). Additionally, climate change has further intensified conflicts and casualties in recent years.

Figure: 10.3 Intensity of HWC in Kerala, 2022

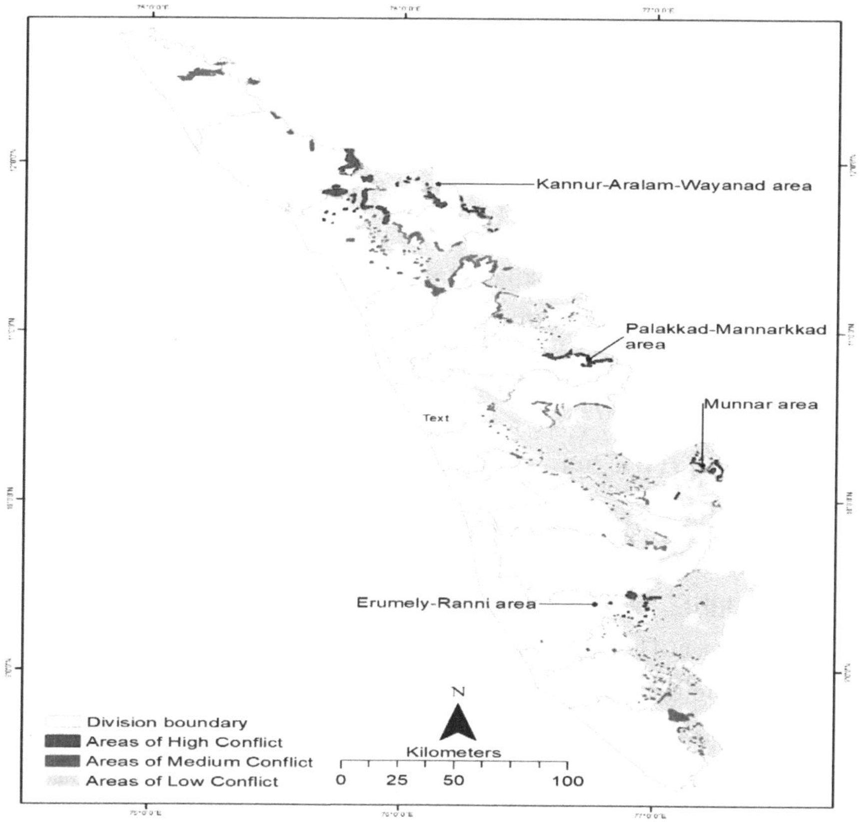

Source: SPB, 2022

The Kerala Forests and Wildlife Department addresses HWC through physical barriers to keep animals away from farmlands and settlements. These measures include 511.22 km of elephant-proof trenches, 2,348.14 km of solar-powered fences, and over 2,500 km of additional fencing (KFD, 2023). It was reported that Kerala struggles with the financial burden of installing permanent barriers against wildlife and needs Central government support (Ramakumar, 2025). For example, constructing stone walls costs around ₹1.5 crore per kilometer, while solar fencing requires ₹1.3 lakh per kilometer—making effective HWC management economically challenging. The department has also initiated voluntary relocation programs for communities near wildlife corridors, with some areas already vacated—supported in part by NGOs that help secure land in critical zones.

To manage problematic animals, the department employs innovative capture-and-translocation techniques for elephants and tigers, along with deploying Rapid Response Teams (RRTs) for emergencies. A KIIFB-funded fencing project is underway, with Phase I covering 101.50 km of solar fences and barriers in targeted areas. Phase II will add 136.70 km of solar fences, 48 km of steel rope crash barriers, and 185 km of elephant-proof walls across multiple forest divisions (SPB, 2022).

Additional HWC mitigation strategies include:

i. Landscape-based management (Physical barriers, early warning systems, drones, radio-collaring elephants).
ii. Wildlife corridor development (where human settlements intersect forests).
iii. Strengthening community involvement through Primary Response Teams (PRTs), RRTs, and relocation initiatives.

Currently, 15 RRTs (8 permanent, 7 temporary) operate in high-conflict zones, with 25 more planned. The department collaborates with 427 Vana Samrakshana Samithis (VSS) and 213 Eco-Development Committees (EDC), ensuring local participation in managing HWC hotspots (KFD, 2023).

To tackle the increasing HWC, the Kerala government has implemented several strategies as part of the recommendations of the 14th Five Year Plan Working Group recommendations (SPB, 2022):

i. *Traditional Methods*: Communities in Kerala have long used various methods to try and keep wild animals away from their crops. These include labor-intensive practices like guarding from raised platforms and making noise. Fences made of sarees or bamboo are somewhat effective against wild boars but become less so as plants grow on them. Using fire and sounds of predators to scare animals has had inconsistent results because animals often get used to them. Despite these challenges, some communities have developed creative solutions like rooftop shelters and trenches, showing their resilience in dealing with this ongoing issue.

ii. *Technological Interventions:* The government has also embraced technology to find solutions and launched 'Safe Habitat Hack,' a hackathon aimed at developing innovative tools for reducing HWC, such as real-time monitoring systems. Artificial intelligence-based tracking of wildlife movements, like the Project Elephant initiative, has helped in lessening conflict. Solar-powered fences are also being used to deter elephants (KFD, 2023).

iii. *Community Engagement:* Recognizing the importance of involving local people, the government has organized training programs in collaboration with different departments. These programs educate communities on how to prevent conflict and provide first aid, especially for snakebites. Participatory Forest Management, which involves tribal communities, has been very successful in Kerala. Early warning systems that send SMS alerts about elephant movements have also proven effective.

Box: 10.1 HWC in Wayanad

The HWC in Wayanad stem from a complex history shaped by agricultural expansion, forest conservation policies, and socio-political struggles. These conflicts intersect with tourism, tribal rights, government conservation efforts, and environmental activism. Wayanad's forests have long been a contested space—exploited for timber, elephants, and minerals. Post-independence, food shortages and agrarian demands led to large-scale forest encroachment, particularly by settler farmers from central Kerala. The mid-20th century saw aggressive land conversion for commercial agriculture, often supported by the revenue department, while private forests remained under landlords and temples (Armstrong, 1991). Between the 1940s and 1970s, settlers responded to harsh conditions—malaria, wildlife threats, and an unfamiliar environment—with deforestation, hunting, and fires. By the 1980s, Wayanad was a hotspot for illegal activities like sandalwood smuggling and elephant poaching. Despite this, elephants had sufficient space to migrate without frequent human encounters.

The establishment of the Wayanad Wildlife Sanctuary (1973) and national forest policies restricted human access to core forest areas. However, monoculture plantations degraded wildlife habitats, forcing animals to venture into human settlements for food. The first recorded human death due to wildlife conflict occurred in 1982. In the 1990s, Wayanad was included in Project Elephant, leading to stricter measures like fencing and trenches. While these efforts aimed to reduce conflicts, they failed to prevent escalating casualties and crop losses (paddy, banana, tapioca, etc.). This sparked tensions between farmers and the forest department, with disputes over fence maintenance and delayed compensation. Frustrated farmers resorted to violent retaliation—poisoning elephants, electrocution, and arson—giving rise to anti-wildlife activism. Today, Wayanad's landscape remains a battleground between conservation and agrarian survival, reflecting deeper tensions over land use and ecological justice.

Source: Munster & Vishnudas, 2011

Furthermore, the government has identified and mapped areas where conflicts leading to human or animal deaths, injuries, and property damage frequently occur. Joint patrols involving local community members are conducted in these 'hotspots' at the local forest range and station levels. A state-level record of these hotspots is maintained on a secure, online mapping system overseen by the chief wildlife warden, with access for all local wildlife wardens.

To enhance early warning capabilities, the government is currently using alert systems in several forest divisions known for high elephant conflict, including Punalur, Konni, Marayoor, Palakkad, Thiruvananthapuram, Munnar, and Wayanad. These systems have been effective, and the Department plans to establish 42 more units across the state (KFD, 2023). Recognizing the crucial role of local governing bodies, 246 Joint Forest Management Committees (JFMC) have been formed at the Panchayat level, comprising elected officials, farmers' representatives, and forest officers. Initiatives to create ward-level committees are also underway (SPB, 2022). These local committees are valuable because they allow for detailed discussion of conflict issues and the development of solutions, while also securing public support in addressing the challenges.

10.4 Conclusion

HWC in Kerala is a complex issue that necessitates a comprehensive approach integrating infrastructure development, technological advancements, community engagement, and policy reforms. Achieving sustainable coexistence requires coordinated efforts to tackle the underlying causes of the conflict. Addressing HWC in Kerala demands a collaborative strategy involving government agencies, local communities, and conservationists. Enhancing forest corridors, refining compensation systems, and utilizing technology can help alleviate conflicts while promoting wildlife conservation. However, challenges remain due to habitat fragmentation, insufficient compensation frameworks, and limited involvement from the community. The following recommendations can help address these issues:

i. *Habitat Restoration*: Habitat destruction, primarily caused by human activities, is a significant factor contributing to HWC. It is essential to encourage viable conservation initiatives and ensure that local communities benefit from conservation efforts. Reforestation and the protection of wildlife corridors can help minimize animal encroachment into human areas.

ii. *Enhanced Surveillance*: Implementing advanced monitoring systems will allow for early detection of wildlife movements. Continuous monitoring of crops and livestock is also necessary.

iii. *Policy Reforms*: Existing wildlife protection laws should be reviewed and amended to strike a balance between conservation and human safety. Eco-restoration efforts should aim to reconnect fragmented habitats.

iv. *Forest Fringes*: Land subdivision and fencing in villages near forests should be discouraged, as these practices hinder wildlife movement through established corridors.

v. *Separating Human Settlements*: Government policies should focus on zoning regulations to create clear separations between human settlements, wildlife habitats, and livestock grazing areas.

vi. *Livestock Protection*: Constructing predator-proof enclosures can help safeguard livestock. Given that most livestock losses occur during droughts, farmers should be advised to reduce their herd sizes to maintain population stability over the long term.

vii. *Disbursement of Compensation*: Timely and fair compensation should be provided to victims and their families to foster positive relationships with wildlife. Compensation schemes should be revised for quicker payouts.

viii. *Summer Crops*: Planting early-maturing crops can help reduce wildlife raids during the summer months, as well as cultivating crops that are less appealing to wildlife.

References

1. Armstrong, Allen (1991), 'Resource frontiers and regional development: the role of refugee settlement in Tanzania,' *Habitat International*, Vol. 15, No. 1-2, pp. 69-85.
2. Forest Survey of India (FSI). (2023). *India State of Forest Report*.
3. Kerala Agriculture Department. (2023). *Crop Damage and Compensation Data*.
4. Kerala Forest Department. (2023). *Annual Report on HWC*.
5. Mahanti, P & S. Kumar (2018), 'HWC: A Case Study in Kerala, India,' *Journal of Biodiversity and Conservation*, Vol. 1, No. 2, pp. 42-52.
6. Munster, Daniel, and Ursula Munster (2012), "Human-Animal Conflicts in Kerala: Elephants and Ecological Modernity on the Agrarian Frontier in South India." In: "Fields and Forests: Ethnographic perspectives on Environmental Globalization," edited by Daniel Munster, Ursula Munster, and Stefan Dorondel, *RCC Perspectives*, No. 5, pp. 41–49

7. The New Indian Express. (2024, October 15). *Kerala forest dept reveals 2,771 man-wild conflict cases in last six months.* https://www.newindianexpress.com/states/kerala/2024/Oct/15/kerala-forest-dept-reveals-2771-man-wild-conflict-cases-in-last-six-months-months
8. Onmanorama. (2024, October 10). *915 people lost lives in man-animal conflict in 9 years in Kerala, 7917 injured.* https://www.onmanorama.com/news/kerala/2024/10/10/kerala-wild-animal-man-conflict-deaths-injuries.html
9. The New Indian Express. (2024, November 21). *Government identifies 273 local bodies as critical zones of HWC in Kerala.* https://www.newindianexpress.com/states/kerala/2024/Nov/21/government-identifies-273-local-bodies-as-critical-zones-of-human-wildlife-conflict-in-kerala
10. The Indian Express. (2025, February 14). *HWC claimed 460 lives in Kerala in past 5 years, govt tells Rajya Sabha.* https://indianexpress.com/article/india/human-wildlife-conflict-claimed-460-lives-govt-rajya-sabha-9834609/
11. Mathrubhumi. (2024, December 18). *940 people died in wildlife attacks in Kerala over 8 years.* https://www.mathrubhumi.com/news/kerala/human-wildlife-conflict-940-deaths-in-8-years-1.10175496
12. Ramakumar R. (2025). Human Wildlife Conflicts: Scientific Perspectives and Central Government Stand. *Chintha.* June 13.
13. SPB. (2022). *Working Group Report on HWI in Kerala*, 14th Five Year Plan.
14. SPB (2024). *Economic Review 2023.* Government of Kerala.

15. Sukumar, R (2003), *The living elephants: evolutionary ecology, behaviour and conservation*, Oxford university press, New York.
16. WWF-India. (2023). *Mitigating Human-Elephant Conflict in Kerala.*

CHAPTER: 11
CONCLUSION AND RECOMMENDATIONS

HWC is a worldwide problem that arises when wild animals' needs and behaviors clash with human populations, leading to negative interactions. As people spread out and natural habitats shrink due to deforestation, urbanization, and farming, animals are increasingly forced into human-dominated areas to find food, water, and shelter. This closeness often causes conflict, showing up as destroyed crops, animals killed for food, damaged property, and sometimes people getting hurt or killed. On the other hand, wildlife also suffers, facing revenge attacks, broken-up habitats, and often declining numbers because of human aggression.

Around the world, the specifics and intensity of HWC differ depending on the region and the animals involved. In Africa, elephants and lions often clash with rural communities, with elephants raiding farms and lions attacking livestock (Patterson, et al. 2004). In Asia, especially in countries like India, Sri Lanka, and Nepal, conflicts with elephants, leopards, and tigers are common near the edges of forests (Sukumar, 2003). In North America, bears and wolves sometimes threaten farm animals and wander into cities, especially as human development pushes further into wild areas (Conover, 1997). In Australia, kangaroos and wild dogs can cause problems for farmers, while in South America, jaguars are often targeted for killing livestock (Bautista, 2019). These conflicts not only lead to financial losses but also cause emotional distress, create fear and anger, and reduce public support for protecting wildlife.

The global effects of HWC are significant, as they directly impact the conservation of different species, local economies, food availability, and human safety. They also highlight deeper environmental problems like habitat loss, climate change, and unsustainable land use. The increase in conflicts strongly indicates a growing imbalance between human development and natural ecosystems. Efforts to lessen HWC worldwide include conservation work involving local communities, restoring habitats, using deterrents and barriers, and providing compensation to affected communities (MET/NACSO, 2019). Furthermore, promoting coexistence through education, scientific research, and policy changes is essential for creating long-term, sustainable solutions.

Ultimately, HWC is not just a conservation issue but a social and environmental problem that requires global cooperation and local solutions. It demands finding a balance between protecting wildlife and safeguarding human interests, ensuring that both can thrive in a shared environment (Western, 2009). Without such a balance, the continuation of these conflicts threatens not only the survival of species but also the stability and well-being of communities around the world.

In India, HWC has become a major environmental and socio-economic challenge, affecting both the protection of biodiversity and people's livelihoods. As human populations grow and natural habitats decrease, encounters between people and wild animals have become more frequent, leading to damaged crops, killed livestock, destroyed property, and even human deaths. India, with its rich variety of life and dense human populations, faces unique difficulties in balancing conservation efforts with the needs of local communities. The conflict is particularly serious in states like Kerala, Karnataka, West Bengal, and Uttarakhand, where forests border farmland and villages (MoEFCC, 2023).

A major contributor to HWC is the loss and fragmentation of habitats. Urban expansion, deforestation, and agricultural development have invaded wildlife territories, compelling animals such as elephants, leopards, and tigers to enter human-populated areas in search of food and shelter. Large infrastructure projects, including highways and railways that cut through forests, further disrupt animal movements, heightening the chances of conflicts. For example, elephants, which need extensive ranges, often raid crops when their traditional migration paths are obstructed by human settlements (WWF, 2023). Likewise, diminishing forest cover leads to a decline in prey for predators, driving them to attack livestock, which in turn triggers retaliation from farmers.

Another critical factor is the changing patterns of land use and agricultural methods. Monoculture plantations, such as those for tea, coffee, and rubber, replace natural forests, leading to a loss of biodiversity and altered ecosystems (UNEP, 2023). These transformations impact the availability of food and water for wildlife, forcing animals to venture into nearby villages in search of resources. Furthermore, inadequate waste management in both rural and urban settings attracts scavengers like monkeys, wild boars, and even leopards, resulting in frequent encounters. In regions like Himachal Pradesh and Maharashtra, monkeys pose significant problems in urban areas by raiding homes and markets for food, raising public safety concerns (Goayal, et al. 2000).

Climate change has also intensified HWC by modifying natural habitats and resource availability. Irregular rainfall patterns, prolonged droughts, and rising temperatures drive animals to migrate outside their usual territories in search of water and food. For instance, during dry spells, elephants often wander into villages to access wells and ponds, causing property damage and human fatalities (GoI, 2008). Similarly, dwindling water sources in forests push herbivores into agricultural lands, followed closely by predators, escalating tensions between humans and wildlife.

The economic and psychological repercussions of these conflicts are profound, particularly for rural populations. Farmers experience substantial crop losses due to raids by elephants, wild boars, and deer, leading to financial strain. Livestock losses from leopards, wolves, and tigers exacerbate the situation, plunging struggling families into deeper poverty. In retaliation, some communities resort to lethal measures such as poisoning, electrocution, or hunting, which endangers vulnerable species and undermines conservation efforts (Athreya, 2013). The constant fear of animal attacks also inflicts psychological distress on affected populations.

Despite government efforts, including compensation schemes, wildlife corridors, and awareness initiatives, the effectiveness of these strategies is often limited. Compensation processes can be slow, bureaucratic, and inadequate, leaving victims dissatisfied. While relocating problematic animals is occasionally attempted, it is not a sustainable solution, as it simply shifts the issue to different areas (Butler, 2000). A more comprehensive approach, involving community engagement, improved land-use planning, habitat restoration, and innovative mitigation strategies like early warning systems and eco-friendly barriers, is crucial for achieving long-term solutions.

Resolving HWC in India demands a well-rounded strategy that gives importance to both protecting wildlife and ensuring human well-being. Actions like making protected areas stronger, encouraging ways for humans and animals to live together, and providing prompt payment for damages can help lessen conflict. Raising public awareness and educating people about wildlife behavior and how to prevent conflicts are also very important. By encouraging peaceful coexistence between people and wildlife, India can safeguard its diverse natural heritage while also protecting the livelihoods of its people.

Recommendations

Addressing HWC is a multifaceted endeavor, requiring solutions to be developed at various levels. Based on the discussions in previous chapters following recommendations are proposed for important stakeholders, including the international community, national governments, business organizations, non-governmental organizations, research and academic institutions, affected communities, media, and other relevant parties.

International community

For the international community, it is essential to recognize human-wildlife coexistence as a key target within the Convention on Biological Diversity (CBD) process aimed at achieving a harmonious relationship with nature by 2050 (Daneil, 2002). Additionally, integrating human-wildlife coexistence into the Sustainable Development Goals (SDG) framework is crucial for effective wildlife conservation and the pursuit of sustainable development.

Governments

At the national government level, incorporating human-wildlife coexistence into environmental policies and programs is vital, along with ensuring adequate financial support for these initiatives. HWC should be recognized as a global challenge that threatens sustainable development, food security, and conservation efforts within international conventions. Development plans in areas affected by HWC should prioritize coexistence, natural resource management, and biodiversity conservation through integrated spatial planning for long-term benefits. Local and regional governments should adopt a participatory approach involving stakeholders to manage HWC effectively. Furthermore, it is important to establish laws and regulations governing HWC management to ensure fair and local sharing of the benefits associated with living alongside wildlife. Lastly, initiating education and awareness programs focused on HWC management, particularly targeting media and decision-makers, can foster greater tolerance and understanding of wildlife among communities.

Private sector Companies

The commodities sector should prioritize creating and implementing industry-wide innovations aimed at improving the working conditions for all staff, with a particular focus on those who are most susceptible to the negative impacts of HWC. It is crucial to develop and support projects that actively promote coexistence between humans and wildlife, especially in regions where HWC is particularly challenging to manage (FAO, 2023). These initiatives should be designed to be HWC management-friendly and should strongly involve and be supported by local communities. To ensure their effectiveness and adoption, innovations intended to manage HWC should be co-designed with the individuals and communities who will ultimately be using them. This collaborative approach will help ensure the solutions are practical and meet the needs of the end-users. Within the commodities sector, it is necessary to establish management practices that actively maintain natural habitat corridors across production sites. These corridors are essential to allow for the safe movement of wildlife and to help mitigate habitat fragmentation. Efforts should be made to integrate standards that promote human-wildlife coexistence into the certification processes for products originating from agriculture, forestry, fishery, and aquaculture. This will help to incentivize and recognize practices that minimize conflict. Finally, it is important to implement measures that clearly demonstrate the tangible benefits of minimizing HWC throughout various value chains. Highlighting these advantages can encourage wider adoption of conflict-reducing strategies.

International donor agencies

It is important to prioritize human-wildlife coexistence in the development of relevant programs. This includes identifying funding opportunities within development plans and regional projects to effectively implement and integrate HWC management systems. Additionally, creating a pipeline of site-specific projects that take into account local environmental needs for HWC management is essential, especially when anticipating future hotspots for HWC. A strong emphasis should be placed on participatory and community-based approaches, as managing HWC necessitates long-term commitments from all stakeholders involved (Gross, 2019). Furthermore, it is crucial to establish internal safeguards to ensure that no funding is allocated to activities that could negatively impact HWC, such as habitat alteration or infrastructure development.

Civil Society Organizations/Community-Based Organizations/ Nongovernmental Organizations

Governments and relevant stakeholders require organizational and technical support to effectively integrate human-wildlife coexistence principles into their planning and management processes. To achieve both socio-economic and biodiversity goals, it is essential to incorporate coexistence safeguards into existing development and conservation programs (IUCN, 2022). Furthermore, there is a need to standardize HWC information systems, track trends, and coordinate monitoring efforts through established networks. Best management practices should be institutionalized across relevant sectors following the exchange and review of successful approaches. Mainstreaming HWC management strategies into all development and conservation programs is crucial for holistic and sustainable outcomes. To create beneficial synergies in addressing HWC, the promotion of strategic partnerships between development and conservation organizations is vital. Finally, maintaining gender equality and upholding human rights must be integral considerations in all aspects of HWC management.

Affected Communities

To enhance the management of HWC, it is essential to provide information to organizations working in the field, enabling them to gain a clearer understanding of the local HWC dynamics. Engaging in capacity-building initiatives is also crucial for effectively managing HWC and promoting coexistence among communities and wildlife (Letty, 2007). Additionally, implementing standardized HWC management strategies will contribute to more consistent and effective approaches in addressing these conflicts.

Researchers/Research institutions

Encouraging research that spans across and integrates various academic disciplines, including the social sciences, is crucial for a comprehensive understanding of HWC and coexistence. These researches should emphasize the underlying processes, driving factors, and broader impacts of both conflict and coexistence within larger ecological and social contexts (Koning, 2020). Furthermore, it is essential to conduct evidence-based research to rigorously evaluate the success or failure of different coexistence strategies. Ultimately, the goal of this research should be the development of innovative strategies that yield positive outcomes for both communities and wildlife populations.

Public awareness/Educational institutions/Media

It is important to ensure the distribution of accurate information and updates regarding human-wildlife interactions. This includes implementing targeted educational programs that highlight the significance of wildlife and ecosystems, as well as the advantages of coexisting with wildlife. Additionally, there should be a focus on creating tailored education and information systems aimed at safeguarding individuals and their property (MoEFCC, 2017). Furthermore, addressing misconceptions related to wildlife and the management of HWC is essential for fostering better understanding and cooperation.

Stakeholders

HWC should be recognized and addressed as a matter of human rights, acknowledging the profound impacts it can have on the safety, livelihoods, and well-being of individuals and communities affected (Nyhus, 2016). Consequently, the management of HWC should adopt rights-based approaches, ensuring that the rights of all stakeholders, including those living with or near wildlife, are respected, protected, and fulfilled in the development and implementation of mitigation strategies.

References

1. Athreya V, et. al. (2013), 'Big cats in our backyards: Persistence of large carnivores in a human dominated landscape in India', *PLoS ONE*, Vol. 8, No.3, pp. 57-72
2. Bautista C., et al. (2019), 'Large carnivore damage in Europe: Analysis of compensation and prevention programs,' *Biological Conservation*, No. 235, pp. 308-316.
3. Butler, J.R., 2000, 'The economic costs of wildlife predation on livestock in Gokwe communal land, Zimbabwe', *African Journal of Ecology*, Vol. 38, No. 1, pp.23–30.
4. Conover (1997), 'Monetary and intangible valuation of deer in the United States,' *Wildlife Society Bulletin,* Vol. 25, pp. 298–305.
5. Daniel J. Decker, et. al. (2002), *HWC Management: A Practitioners Guide,* Human Dimensions Research Unit, Cornell University, Ithaca, New York.
6. FAO. (2023). *Global Forest Resources Assessment.*
7. Government of India (2008), *The Wild Life (Protection) Act, 1972: (53 of 1972) as amended by the Wild Life (Protection) Amendment Act, 2006 (39 of 2006),* Universal Law Publishing Co., Delhi, India.
8. Goyal, S P, eta. al (2000), 'A Study on Distribution, Relative Abundance and Food Habits of Leopard (Panthera pardus) in Garhwal Himalayas,' *Technical Report*, Wildlife Life Institute of India, Dehradun.
9. Gross E.M (2019), *Tackling routes to coexistence. Human-elephant conflict in sub-Saharan Africa*, GIZ Partnership against Poaching and Illegal Wildlife Trade, Eschborn, Germany.
10. Hazzah, L.N (2006), *Living among Lions: Coexistence or Killing? Community Attitude towards Conservation Initiatives and the Motivations behind Lion Killing in Kenyan Maasailand*, University of Wisconsin-Madison .
11. IUCN. (2022). *HWC Solutions in Asia.*

12. Konig H.J., et. al. (2020), 'Human-wildlife coexistence in a changing world,' *Conservation Biology*, Vol. 34, No. 4, pp. 786-749.
13. Letty J, et. al. (2007), 'Problems Encountered by Individuals in Animal Translocations: Lessons from Field Studies, *Eco science*, Vol. 14, pp. 420 -431.
14. MET/NACSO (2019), 'The State of Community Conservation in Namibia,' *Annual Report 2019*, Windhoek, Namibia.
15. MoEFCC (2017), *India's National Wildlife Action Plan 2017-2031*., Ministry of Environment, Forests and Climate Change, New Delhi, India.
16. MoEFCC. (2023). *Human-Elephant Conflict Report*. New Delhi: Government of India.
17. Ministry of Environment, Forest and Climate Change (MoEFCC), Government of India. (2023). *Elephant Census Report*.
18. Nyhus, P. J. (2016). *HWC: The Basics*.
19. Patterson B D, et. al. (2004), 'Livestock Predation by Lions and Other Carnivores on Ranches Neighbouring Tsavo National Park, Kenya,' *Biological Conservation*, Vol. 119, pp. 507-516.
20. Sukumar, R (2003), *The living elephants: evolutionary ecology, behaviour and conservation*, Oxford university press, New York.
21. UNEP. (2023). *Climate Change and HWC*.
22. Western, et. al. (2009), The Status of Wildlife in Protected Areas Compared to Non-protected Areas of Kenya, PLoS One, Vol. 4, No. 7 https://doi.org/10.1371/journal.pone.0006140.
23. WWF. (2023). *Living with Wildlife: Mitigation Strategies*.

APPENDICES

Appendix – 1 Different discipline dealing HWC and their application

Disciplines	*Key Concepts*	*HWC application*
1. Environmental history	Changes in the interactions between nature, humans and natural world	Places contemporary conflicts in their historical context, and reveals 'tipping points', shifts and events that led to conflict escalation or de-escalation
2. Human-animal geography	Relation of geography of animals to human use of space	Helpful in predicting where conflicts may occur, or where there may be high incidence of human-animal interactions.
3. Ethics	Justification of moral values and nature on decision making	Helping to understand values and norms, and their role in decision-making and conflicts. Also ethical considerations for management practices.
4. Ethnography	Documentation of human behaviours, sociability, cultures and emotional states	Useful for depth analysis of human perspectives, social issues, and cultures that may influence HWC. Can be used to uncover hidden impacts. Valuable in sensitive situations that require a longer-term, less intrusive approach.
5. Psychology	Recognising, understanding and predicting human behavioural or cognitive patterns, attitudes and motivations	Aids in comprehending and predicting behaviour of stakeholders towards wildlife or other stakeholders in a conflict situation, and reactions to management interventions.
6. Anthropology	Study of human behaviour	Can explain people's behaviours towards wildlife or conservation interventions. Lends insight in to

		different cultures, values and norms.
7. Sociology	Scientific study of human and societal relationships	Understand interaction at all levels, individual, institutional, and community.
8. Economics	Understanding economic agents and the consequences of their interactions	Measure cost and benefits to different parties, and mitigation of conflicts using the knowledge. Also use of incentives as management strategies.
9. Criminology	Study of crime, explanations for crime and social reactions to crime	Help to understand people's engagement in illegal activities, underlying socio-political causes, and classification of such crimes.
10. Social-ecological system	Considers relationship between the social and ecological components of a system	Help to integrate social consideration into conservation, and emphasizes the dynamic and unpredictable nature of such systems.
11. Political ecology	Attention to inequalities and structures that influences conflict dynamics. Focus on power dynamics and social justice	Identifies social and political inequalities that shape relations and changes required to transform the situations
12. International relations	Study of politics, economics and law and their relations at the global level	Understanding of trans-boundary conflicts, global political dynamics and the theories of peace building on an international scale.
13. Peace studies	Analysis of roots and structural causes of conflict, for its prevention and resolution	Seeks to understand and address complex, underlying structural factors that produce conflict. Looks for general and global patterns.
14. Power theory	Theory and understanding of power structure and their development or institutionalisation. Changes in power distribution over time	To overcome structural causes of conflicts. Understanding of development power dynamics and their changes. Highly relevant to changes.

15. Geopolitics	Influence of geography, economics, demography on politics, or combination of political and geographic factors	In the present period conflicts are seen through this angle.
16. Human dimension research	Human valuation of natural resources, their management and influence of natural resources management decisions on humans	Focuses on human attitudes towards wildlife and how to improve tolerance.

Source: Luc Hoffmann Institute (2020), The state of knowledge and practice on HWC

Appendix 2 Gravity of HWC and threatened Species

Threatened wild animals	*Gravity of HWC*	*References*
African lion - Panthera leo	Lions are killed in retaliation for damage to livestock – due to misperceptions when other species are, in fact, responsible for the livestock predation – or out of fear.	Woodroffe R., Frank L.G (2005), 'Lethal control of African lions (Panthera leo): local and regional population impacts,' *Animal Conservation*, Vol. 8, No. 1, pp.91-98.
Cheetah - Acinonyx jubatus	Although cheetahs seldom prey on livestock, 48% of cheetah mortality in Namibia has been attributed to retaliatory killing.	Marker L.L., Dickman A.J., Mills M.G.L., Macdonald D.W (2003), 'Aspects of the management of cheetahs, Acinonyx jubatus trapped on Namibian farmlands', *Biological Conservation,* Vol. 114, No. 3, pp. 401-412.
African elephant - Loxodonta africana	African elephants are a far-ranging species and can cause damage in areas where farmland and human habitation have replaced natural habitat. Depending on the jurisdiction, they can be legally killed as problem animals when damage is high, and they are sometimes illegally killed in retaliation.	Nyirenda V.R., Lindsey P.A., Phiri E., Stevenson I., Chomba C., Namukonde N., et al. (2015), 'Trends in Illegal Killing of African Elephants (Loxodonta africana) in the Luangwa and Zambezi Ecosystems of Zambia,' *Environment and Natural Resources Research* Vol. 5, No. 2, pp. 24-36.
Gorilla - Gorilla spp.	Gorillas consume fruits and leafy vegetables cultivated by communities living adjacent to their forest habitats. When they leave protected areas to consume crops, they become the target of retaliation.	Seiler N., Robbins M.M (2015), 'Ranging on Community Land and Crop-Raiding by Bwindi Gorillas,' *Gorilla Journal* No.50, pp. 11-13.

Mauritius fruit bat - Pteropus niger	Fruit bats feed on wild fruits but are also attracted to fruit trees on farms and in orchards, where they are culled due to fear of disease transmission.	IUCN (2018), *IUCN SSC Position Statement on the Culling of the Mauritius Fruit Bat Pteropus Niger*, IUCN Gland, Switzerland).
Asian elephant - Elephas maximus	Asian elephants migrate long distances and can cause crop and property damage and threaten lives, which often results in retaliatory killing. HWC is a significant threat to this species and has caused population declines in the past few decades.	Thirgood S., Woodroffe R., Rabinowitz A (2005), 'The impact of HWC on human lives and livelihoods,' In: *People and Wildlife: Conflict or Coexistence?* 1st edition (eds. R. Woodroffe, S. Thirgood, A. Rabinowitz), pp. 13-26, Conservation Biology, Cambridge University Press, UK.
Tiger - Panthera tigris	Tigers generally avoid encounters with people but can prey on livestock or attack humans. Retaliatory killing by people makes up 50% of tiger mortality.	Miquelle D., Nikolaev I., Goodrich J., Litvinov B., Smirnov E., Suvorov E., et al. (2005), 'Searching for the coexistence recipe: a case study of conflicts between people and tigers in the Russian Far East,' In: *People and Wildlife: Conflict or Coexistence?* 1st edition (eds. R. Woodroffe, S. Thirgood, A. Rabinowitz), pp. 305-22. (Conservation Biology. Cambridge University Press, UK).
Philippine crocodile - Crocodylus mindorensis	Rural fishing communities in the Philippines regard crocodiles as vermin, as they compete for fish and may attack people. Deliberate killing of crocodiles is a major threat to their survival.	Corvera M.D, Manalo R.I., Aquino M.T.R. (2017), 'People and Crocodiles Sharing One Environment: An Analysis of Local Human-Crocodile Conflict Management Strategies in the Philippines,' *Journal of Animal Science and Research*, Vol. 1.
King cobra - Ophiophagus hannah	The king cobra, the longest venomous snake in the world, is indiscriminately killed by people. Deaths from snake bites and misperceptions about	Bharadwaj A.R., Prasad A.D(2019), ' Human-King Cobra Conflict in Western Ghats Region of Sringeri, Karnataka, India,' *Journal of Biodiversity Management & Forestry*, Vol. 8, No. 2.

	snakes make coexistence difficult in most parts of the world.	
Snow leopard - Panthera uncia	Snow leopards increasingly come into conflict with herders due to livestock predation. Of all snow leopard killings worldwide, 55% resulted from HWC.	Nowell K, Li J, Paltsyn M, Sharma RK (2016), *An Ounce of Prevention: Snow Leopard Crime Revisited*, TRAFFIC, Cambridge, UK.
Common leopard - Panthera pardus	Leopards frequently stray close to human habitations, prey on dogs and livestock, and occasionally kill people. In Pakistan, their numbers have significantly declined as a result of retaliation.	Shehzad W., Nawaz M.A., Pompanon F., Coissac E., Riaz T., Shah S.A., et al. (2014), 'Forest without prey: livestock sustain a leopard Panthera pardus population in Pakistan,' *Oryx*, Vol. 49, No. 2, pp. 248-53.
Great white shark - Carcharodon carcharias	There is a significant tension in Australia between the need to conserve and recover depleted shark populations and the issue of human safety, particularly because frequent high-profile shark attacks have occurred in recent years.	Le Busque B., Dorrian J., Litchfield C (2021), 'The impact of news media portrayals of sharks on public perception of risk and support for shark conservation,' *Marine Policy*, Vol. 124.
Jaguar - Panthera onca	Jaguars tend to prey on livestock; 88% of ranchers interviewed in the Brazilian Pantanal believe that jaguars are shot to prevent cattle losses. Local extinctions, like those in El Salvador and Uruguay, are a result of such killings.	Zimmermann A., Walpole M.J., Leader-Williams N. (2005), 'Cattle ranchers' attitudes to conflicts with jaguar Panthera onca in the Pantanal of Brazil,' *Oryx, Vol.* 39, No. 4.
Amazon river dolphin - Inia geoffrensis	Dolphins break artisanal fishing nets and feed on the fish, causing economic losses for fishers. In the Amazon, fishers kill	Campbell E., Mangel J.C., Alfaro-Shigueto J., Mena J.L., Thurstan R.H., Godley B.J. (2020), 'Coexisting in the Peruvian Amazon: Interactions between

	river dolphins in retaliation, which places further pressure on the threatened population.	fisheries and river dolphins,' *Journal for Nature Conservation,* Vol. 56.
Polar bear - Ursus maritimus	Polar bears are now more frequently found close to human settlements along the coast due to the loss of sea ice habitat. Conflict leads to the death of people and polar bears.	Wilder J.M., Vongraven D., Atwood T., Hansen B., Jessen A., Kochnev A., et al. (2017), 'Polar bear attacks on humans: Implications of a changing climate,' *Wildlife Society Bulletin,* Vol. 41, No. 3, pp. 537-547.
Grey wolf - Canis lupus	In several European countries, the wolf had been eradicated due to HWC. Wolf populations are now making a comeback, but because of deep-rooted intolerance, they are still illegally killed.	Liberg O., Chapron G., Wabakken P., Pedersen H.C., Hobbs N.T., Sand H (2012), 'Shoot, shovel and shut up: cryptic poaching slows restoration of a large carnivore in Europe,' *Proceedings of the Royal Society*, Vol. 279, pp. 910-915.
European hornet - Vespa crabro	Population dynamics and conservation status of insect species are poorly monitored. The hornet in Germany is an exception; it has been placed under strict protection to avoid its extinction due to nest destruction by people who are afraid of hornets.	Hoffmann W.R.E., Neumann P., Schmolz E (2000), 'Technique for rearing the European hornet (Vespa crabro) through an entire colony life cycle in captivity,' *Insectes sociaux*, Vol. 47, No. 4, pp351-353.
Mediterranean monk seal - Monachus monachus	The Mediterranean monk seal, the only seal species in the region, is under threat; 20% of the species' mortality is attributed to deliberate killing by fishers who see them as competitors.	Karamanlidis A., Adamantopoulou S., Kallianiotis A.A., Tounta E., Dendrinos P (2020), 'An interview-based approach assessing interactions between seals and small-scale fisheries informs the conservation strategy of the endangered Mediterranean monk seal,' *Aquatic Conservation: Marine and Freshwater Ecosystems,* Vol. 30, no. 5, pp. 928-936.

Bearded vulture - Gypaetus barbatus	These vultures only consume the bones of carcasses but have been hunted to extinction in the Alpine region due to the misperception that they prey on lambs and small children.	Robin K. (2001), 'Die Wiederansiedlung des Bartgeiers in den Alpen: ein Positivbeispiel,' *Forest Snow and Landscape Research,* Vol. 76, No. 1-2, pp.41-52.

Source: Gross E, et. al, 2021, A Future for All: The Need for Human-Wildlife Coexistence, WWF, Gland, Switzerland.

Appendix – 3 Main Approaches to HWC Management

Category	*Sub-category*	*Approaches*	*Strength*	*Weakness*	*Evidences*
Technical	Lethal control	Regulated harvest/cull of conflict species. Selective or targeted killing of problem individuals	Considered cheap and cost effective. Linked to reduced human–wildlife impacts (e.g. predation) and increased tolerance. Can bring additional revenue to communities, e.g. trophy hunting	Could be considered unethical; limited social acceptability. Unwanted ecological impacts. Evidence of link to tolerance inconclusive	Hunting of cougars in North America and brown bear in Sweden
	Non-lethal control	Translocation of problem individuals. Reproductive control	Can reduce predation and attack rates. More ethical and socially acceptable method of control	Resource heavy. Translocation rarely successful; animal dies, is replaced, or returns to site of capture. Effectiveness is species dependent	Translocation of problem elephants in Africa. Brood management of hen harriers in UK
	Deterrents	Olfactory (chilli, surfactants), visual (lighting, fladry), biological (bees), auditory (acoustic deterrent devices) animal repellents	Shown to reduce incidences of crop raiding and predation. Often cheap and culturally appropriate method	Effective in areas with infrastructure, e.g. sufficient electricity. Seen as a panacea. Animals can become habituated	Elephants and Bees project, Save The Elephants
	Physical barriers	Fencing and reinforced biomass	Sometimes successful at reducing	Fail in long term. Responsibility	Implemented in Amboseli region (east

			predation, crop raiding or property damage	of maintenance falls to local communities	Africa) by Born Free Foundation and African Wildlife Society
	Livestock husbandry	Guard animals, alternative practices	Guards effectively deter solitary species. Changes to practice limit human–wildlife interaction and thus reduce impacts. Financially feasible	Financial limitations of training and feeding guards. Changes to practice may not be possible or culturally acceptable	Anatolian guard dog scheme by Cheetah Conservation Fund (CCF) in Namibia
Technical	Land use planning	Spatial separation of humans and wildlife. Zonation, corridors, habitat modification	Allows people to co-occur with wildlife at high densities (in theory). Wildlife undisturbed; allows for normal behaviours	Limited empirical evidence. Relies on extensive data of species movements and home ranges. May require political support (planning permission)	Niche partitioning in Kenya
	Predictive measures	Behavioural and spatial analyses of human–wildlife interactions	Techniques used to detect presence and movements of wildlife and prevent negative incidents. Some evidence to show decline in attack rates and predation	Require expensive technologies and thus technical knowledge. Some methods (e.g. surveillance) rely on human compliance	Shark Spotters programme in False Bay, South Africa
Cognitive	Education schemes	Providing information and	Improve tolerance and	Not well represented by	Bear Aware programme in

		training to local communities on animal movements, behaviours and conflict prevention	attitudes through enhanced knowledge and capacity to deal the impacts. Provides additional benefits to communities through training	reviews; effectiveness largely unknown. Can encounter problems of legitimacy	Aspen, Cheetah Conservation Fund field research and education centre in Namibia
	Social marketing or awareness campaigns	Encourage collective action and pro-conservation behaviours through communication	Can encourage pro-environmental behaviours. Evoke positive emotions towards species	Few evaluations of effectiveness. Only effective in societies with the infrastructure to deliver campaigns (e.g. television and social media).	Heads up for Harriers! campaign, UK
Structural	Economic or livelihood	Compensation, wildlife utilisation	Helps to reduce costs incurred by wildlife. Provides incentive to engage in conservation. Additional benefits to communities	Subject to issues associated with poor governance structures, e.g. corruption, insufficient rates, unequal distribution of benefits	Predator conservation fund, Amboseli
	Legal mechanisms	Binding (international, national, regional law). Non-binding (guidelines, codes of conduct)	Multiple and varied. Can be necessary when species are endangered	Effectiveness difficult to ascertain; attitude change influenced by many other factors. Often multiple laws in place that contradict one another	Code of Conduct among fishermen in Purse Seine. EU Habitats Directive (1992) and Natura 2000.

	Socio-political dimensions	Participatory processes, community based conservation	Can build dialogue and trust. Improve tolerance towards wildlife, while providing benefits to local communities	Subject to politics of participation. Problems of corruption and poor governance	Partnership Against Wildlife crime Scotland. Wildlife Management Areas in Tanzania

Source: Luc Hoffmann Institute (2020), The state of knowledge and practice on HWC

Appendix: 4 Direct and Indirect Interventions to Mitigate HWC & Design Criteria for Feasibility

Type of Intervention	*Methods*	*Feasibility Criteria*		
		Cost Effectiveness	*Wildlife Specificity*	*Socio-political Acceptability*
I. Direct interventions				
1. Barriers	1. Buffer Zones 2. Fences 3. Nets 4. Trenches 5. Walls	Consider placement, size, permeability, and materials/labour/maintenance costs; can include escape paths, alarms, and deterrents (e.g. electricity, thorns, and non-palatable crops)	With time intelligent, motivated animals may penetrate, consider impact on migration/dispersal movements	Generally familiar and popular among those who feel threatened; consider impact on local people's access to resources; metals fence wires have been used as snares; livestock may injure themselves on barriers; 3 wide

				barriers (e.g buffers) must be profitable if land is scarce.
2. Guards	1. Supervision by Dogs 2. Supervision by Humans 3. Supervision by other animals	Consider timing relative to wildlife activities; guards may be exposed to disease, attack, or weather; consider behaviour of guards: feeding, health, ranging, social system, vigilance, and vocal	Consider risk of disease transmission between guard and wildlife; consider whether guard competes with or preys on wildlife; human guards may fail to deter habituated wildlife; hence, more effective in areas with hunting.	Generally familiar, but acceptance of loud sounds, lights at night, noxious orders, toxic chemicals, and attraction of predators vary.
3. Repellents	1. Acoustic i. Sirens ii. Explosions iii. Predator sounds 2. Chemical i. Odour/Taste repellents ii. Conditional Taste aversion 3. Visual i. Colours ii. Lights iii. Predator mimicry	From most to least effective: behaviour contingent, motion-activated, unpredictably mobile, or stationary; chemical, consider persistence in various climates; determine whether predatory response is inhibited or simply feeding	Consider chemical toxicity; consider circadian behaviour, intelligence, and the visual and acoustic acuity of target, non-target wildlife, people and domestic animals.	Generally familiar, but acceptance of loud sounds, lights at night, noxious odours, toxic chemicals, and attraction of predatory vary.
4. Manipulate problematic animals	1. Culling 2. Eradication	Selective removal of culprits difficult; goals of hunters (e.g. food and sport) may not match	Risky for endangered species; generally	Generally familiar, but certain methods

	3. Hunting 4. Relocate to captivity 5. Selective removal 6. Sterilization	those of complainants (e.g. safety and income) or managers (e.g. conservation and revenue); complex methods of capture and animal handling demand professional supervision and are costly; public collaboration (e.g. hunting) demands professional communications, monitoring, and enforcement.	possible to target problematic species, but varies by method (shooting vs. traps, explosive or poison); selection of individual culprits is difficult; if released, consider disease transmission and capture-related injury.	(e.g. poison and traps), certain sites (private lands and densely settled areas), and certain targets (social, intelligent, and charismatic species) provoke opposition by common interest groups.
5. Manipulate problematic animals (Non-lethal/temporary)	1. Capture followed by deterrence (Punish or affix electric shock collar) 2. Release 3. Relocate	Selective removal of culprits difficult; released animals often return or cause problems at new site; complex methods or capture and animal handling demand professional supervision and are costly.	Risky for endangered species. Generally possible to target problematic species, but varies by method; selection of individual culprits is difficult; if released, consider disease transmission and capture-related injury.	Capture of problematic animals familiar, but subsequent handling may not be; generally more acceptable to urban, wealthy populations; affected communities may distrust release.
6. Manipulate habitat or other wildlife	Alter resources required by problematic wildlife	Demands information on behavioural ecology of problematic wildlife or comparisons of affected and unaffected	Suitable for endangered wildlife if habitat is improved (e.g.	Improvement may be unfamiliar; degradation of habitat is

	(food, shelter, breeding sites, etc.) to discourage use of human areas.	properties/people; improvement of habit through remediation and restoration activities may discourage wildlife damage to property or degradation of habitat may diminish wildlife abundance.	restoring wild prey); unpredictable consequence for wider ecosystem.	generally familiar; little data on acceptability; biodiversity interest may oppose degradation.
7. Protect Wildlife or Habitats.	Prevent retaliation against Wildlife habitat destruction via law enforcement, interdiction, or physical barriers to access.	Depends on frequent and sensitive monitoring or surveillance at local sales; clear rules that govern access and te use of natural resources; physical barriers and obvious delimiters; trained staff to communicate, enforce, and prosecute.	Far ranging animals that cross jurisdiction elude protection; if retaliation and habitat destruction are inconspicuous activities, interdiction and enforcement will be difficult.	Generally familiar but opposed when traditions or broader policies allow access to and the use of natural resources; enforcement may generate political clashes and local ill will.
8. Reduce Attractiveness of Property/people	1. Remove attractant (e.g. food and garbage 2. Relocate property or activities, 3. Switch contested resources to less desirable varieties.	Reduce attractiveness of property/people; demands information on behavioural ecology of problematic wildlife and comparisons of affected and unaffected properties/people; change in locations, timing, or attributes or vulnerable property/people.	Suitable for endangered wildlife if the habitat is improved (removing human influences); difficult for damage patterns that are uniform, extremely variable in space or time,	Few people like to change their livelihood practices or living conditions; cost-benefit analyses and opportunity costs are key; high potential

			or difficult to ascribe to target wildlife.	risk for vulnerable people.
II. Indirect Interventions				
1. Co-management (Collaboration in planning, intervention, or monitoring)	Involve interest groups or stakeholders in planning, implementation, or monitoring	Should include households, consensus, social-learning, long-term investment in relationships, fair representation of affected households, technical experts, and legal owners of wildlife	Most effective for wildlife with value (material or non-material); less effective for inconspicuous wildlife or those with little value to any interest group.	Generally familiar, but acceptance depends on whether participants and processes are seen as legitimate, representative, and fair; majority views may dominate and mislead planners.
2. Compensation/ Insurance re-imbursements	Payments for damaged property or injury to people (Cash or equivalent).	Vulnerable to fraud, corruption, inefficiencies, and moral hazards; difficult to phase-out; administration may demand training.	Most effective for rare wildlife or small populations or costs rise; demands generous donor base so most effective for charismatic wildlife.	Generally familiar, but acceptance varies with political clashes between donors, payers, and recipients; acceptance may decline as costs rise; payments do not turn recipients into pro-wildlife advocates; some recipients

				may reject payments in favour of wildlife control.
3. Incentives/ Performance payments	Add value to live wildlife as a commodity or through direct payments for live wildlife	Vulnerable to fraud, corruption, inefficiencies, and moral hazards; difficult to phase-out; administration may demand training. Link to wildlife survival is key; tourism can hav negative impacts on wildlife if not designated with behavioural ecology of wildlife in mind.	Demands a market or donors, so most effective for valued wildlife	Unfamiliar to most except for tourism revenue sharing; some recipients may reject payments in favour of wildlife control; market volatile and complex.
4. Information sharing	Communication of information generated by research via environmental education, consulting, media, training, and wirings.	Salience to target audience, clarity, novelty, and communication medium are the key; broadcast may reach many but persuade few; interpersonal communication may reach few but persuade effectively; goal is often to change behaviour among receivers.	Works for any wildlife, but dissemination/ persuasion for non-charismatic species difficult.	Generally familiar, but acceptance improves with trusted messengers; unfamiliar advocates may engender scepticism; deeply held values and beliefs change slowly.
5. Policy/ Legal reform or devolution of authority	Changing legal relationships to wildlife or habitats (tenure and rights of	Ownership may enhance perceived control over wildlife and their damages; use rights may enhance the perceived value of wildlife and habitats;	Most effective for wildlife with value (material or non-material); less effective for	Generally familiar, but acceptance varies with the rules of uses and

	property, use access, etc.)	policy and legal reforms must be communicated stakeholder effectively and clearly; miss-incentives for overharvesting or misuse common; regulation of use/ access may still be needed; vulnerable to fraud, corruption, inefficiencies, and moral hazards.	inconspicuous wildlife or those with no traditional value to affected households.	ownership; political clashes between past and current owners likely.

Source: Treves, Adrian, et. al. (2009)

BIBLIOGRAPHY

Aber, J., et al. (2001), Forest processes and global environmental change: predicting the effects of individual and multiple stressors. *Bio Science*, Vol. 51, pp. 735–751.

Ale, S (1998), 'Culture and Conservation: the Snow Leopard in Nepal,' *International Snow Leopard Trust Newsletter*, Vol. 16, p.10.

Amy Newsom, Zita Sebesvari, Ine Dorresteijn. (2023). Climate change influences the risk of physically harmful human-wildlife interactions. *Biological Conservation.* Volume 286, October 2023. https://www.sciencedirect.com/science/article/pii/S0006320723003567

Anderies, et. al. (2004), 'A Framework to Analyse the Robustness of Social-ecological Systems from an Institutional Perspective,' *Ecology and Society*, Vol. 19, p. 18.

AP News. (2025). *Zimbabwe is full of elephants and conflict with villagers is growing.* Retrieved from https://apnews.com/article/e0685f64a82be3847730bbad66d4dcfd

Armstrong, Allen (1991), 'Resource frontiers and regional development: the role of refugee settlement in Tanzania,' *Habitat International*, Vol. 15, No. 1-2, pp. 69-85.

Athreya V, et. al. (2010), 'Translocation as Tool of Mitigating Conflict with Leopards in Human-dominated Landscapes of India,' *Conservation Biology*, pp.1-10.

Athreya V, et. al. (2013), 'Big cats in our backyards: Persistence of large carnivores in a human dominated landscape in India', *PLoS ONE*, Vol. 8, No.3, pp. 57-72

Atwood T., et al. (2016), 'Rapid Environmental Change Drives Increased Land Use by an Arctic Marine Predator, *PLoS One*, Vol. 11, No. 6.

Atwood T.C (2017), 'Implications of Rapid Environmental Change for Polar Bear Behavior and Sociality,' in *Marine Mammal Welfare: Human Induced Change in the Marine Environment and its Impacts on Marine Mammal Welfare* (ed. A. Butterworth), Springer International Publishing, pp. 445-462.

Atwood, T. C., et al. (2020). *Nature Climate Change*. Vol. 10. No. 9. Pp. 844-850.

Barua, et. al. (2013), 'THe Hidden Dimensions of HWC: Health Impacts, Opportunity and Transaction Costs,' *Biological Conservation*, Vol. 157, pp. 309-316.

Baruch-Mordo, S., et al. (2021). *Global Ecology and Conservation*. 25, e01413.

Bautista C., et al. (2019), 'Large carnivore damage in Europe: Analysis of compensation and prevention programs,' *Biological Conservation*, No. 235, pp. 308-316.

Bluwstein, J., Moyo, F., Kicheleri, R (2016), 'Austere conservation: Understanding conflicts over resource governance in Tanzanian wildlife management areas,' Conservation and Society, Vol. 14 No. 3, p. 218.

Boitani L., Powell R.A. (2012), *Carnivore Ecology and Conservation: A Handbook of Techniques*, Oxford University Press, New York, USA.

Bourdillon, et. al. (1985), *Studies on the Fishing on Lake Kariba, Zimbabwe*, Mambo Press, Gweru, pp. 3-35.

Brown, J, R, et. al (2009), 'Effectiveness of Short-distance Translocation and its Effects on Western Rattlesnakes,' *Journal of Wildlife Management*, Vol. 73, pp. 419-425.

Bulte, E.H., Rondeau, D (2005), 'Why compensating wildlife damages may be bad for conservation,' *Journal of Wildlife Management*, Vol. 69, pp. 14–19.

Butler, J.R., 2000, 'The economic costs of wildlife predation on livestock in Gokwe communal land, Zimbabwe', *African Journal of Ecology*, Vol. 38, No. 1, pp.23–30.

Caro, T., Riggio, J (2013), 'The Big 5 and conservation,' *Animal Conservation*, Vol. 16, pp. 261–262.

Carpenter et al. (2000), 'Stakeholder acceptance capacity in wildlife management,' *Human Dimensions of Wildlife*, vol. 5, pp. 5–19.

Carter, M (1997), 'Environment, Technology and Social articulation of Risk in West African Agriculture,' *Economic Development and Cultural Change*, Vo.45, pp. 557-590.

Carter, N H & Linnell, J D C (2016), 'Co-adaptation is key to co-existing with large carnivores,' *Trends in Ecology and Evolution*, Vol. 31, No.8, pp. 575-578.

Chartier, et. al (2011), 'Habitat Loss and Human-elephant Conflict in Assam, India: Does a Critical Threshold Exist?,' *Oryx*, Vol. 45, pp.528-533.

Chaturvedi, R. K, et. al. (2011), 'Impact of climate change on Indian forests: a dynamic vegetation modeling approach,' *Mitig Adapt Strateg Glob Change*, Vol. 16, pp.119–142.

Chen, S., Yi, Z-F., Campos-Arceiz, A., Chen, M-Y.,Webb, E.L (2013), 'Developing a spatially-explicit, sustainable and risk-based insurance scheme to mitigate human–wildlife conflict,' *Biological Conservation*, Vol. 168, pp. 31–39.

Chettri, N., et al. (2022). *Biological Conservation*. 265, 109399.

Chiyo, P I, et. al. (2011a), 'Using Molecular and Observational Techniques to Estimate the Number and Raiding Patterns of Crop-raiding Elephants,' *Journal of Applied Ecology*, Vol. 48, pp. 788-796.

Chiyo P.I., et.al. (2011b), 'No risk, no gain: effects of crop raiding and genetic diversity on body size in male elephants,' *Behavioral Ecology*, Vol. 22, No. 3, pp. 552-558.

Chomba C, et. al. (2012), 'Pattern of HWCs in Zambia, Causes, Consequences and Management Responses,' *Journal of Ecology and the Natural Environment*, Vol. 4, No. 12, pp. 303-313.

Cisneros-Montemayor, A., Barnes-Mauthe, M., Al-Abdulrazzak, D., Navarro-Holm, E., Sumaila, U (2013), 'Global economic value of shark ecotourism: Implications for conservation,' *Oryx*, Vol. 47, No. 3, pp. 381–388

Climate Fact Checks. (2025). *Human-Wildlife conflict in Kerala: Over 100 deaths in the past year, experts cite Climate Change as a factor.* Retrieved from https://climatefactchecks.org/human-wildlife-conflict-in-kerala-over-100-deaths-in-the-past-year-experts-cite-climate-change-as-a-factor/

Conover, et al. (1995), 'Review of human injuries, illness, and economic losses caused by Wildlife in the United States,' *Wildlife Society Bulletin*, Vol. 23,m pp.407-414.

Conover (1997), 'Monetary and intangible valuation of deer in the United States,' *Wildlife Society Bulletin,* Vol. 25, pp. 298–305.

Conover, M.R (1998), 'Perceptions of American Agricultural Producers about Wildlife on their Farms and Ranches,' *Wildlife Society Bulletin*, Vol. 26, pp.597-604.

Conover, M.R (2002), *Resolving HWCs: the Science of Wildlife Damage Management,* Lewis Publishers, Boc Raton, Florida, USA.

Cromsigt, Joris P.G.M, et. al. (2013), 'Hunting for fear: Innovating management of HWCs,' *Journal of applied ecology*, No. 50, pp.544-549, British Ecological Society.

Curtin. C.G (2002), 'Integration of Science and Community based Conservation in Mexico, US borderland, *Conservation Biology*, Vo. 16, No.4, pp.880-886.

Daniel J. Decker, et. al. (2002), *HWC Management: A Practitioners Guide,* Human Dimensions Research Unit, Cornell University, Ithaca, New York.

Dave, C., & Jhala, Y. (2023). *Journal of Applied Ecology*. Vol. 60. No. 2. pp. 301-312.

Defenders of Wildlife. (2023). *Range Rider Programs in North America.*

DeMotts, R and P. Hoon (2012), 'Whose Elephants? Conserving, Compensating, and Competing in Northern Botswana,' *Society and Natural Resources*, Vol. 25, No. 9, pp.837-851.

Dickman AJ (2010), 'Complexities of Conflict: the Importance f Considering Social Factors for Effectively Resolving HWC,' *Animal Conservation*, Vol. 13, pp.458-466.

Dickman et al. (2014), 'Carnivores, culture and 'contagious conflict: Multiple factors influence perceived problems with carnivores in Tanzania's Ruaha landscape', *Biological Conservation,* Vol. 178, pp.19-27.

Dickman, A.J., Hazzah, L. (2016). 'Money, myths and man-eaters : Complexities of human–wildlife conflict,' In: Angelici, F.M. (editor), *Problematic wildlife*, Cham: Springer, pp. 339–356.

DNPWC, DFSC (2018), *Status of Tigers and Prey in Nepal*, Department of National Parks and Wildlife Conservation & Department of Forests and Soil Conservation, Ministry of Forests and Environment, Kathmandu, Nepal.

Duncan, C, et. al. (2014), 'Oil in the Sahara: Mapping Anthropogenic Threats to Saharan Biodiversity from Space,' *Philosophical Transactions of the Royal Society* B369:20130191.

Dwitvedi O.P (2001), 'Satyagraha for Conservation: Awakening the Spirit of Hinduism,' in L.P Pojman (Ed.), *Environmental Ethics*, Wadsworth/Thomson Learning, Belmont, pp. 29-50.

Fagerstone , K A (2010), 'Review of Issues Concerning the Use of Reproductive Inhibitors with Particular Emphasis on Resolving HWC in North America,' *Integrative Zoology*, Vol.1, pp.15-30.

Folke, C, et.al. (2010), 'Resilience thinking: Integrating resilience, adaptability and transformability,' *Ecology and Society*, Vol.15, No.4, p.20

Fontorbel FE & Simoetti JA (2011), 'Translocations and Human-carnivore Conflicts: Problem Solving or Problem Creating?,' *Wildlife Biology*, Vol. 17, pp.217-224.

Food and Agriculture Organization of United Nations (FAO, 2010), *Global forest resources assessment*, Rome, Italy: Food and Agriculture Organization of United Nations.

Food and Agriculture Organization of United Nations (FAO, 2012), S*tate of the World's forests,* Rome, Italy: Food and Agriculture Organization of United Nations.

FAO. (2022). *Crop Damage by Wildlife: Global Assessment*. Rome: FAO.

FAO. (2023). *Global Forest Resources Assessment.*

FAO. (2023). *HWC and Food Security.*

FAO. (2023). *Global Assessment of HWC Impacts on Agriculture.*

Food and Agriculture Organization (FAO). (2023). *Global Trends in HWC.*

Frank, Beatrice (2016), 'Human–Wildlife Conflicts and the Need to Include Tolerance and Coexistence: An Introductory Comment,' *Society and Natural Resources*, Vol. 29, No. 6, pp. 738-743.

Franks P., Twinamatsiko M (2017), *Lessons learnt from 20 years of revenue sharing at Bwindi Impenetrable National Park, Uganda*, International Institute for Environment and Development (IIED), London, UK.

Fritz H (2017), 'Long-term field studies of elephants: understanding the ecology and conservation of a long-lived ecosystem engineer,' *Journal of Mammalogy*, Vol. 98, No. 3, pp.603-611.

Frontiers. (2024). *Editorial: Climate change, human-wildlife interactions and sustainable tourism nexus in protected areas.*

Fulton, et. al. (1996), 'Wildlife Value Orientations: A Conceptual and Measurement Approach,' *Human Dimensions of Wildlife*, Vol. 1, No. 2, pp. 24-47.

Gillingham, S (2001), 'Social Organization and Participatory Resources Management in Brazilian Ribeirinho Communities: A Case Study of the Mamiraua Sustainable Development Reserve, Amazonas,' *Society and Natural Resources,* Vol. 14, PP.803-814.

Gnacadja and Lesch (2009), *Running dry- Climate change in dry lands and how to cope with it.* Germany: M€unchen.

Goldman M.J., Roque De Pinho J. Perry J (2010), 'Maintaining Complex Relations with Large Cats: Maasai and Lions in Kenya and Tanzania,' *Human Dimensions of Wildlife*, Vol. 15, No. 5, pp. 332-346.

Gompper, ME (2014), *Free-ranging Dogs and Wildlife Conservation*, Oxford University Press, Oxford.

Government of India (2008), *The Wild Life (Protection) Act, 1972: (53 of 1972) as amended by the Wild Life (Protection) Amendment Act, 2006 (39 of 2006),* Universal Law Publishing Co., Delhi, India.

Goyal, S P, eta. al (2000), 'A Study on Distribution, Relative Abundance and Food Habits of Leopard (Panthera pardus) in Garhwal Himalayas,' *Technical Report*, Wildlife Life Institute of India, Dehradun.

Graham M.D., et. (2010), 'Patterns of crop-raiding by elephants, Loxodonta africana, in Laikipia, Kenya, and the management of human-elephant conflict,' *Systematics and Biodiversity*, Vol. 8, No. 4, pp. 435-445.

Gross E.M (2019), *Tackling routes to coexistence. Human-elephant conflict in sub-Saharan Africa*, GIZ Partnership against Poaching and Illegal Wildlife Trade, Eschborn, Germany.

Gross E, et.al. (2021), *A Future for All: The Need for Human-Wildlife Coexistence*, WWF, Gland, Switzerland.

Guerra, A.S. (2019), 'Wolves of the sea: Managing human–wildlife conflict in an increasingly tense ocean', *Marine Policy*, Vol. 99, pp. 369–373.

Guthrie, RD (2005), *The Nature of Paleo-lithic Art*, University Chicago Press, Chicago, IL.

Guynn, D.E (1997), 'Miracle in Montana- Managing Conflicts over Private Lands and Public Wildlfe Issues,.' *Transactions of the North American Wildlife and Natural Resources Conference,* Vol. 62, pp.146-154

Hanley, N. (2015). 'Understanding conservation conflicts: An economic perspective', In: Redpath, S. M., Gutiérrez, R.J., Wood, K.A., Young, J.C. (editors*), Conflicts in conservation: Navigating towards solutions*, Cambridge: Cambridge University Press, pp. 79–93.

Hart D & Sussman, W (2009), Man the Hunted: Primates, *Predators and Human Evolution*, Westview Press, Boulder.

Hazzah, L.N (2006), *Living among Lions: Coexistence or Killing? Community Attitude towards Conservation Initiatives and the Motivations behind Lion Killing in Kenyan Maasailand*, University of Wisconsin-Madison .

Hedges, S & Gunaryadi D (2010), 'Reducing Human-elephant Conflict: Do Chillies Help Deter Elephants from Entering Crop Fields?,' *Oryx*, Vol. 44, pp.139-146.

Hemson, G., Maclennanan, S., Mills, G., Johnson, P., Macdonald, D (2009), 'Community, lions, livestock and money: A spatial and social analysis of attitudes to wildlife and the conservation value of tourism

in a human–carnivore conflict in Botswana,' *Biological Conservation,* Vol. 142, No. 11, pp. 2718–2725.

Hill, C.M (2004), 'Farmers' perspectives of conflict at the wildlife-agriculture boundary: Some lessons learned from African subsistence farmers,' *Human Dimensions of Wildlife*, Vol.9, pp.279-286.

Hillman G, et. al. (2016), 'New evidence of Late Glacial cereal cultivation at Abu Hureyra on the Euphrates,' *The Holocene,* Vol. 11, No. 4, pp. 383-393.

Hlasny, T, et. al. (2011), Expected impacts of climate change on forests: Czech Republic as a case study, *Journal of Forest Science*, Vol. 57, No. 10, pp. 422–431.

Hoare, R. (2015), 'Lessons from 20 years of human–elephant conflict mitigation in Africa,' *Human Dimensions of Wildlife,* Vol. 20, No. 4, pp. 289–295.

Holling, C.S (2001), 'Understanding the complexity of economic, ecological, and social systems,' *Ecosystems*, Vol. 4, pp. 390–405.

Ingold T (1994), 'From Trust to Domination: An Alternative History of Human-animal Relations,' in A. Manning & J. Serpell (eds.), *Animals and Human Society*, Routledge, New York, pp. 1-22.

Inskip C & Zimmermann A (2009), 'Human-Felid Conflict: A Review of Pattern and Priorities Worldwide,' *Oryx*, Vol.43, pp. 18-34.

IPCC. (2022). *Climate Change 2022: Impacts, Adaptation, and Vulnerability.*

Intergovernmental Panel on Climate Change (IPCC). (2023). *Climate Change 2023: Impacts, Adaptation, and Vulnerability.*

IUCN. (2020). *Mitigating HWC in Africa.* International Union for Conservation of Nature.

International Union for Conservation of Nature (IUCN). (2021). *Guidelines for HWC Management.*

IUCN. (2022). *HWC Resolution Strategies.*

IUCN. (2022). *HWC Solutions in Asia.*

IUCN (2023), *IUCN SSC guidelines on HWC and coexistence*, First Edition, Gland, Switzerland: IUCN.

IUCN. (2023). *Red List of Threatened Species*. Gland, Switzerland.

IUCN Species Survival Commission (SSC) HWC Task Force. (2020). *IUCN SSC position statement on the management of HWC.* HWCTF.

IUCN (2023), *IUCN SSC guidelines on HWC and coexistence*, First Edition, Gland, Switzerland: IUCN

Jadhav S., Barua M (2012), 'The Elephant Vanishes: impact of human-elephant conflict on people's wellbeing,' *Health Place*, Vol. 18, No. 6, pp. 1356-1365.

Jones K.E., et al. (2008), 'Global trends in emerging infectious diseases', *Nature* Vol. 451, No. 7181, pp. 990-993.

Jones B.T.B., Diggle R.W., Thouless C (2015), 'From Exploitation to Ownership: Wildlife-Based Tourism and Communal Area Conservancies in Namibia,' in *Institutional Arrangements for Conservation, Development and Tourism in Eastern and Southern Africa: A Dynamic Perspective* (eds. R. van der Duim, M. Lamers, J. van Wijk), Springer Netherlands, Dordrecht, pp. 17-37.

Karanth, K.U & Madhusudan, M. D (2002), Mitigating HWCs in Southern Asia, in J. Terborgh, C.P Van Schaik, M. Rao & L. C Davenport (eds.), *Making park work: identifying key factors to implementing parks in the tropics* (pp. 250-264). Convelo, CA: Island Press.

Kaswamila A & A. N Songorwa (2009), 'Participatory Land-use Planning and Conservation in Northern Tanzania Rangelands,' *African Journal of Ecology*, Vol. 47, pp.128-134.

Keith, D. A, et. al. (2011), 'Uncertainty and adaptive management for biodiversity conservation,' *Biological conservation*, Vol. 144, No. 4, pp. 1175-1178.

Kenya Wildlife Service (KWS). (2023). *Annual HWC Report.*

Khaine, Inkyin & Su Young Woo (2015), 'An overview of interrelationship between climate change and forests,' *Forest Science and Technology*, Vol. 11, No. 1, March, Taylor and Francis.

Khumalo K E & Young L A (2015), 'Women, HWC, and CBNRM: Hidden Impacts and Vulnerabilities in Kwandu Conservancy, Namibia,' *Conservation and Society*, Vol. 13, No.3, pp. 232-243.

King, L E, et. al. (2011), 'Beehive Fences as Effective Deterrents for Crop-raiding Elephants: Field trials in Northern Kenya,' *African Journal of Ecology*, Vol. 49,pp. 431-439.

Knight, J (2000), 'Culling Demons: the Problem of Bears in Japan,' *Natural enemies- People-wildlife Conflicts in Anthropological Perspective*, Routledge, London, pp.145-169.

Knight et al., (2009), 'Deer facilitate invasive plant success in a Pennsylvania forest under-story', Natural Areas Journal, No. 29, pp. 110-116.

Konig H.J., et. al. (2020), 'Human-wildlife coexistence in a changing world,' *Conservation Biology*, Vol. 34, No. 4, pp. 786-749.

KWS (2000), *Wildlife-Human Conflicts: Sources, Solutions and Issues*, Wildlife Service, Nairobi.

Lambert CMS, et. al. (2006), 'Cougar Population Dynamics and Viability in the Pacific Northwest,' Wildlife Management, Vo. 70, pp. 246-254.

Lamichhane B.R., et al. (2019), 'Contribution of Buffer Zone Programs to Reduce Human-Wildlife Impacts: the Case of the Chitwan National Park, Nepal', *Human Ecology*.

Lapidge S, et. al. (2007), 'Global Harmonisation in the field of invasive species management product development,' *Proceeding of the International Symposiums* on Managing Vertebrate Invasive Species, Vol. 7-9, August, Fort Collins, Co, USA, pp. 34-41.

Leong, K.M (2009), 'The tragedy of becoming common: landscape change and perceptions of wildlife,' *Society and Natural resources*, No. 23, pp. 111-127.

Letty J, et. al. (2007), 'Problems Encountered by Individuals in Animal Translocations: Lessons from Field Studies, *Eco science*, Vol. 14, pp. 420 -431.

Lute, M.L & Gore, M L (2014), 'Knowledge and power in wildlife management,' *The Journal of Wildlife Management,* Vol. 78, No. 6, pp.1060-1068.

Mahanti, P & S. Kumar (2018), 'HWC: A Case Study in Kerala, India,' *Journal of Biodiversity and Conservation*, Vol. 1, No. 2, pp. 42-52.

Madden, F., McQuinn, B. (2014), 'Conservation's blind spot: The case for conflict transformation in wildlife conservation,' *Biological Conservation*, Vol. 178, pp. 97–106.

Madhusadan, M.D. (2003), 'Living amidst large wildlife: Livestock and crop depredation by large mammals in the interior villages of Bhadra Tiger reserve, South India,' *Environmental Management,* Vol. 31, No. 4, pp. 466–475.

Manfredo, M J & Ashley A D (2004), 'Concepts of Exploring the Social Aspects of HWC in a Global Context,' *Human Dimensions of Wildlife*, Vol. 9, pp. 317-328.

Manfredo, M J, et. al. (2009), 'Linking society and environment: A multilevel model of shifting wildlife value orientations in the western US,' *Social Science Quarterly*, Vol. 90, No. 2, pp. 407-427.

Marchini S & P. G Crawshaw (2015), 'HWCs in Brazil: A Fast-growing Issue,' *Human Dimensions of Wildlife*, Vol. 20, pp. 323-328.

Marker, L (2005), *Aspects of Cheetah – Biology, Ecology and Conservation Strategies on Namibian Farmlands*, University of Oxford, Oxford.

Marker LL, et. al. (2005), 'Perceived Effectiveness of Livestock-guarding Dogs Placed on Namibian Farms,' *Rangeland Ecology Management*, Vol. 58, pp. 329-339.

Marker L (2019), 'Cheetahs Race for Survival: Ecology and Conservation' *IntechOpen*.

Mason et al., (2018), 'Wicked conflict : Using wicked problem thinking for holistic management of conservation conflict,' Conservation Letters, Vol.

Massei, Giovanna (2010), 'Can translocations be used to mitigate human–wildlife conflicts?' *Wildlife Research*, Vol. 37, No. 5, pp. 428-439.

McManus etal. (2015), 'Dead or alive? Comparing the costs and benefits of lethal and non-lethal human–wildlife conflict mitigation on livestock farms,' *Oryx*, Vol. 49, No. 4, pp. 687–695.

Mesmer, et al. (1999), 'United States Public Attitudes regarding Predators and their Management to Enhance Avian Recruitment,' *Wildlife Society Bulletin*, Vo. 27, pp.75-85.

MET/NACSO (2018), 'The State of Community Conservation in Namibia,' *Annual Report 2018*, Windhoek, Namibia.

MET/NACSO (2019), 'The State of Community Conservation in Namibia,' *Annual Report 2019*, Windhoek, Namibia.

Michalski, et.al. (2006), 'HWCs in a Fragmented Amazonian Forest Landscape: Determinants of Large Felid Depredation on Livestock,' *Animal Conservation*, Zoological Survey of India, Vo..9, pp.179-188.

Mishra C (1997), Livestock depredation by Large Carnivores in the Indian trans-Himalaya: Conflict Perceptions and Conservation Prospects, *Environmental Conservation*, Vol. 24, No. 4, pp. 338-343.

MoEFCC (2017), *India's National Wildlife Action Plan 2017-2031.*, Ministry of Environment, Forests and Climate Change, New Delhi, India.

MoEFCC. (2023). *Human-Elephant Conflict Report*. New Delhi: Government of India.

Ministry of Environment, Forest and Climate Change (MoEFCC), Government of India. (2023). *Elephant Census Report*.

Mosimane, et. al. (2013), 'Using Mental Models in the Analysis of Humn-wildlife Conflict from the Perspective of a Social-ecological System in Namibia,' *Oryx*, Vol. 48, No. 1, pp.64-70.

Mukeka J.M, et. al. (2018), 'Characteristics of HWC in Kenya: Examples of Tsavo and Maasai Mara regions, *Environment and Natural Resources Research*, Vol. 8, No.3, pp.148-165.

Mukeka, J M, et. al. (2019), 'HWCs and their Correlates in Narok County, Kenya,' *Global Ecology and Conservation*, Vol. 18, pp.1-22.

Munster, Ursula and Suma Vishnudas (2011), *In the jungle of the law: The implementation of the Forest Rights Act in Kerala,* European Society for Environmental History Conference, Turku, Finland, 28th June to 2nd July 2011.

Munster, Daniel; and Ursula Munster (2012a), 'Consuming the forest in an environment crisis: nature tourism, forest conservation and neo-liberal agriculture in south India,' Development and Change, Vol. 43, No. 1, pp.205-227.

Munster, Daniel, and Ursula Munster (2012b), "Human-Animal Conflicts in Kerala: Elephants and Ecological Modernity on the Agrarian Frontier in South India." In: "Fields and Forests: Ethnographic perspectives on Environmental Globalization," edited by Daniel Munster, Ursula Munster, and Stefan Dorondel, *RCC Perspectives*, No. 5, pp. 41–49

Mkonyi, F., et al. (2022). "Livestock Predation and Prey Depletion in Tanzania." *Journal of Wildlife Management,* 86(4), 789-801.

National Wildlife Federation (NWF). (2023). *Human-Wildlife Encounters in the U.S.*

Naughton-Treves, Holland and Brandon (2005), 'The role of protected areas in conserving biodiversity and sustaining local livelihoods.,' *Annual Review of Environment and Resources,* Vol. 30, No. 1, pp. 219–252.

NTCA. (2022). *Tiger Conservation in India.*

NTCA. (2023). *India's Tiger Conservation Success.*

Nyhus, P. J. (2016). *HWC: The Basics.*

Nyhus, Philip, J, (2016), HWC and Coexistence, *Annual Review of Environment and Resources,* Vol.41, pp.143-171.

Nyhus, P. (2023). "Climate Change and HWC in Africa." *Conservation Biology*, 37(2), 112-125.

Oerke E.C (2006), 'Crop losses to pests,' *The Journal of Agricultural Science*, Vol. 144, No. 1, pp. 31-43.

Ogra M & R. Badola (2008), 'Compensating HWC in Protected Area Communities: Ground level Perspectives from Uttarakhand, India,' *Human Ecology*, Vol. 36, No. 5, pp.717-729.

Okello, Kiringe and Warinwa (2014), 'Human–carnivore conflicts in private conservancy lands of Elerai and Oltiyiani in Amboseli area, Kenya,' *Natural Resources*, Vol. 5, pp. 375–391.

O'Neill M & Jessica Villat (2020), *The State of Knowledge and Practice on Human–Wildlife Conflicts,* Luc Hoffmann Institute, Switzerland.

Othman N., et. al. (2019), 'Shift of paradigm needed towards improving human-elephant coexistence in monoculture landscapes in Sabah,' *International Zoo Yearbook*, Vol. 53, No. 1, pp.161-173.

Pandey P., Shaner P.J., Sharma H.P (2016), 'The wild boar as a driver of HWC in the protected park lands of Nepal,' *European Journal of Wildlife Research,* Vol. 62, No. 1, pp. 103-108.

Panthera. (2023). *Lion Guardians Program Report.*

Panthera. (2023). *Jaguar-Friendly Beef Initiatives*.

Patterson B D, et. al. (2004), 'Livestock Predation by Lions and Other Carnivores on Ranches Neighbouring Tsavo National Park, Kenya,' *Biological Conservation*, Vol. 119, pp. 507-516.

Peters, B. G (2011), 'Governance as political theory,' *Critical Policy Studies*, Vol. 5, No. 1, pp. 63–72.

Peterson, et. al. (2010), 'Rearticulating the Myth of HWC,' *Conservation Letters,* Vol. 3, pp. 74-82.

Pillai, Nair, Jacob. (2010). *Role of Indigenous communities in Forest Conservation: Lessons from Africa.* Institute of Social Research and Action. Thiruvananthapuram.

Population Connection. (2023). *No place to hide: Climate change is worsening human-wildlife conflict.* Retrieved from https://populationconnection.org/blog/climate-change-is-worsening-human-wildlife-conflict/

Raik, D.B., Wilson, A.L., Decker, D.J (2008), 'Power in natural resources management: An application of theory,' *Society and Natural Resources*, Vol. 21, No. 8, pp. 729–739.

Rai R.P., Ghose P.S., Shresta P (2014), 'Shifting perspectives in HWC: Unheard voices from the Sikkim and Darjeeling Himalaya,' in *HWC in the Mountains of SAARC Region: Compilation of Successful Management Strategies and Practices,* SAARC Forestry Centre Office, Thimphu, Bhutan, pp. 72-82.

Ramakumar R. (2025). Human Wildlife Conflict: The Central Government Viewpoints to be Corrected. *Mathrubhumi.com.* June 14.

Ramakumar R. (2025). Human Wildlife Conflicts: Scientific Perspectives and Central Government Stand. *Chintha.* June 13.

Ravenelle, J., Nyhus, P. J (2017), 'Global patterns and trends in human–wildlife conflict compensation,' *Conservation Biology,* Vol. 31, No. 6, pp. 1247–1256.

Ravindranath N. H, et. al. (2010), *Impact of Climate Change on Forests in India*, Centre for Ecological Sciences, Indian Institute of Science, Bangalore

Redfern J.V., et al. (2013), 'Assessing the risk of ships striking large whales in marine spatial planning,' *Conservation Biology*, Vol. 27, No. 2, pp. 292-302.

Redpath, SM, et.ail. (2013), 'Understanding and Managing Conservation Conflict's, *Trends in Ecology and Evolution*, Vol.28, pp.100-109.

Riley et al. (2002), 'The essence of wildlife management,' *Wildlife Society Bulletin*, Vol. 30, pp. 585-593.

Ripple, WJ, et al. (2015), 'Collapse of the World's Largest Herbivores,' *Scientific Advertising*, Vol. 1.

Roe, E (1998), *Taking Complexity Seriously: Policy Analysis, Triangulation, and Sustainable Development,* Kluwer Academic Publishers, Boston, USA.

Roskaft, et. al. (2003), 'Pattern of Self-reported Fear towards Large Carnivores among the Norwegian Public,' *Evolutionary Human Behaviour*, Vol. 24, pp. 184-198.

SANParks. (2022). *HWC Management Report.*

Save the Elephants. (2022). *Beehive Fences in Kenya.*

Scoones, I (1998), Sustianble Rural Livelihoods: A Framework for Analysis,' *IDS Working Paper*: 72.

Seppala R, Buck A, Katila P (eds) (2009) Adaptation of forests and people to climate change: A Global Assessment Report. *IUFRO World Series,* Volume 22, Helsinki, p.224

Shen Z & K. Ma (2014), 'Effects of Climate Change on Biodiversity,' *Chinese Science Bulletin*,pp.1-2.

Simukonda C (2008), *Aerial Survey Report for Large Mammals: A Report submitted to Zambia Wildlife Authority*, Chilanga.

Smit, B, et al. (2000), 'An anatomy of adaptation to climate change and variability,' *Climatic Change*, Vol. 45, pp. 223–251.

Soffker et al., (2015), The impact of predation by marine mammals on Patagonian tooth -fish longline fisheries', *PLoS ONE*, Vol. 10, No. 3.

SPB. (2022). Working Group Report on HWI in Kerala, 14th Five Year Plan.

Spittlehouse D L & R B. Stewart (2003), 'Adaptation to climate change in forest management,' *BC Journal of Ecosystems and* Management, Volume 4, Number 1. FORREX–Forest Research Extension Partnership.

Sukumar, R & Gadgil M (1988), 'Male-Female Differences in Foraging on Crops by Asian Elephants,' *Animal Behaviour*, Vol. 36, pp.1233-1235

Sukumar, R (1989), *The Asian Elephant: Ecology and Management*, Cambridge University Press, Cambridge.

Sukumar, R (2003), *The living elephants: evolutionary ecology, behaviour and conservation*, Oxford university press, New York.

Surovell, TA, et. al. (2016), 'Test of Martin's overkill Hypothesis using Radiocarbon Dates on Extinct Mega fauna,' *Proceedings of the National Academy of Sciences*, Vol. 113, pp.886-891.

Swanepoel LH, et. al. (2015), 'Functional Responses of Retaliatory Killing verses Recreational Sport-Hunting of Leopards in South Africa,' *PLOS One*, Vol10, No. 4, e0125539.

The Guardian. (2024). *Collapsing wildlife populations near 'points of no return.* Retrieved from https://www.theguardian.com/environment/2024/oct/10/collapsing-wildlife-populations-points-no-return-living-planet-report-wwf-zsl-warns

Thornton, P.K (2010), 'Livestock Production: Recent Trends, Future Prospects,' *Philosophical Transactions of the Royal Society of London Royal Society of Biological Science*, Vol. 365, pp.2853-2867.

Toledo et al. (2011), 'Climate is a stronger driver of tree and forest growth rates than soil and disturbance,' *Journal of Ecology*, Vol. 99, pp. 254-264.

Torres D.F., et. al. (2018), 'Conflicts Between Humans and Terrestrial Vertebrates: A Global Review' *Tropical Conservation Science*, No. 11.

Trefethen. J.B (1975), *An American Crusade for Wildlife*, Boone and Crockett Club, Alexandria, Virginia

Treves, Adrian, et.al. (2006), 'Co-managing HWCs: A Review,' *Human Dimensions of Wildlife,* Vol.11, pp.383-396.

Treves, Adrian, et. al. (2009), 'Participatory Planning of Interventions to Mitigate HWCs,' *Conservation Biology*, pp. 1-11.

Triguero-Mas M., et. al. (2010), 'Urban and rural perceptions of protected areas: a case study in Dandeli Wildlife Sanctuary, Western Ghats, India,' *Environmental Conservation*, Vol. 36, No. 3, pp. 208-217.

Trinkel, M., Angelici, F.M (2016), 'The decline in the lion population in Africa and possible mitigation measures', in: Angelici, F.M. (editor), *Problematic wildlife*, Cham: Springer, pp. 45–68.

Treves, A & Karanth, K.U (2003), 'Human-carnivore Conflict and perception on Carnivore Management Worldwide,' *Conservation Biology*, Vo. 17, pp.1491-1499.

United Nations (2009), *What is good governance?*, Economic and Social Commission for Asia and the Pacific, Bangkok, p.3.

UN. (2023). *World Population Prospects*. New York: United Nations.

UNEP. (2023). *Global Environment Outlook.*

UNEP. (2023). *Climate Change and HWC.*

USDA. (2023). *Wolf Depredation on Livestock Statistics*.

US Fish & Wildlife Service (USFWS). (2023). *Wolf Conflict Statistics*.

Urban Wildlife Institute. (2023). *Coyote Conflicts in Urban America*.

Van Der Hoop, JM, et al. (2013), 'Assessment of Management to Mitigate Anthropogenic Effects on Large Whales,' *Conservation Biology*, Vol. 27, pp.121-133.

Vannelli et al. (2019), Community participation in ecotourism and its effect on local perceptions of snow leopard (Panthera uncia) conservation.,' *Human Dimensions of Wildlife*, Vol. 24, No. 2, pp. 180–193.

Waterfield G & Zilberman D (2012), 'Pest Management in Food Systems: An Economic Perspective,' *Annual Review of Environmental Resources*, Vl. 37, pp.223-245.

Waylen et al. (2015), 'Can scenario-planning support community-based natural resource management? Experiences from three countries in Latin America,' *Ecology and Society*, Vol. 20, No. 4.

Weber M (1948), *The Protestant Ethics and the Spirit of Capitalism*, Scribner, New York.

West, H (2001), 'Sorcery of Construction and Socialist Modernisation-Ways of Understanding Power in Post-Colonial Mozambique,' *American Ethnologist*, Vol. 28, pp. 119-150.

Western, et. al. (2009), The Status of Wildlife in Protected Areas Compared to Non-protected Areas of Kenya, PLoS One, Vol. 4, No. 7 https://doi.org/10.1371/journal.pone.0006140.

White L (1967), 'The Historical Roots of our Environmental Crisis,' *Science*, Vol. 155, No. 3767, pp. 1203-1207.

White, P C. L. & Alastair I. Ward (2010), 'Interdisciplinary approaches for the management of existing and emerging human–wildlife conflicts,' *Wildlife Research*, Vol. 37, No.8, pp. 623-629.

Wiafe E.D. (2019), 'Primates crop raiding situation on farmlands adjacent to South-West of Mole National Park, Ghana,' *Ghana Journal of Agricultural Science,* Vol. 54, No. 2, pp. 58-67.

Wildlife Institute of India (WII). (2022). *National Database on Human-Animal Conflict.*

Williams D.J, et al. (2019), 'Strategy for a globally coordinated response to a priority neglected tropical disease: Snakebite envenoming,' *PLoS Neglected Tropical Diseases,* Vol. 13, No. 2.

Woodroffe, R (2000), 'Predators and People: Using human densities to interpret declines of large carnivores,' *Animal conservation*, Vol. 3, No.2, pp. 165-173.

Woodroffe, RT, et.al. (2005), *People and Wildlife: Conflict or Coexistence*, Cambridge University Press, Cambridge.

Worm, B, (2015), 'A Most unusual Super-predator,' *Science*, Vol. 349, pp.784-785.

World Bank. (2023*). Human-Wildlife Conflict: Global Policy and Perception Insights.* Retrieved from https://www.worldbank.org/en/programs/global-wildlife-program/brief/human-wildlife-conflict-global-policy-and-perception-insights

World Wide Fund for Nature (WWF). (2021). *HWC Overview in Kenya.*

WWF Nepal. (2021). *Rhino-Human Encounters: A Conservation Challenge.*

WWF (2022). *Living with Wildlife: Global Best Practices.*

WWF. (2022). *Living with Wildlife: Reducing HWC.*

WWF. (2023). *Living Planet Report 2023.*

WWF. (2025). *C2C—conflict to coexistence: A global approach to manage HWC.*

WWF. (2023). *HWC: A Global Challenge*. Retrieved from https://www.wwf.org

WWF. (2023). *Living Planet Report*. Gland, Switzerland.

WWF. (2023). *Living with Wildlife: Mitigation Strategies*.

WWF. (2023). *Community-Based Conservation in Namibia*.

WWF India. (2023). *Elephant Human Conflict in Northeast India*.